FRANCE'S

BEST - LOVED

DRIVING

TOURS

Simon & Schuster Macmillan

Revised second edition 1995, published in this format 1997
First published January 1991

Edited, designed and produced by AA Publishing.

Published by AA Publishing

Published in the United States by Macmillan Travel
A Simon & Schuster Macmillan Company
1633 Broadway, New York, NY 10019

Macmillan is a registered trademark of Macmillan, Inc

ISBN 0-02861569-7

Cataloging-in-Publication Data is available from the Library of
Congress.

Color separation: Daylight Colour Art, Singapore

Printed and bound by G. Canale & C. S.P.A., Torino, Italy

Opposite: *lace coiffe, Pont l'Abbé*

CONTENTS

ABOUT THIS BOOK

This book is not only a practical touring guide for the independent traveller, but is also invaluable for those who would like to know more about the country.

It is divided into 6 regions, each containing between 3 and 5 tours which start and finish in major towns and cities considered to be the best centres for exploration.

Each tour has details of the most interesting places to visit en route. Panels catering for special interests follow some of the main entries – for those whose interest is in history, wildlife or walking, and those who have children. There are also panels which highlight scenic stretches of road and which give details of events, crafts and customs.

The simple route directions are accompanied by an easy-to-use tour map at the beginning of each tour, along with a chart showing how far it is from one town to the next in kilometres and miles. This can help you to decide where to take a break and stop overnight, for example. (All distances quoted are approximate.)

Before setting off it is advisable to check with the information centre at the start of the tour for recommendations on where to break your journey and for additional information on what to see and do, and when best to visit.

Banks
Normal banking hours are 9am–noon and 2–4pm weekdays. Banks are closed either Mondays or Saturdays and on Sundays and public holidays. Banks close at noon on the day before a national holiday, and all day on Monday if the holiday falls on a Tuesday.

Camping and Caravanning
For information on camping and caravanning in France see pages 160–5.

Credit Cards
International credit cards are accepted widely throughout France, though not so much in rural areas. They are not accepted at some petrol stations.

Currency
The unit of currency is the franc, divided into 100 centimes. Coins are in denominations of 10, 20 and 50 centimes, and 1, 2, 5, 10 and 20 francs; notes are in denominations of 20, 50, 100, 200 and 500 francs.

Customs Regulations
Since 1 January 1993 there is no limit on the importation into one EU country of tax-paid goods purchased in another, provided that these goods are for personal use. However, all EU customs authorities have fixed indicative limits on alcohol and tobacco.

Beyond these limits the importer must be able to prove that these goods are for personal use.

Electricity
220 volts (50 cycles AC), with the standard continental two-pin round plug, making an adaptor essential for British and American appliances.

Embassies
British Embassy: 35 rue du Faubourg St Honoré, 75008 Paris Cedex 08 tel: (1) 42 66 91 42.
Canadian Embassy: 35 avenue Montaigne, 75008 Paris tel: (1) 44 33 29 00.
US Embassy: 2 avenue Gabriel, 75008 Paris Cedex 08 tel: (1) 42 96 12 02.

Emergency Telephone Numbers
Police tel: 17
Fire tel: 18
Ambulance: 15.

Entry Regulations
No visas are required for nationals of EU countries (except Turkey), USA, Canada, Japan, New Zealand, Singapore and South Korea. Visas are required for all others. Check, though, with a travel agent or the French Government Tourist Office, since visa policy is subject to review.

Health Matters
There are no special health requirements or regulations. Visitors other than EU citizens, where there may be reciprocal medical services available, are advised to take out medical insurance.

Motoring
For information on all aspects of motoring in France, including accidents, breakdowns and speed limits, see pages 158–60.

Post Offices
Normal opening times for main post offices are 8am–7pm on weekdays, and 8am–noon on Saturdays, though some small offices may close for lunch. Stamps may also be bought in tobacco shops (tabacs) or cafés marked with a red cigar sign. Letter boxes are yellow.

Public Holidays
1 January – New Year's Day
Easter Monday
1 May – Labour Day
8 May – VE Day
6th Thursday after Easter – Ascension Day
2nd Monday after Ascension – Whitsun
14 July – Bastille Day
15 August – Assumption Day
1 November – All Saints' Day
11 November – Remembrance Day
25 December – Christmas Day

Route Directions
Throughout this book the following abbreviations are used for French roads:
A – Autoroute
N – Route Nationale
D – Route Départementale
C and V – smaller roads.

Telephones
Insert coin after lifting the receiver; the dialling tone is a continuous tone. To make a local call use a 1 franc coin. Most telephone booths now take phonecards (*télécartes*). Buy them for 50FF or 120FF from post offices, tobacconists and news-agents.

For international calls out of France dial 00, wait for a new tone, then dial the national code, followed by the local code, omitting the initial 0, and then the number.

Time
France follows Greenwich Mean Time (GMT) plus one hour,

Roche Tuilière and Roche Sanadoire, near Le Mont-Dore in the Auvergne

with clocks put forward for a further hour from late March to late September.

Tourist Offices
Where no address is given for a separate tourist information office, enquire at the *Mairie* (mayor's office) in a village or small town, the *Hôtel de Ville* (town hall) in a larger place, or perhaps the *Syndicat d'Initiative* office. In some places the tourist offices open only seasonally, and the *Mairie* or *Hôtel de Ville* will handle enquiries out of season.

Useful Words
The most useful phrase in French is *s'il vous plaît* or please. You will get a lot further using it after every request than if you leave it out. The following words and phrases are helpful in finding your way about.

English *French*
bridge *pont*
bus *autobus*
car park *un parking*
I need petrol *j'ai besoin d'essence*
my car has broken down *ma voiture est en panne*
oil *huile*
petrol *essence*
the road for *la route pour*
traffic lights *les feux*
tyres *les pneus*
underground *Métro*
after *après*
behind *derrière*
before *avant*
here *ici*
left *à gauche*
near *près*
opposite *en face*
right *à droite*
straight on *tout droit*
there *là*
where? *où?*
where is? *où est?*
at what time *à quelle heure?*
I do not understand *je ne comprends pas*
do you speak English? *parlez-vous Anglais?*
help! *au secours!*
how much is it? *ça coute combien?*
I'm sorry *pardon*
thank you very much *merci beaucoup*
do you accept credit cards? *acceptez-vous des cartes de crédit?*
money *argent*

NORMANDY & BRITTANY

Normandy has rebuilt itself after World War II into a region of cheerful holiday resorts, attractive farmlands and archetypal rustic villages. Here and there, you will pick up eerie echoes of an earlier invasion which went from Normandy across the English Channel. The original Normans were Norsemen – Vikings who swept down from Scandinavia and, in the 10th century, created the dukedom of Normandy. William the Conqueror was Duke of Normandy, with a legal claim to the English throne, long before he invaded England in 1066. From that point on, the histories of Normandy and England intertwined.

The Normandy coastline is a succession of resorts. Look for the seafood restaurants in the fishing ports. Inland, the livestock farms supply a cuisine which is rich in butter, cheeses, cream and hefty helpings of meat. Apples and pears are major crops. The wooded farmlands of Normandy create some of the most beautiful landscapes in northern France.

Brittany becomes more Breton as you move further west. A wonderful coastline and an airy, high-level interior are linked by a wooded middle district which could easily be in Devon or Cornwall.

Waves of colonists from Britain started arriving in the 5th century. Britain and Brittany, Briton and Breton are all from the same basic word; but the close connection was lost long ago.

Bretons, particularly in the west, retain a feeling of 'apartness' from the rest of France, and you will not be long there before being aware of something Celtic in the air. Traditional costumes and religious processions, not always as well supported as they have been in the past, underline the differences in culture and background.

In both Brittany and Normandy, regional nature parks are very well organised, with wildlife reserves, museums of traditional ways of life and places where you can see products such as bread and cider being made in the old pre-industrialised way.

Caen
You cannot miss William the Conqueror's influence on Caen, which has risen again from the devastation of 1944. Its centrepiece is the château of the dukes of Normandy. Inside this massive fortress, founded by William in 1060, you will find the Musée des Beaux-Arts with its splendid collection of French and Italian paintings, and the Musée de Normandie, devoted to archaeology, history and traditional life. William also endowed the monastery of the Abbaye aux Hommes, just as his wife built the original convent of the Abbaye aux Dames. William's tomb is in the Church of St-Étienne at the Abbaye aux Hommes, which now serves as Caen's Hôtel de Ville.

The Musée de la Nature here concentrates on the wildlife of coast and country. The Mémorial-Musée pour la Paix has impressive displays and audio-visual presentations charting the rise of Facism, the collaboration of the Resistance and the D-Day landings through to the present day.

Dieppe
Like Caen, Dieppe has erased most of the scars of World War II. Its harbour area includes ferry, freight, fishing and pleasure ports. Morning fish stalls are set up by the roadside.

The best view of Dieppe is from the 15th-century hillside château. It houses a fine museum and art gallery with extensive maritime rooms and a glorious collection of ivories, including a full-rigged ship with billowing sails.

Rennes
Rennes is the historic and flourishing provincial capital of Brittany. The River Vilaine runs through it, but, from the tourist office in the Quai Lamartine, there is no water to be seen. Here, the Vilaine has been roofed over to provide a car park.

Another quay, this time named after the writer Émile Zola, is the address of the Musée des Beaux-Arts, with its rich display of paintings, drawings, engravings and sculptures, many confiscated from religious houses during the Revolution. Rubens,

Opposite: Le Mont-St-Michel, steeped in magic and history
Above: brightly painted fishing boats in the harbour at Dieppe

Gaugin, Sisley, Boudin and Picasso are all represented. In the same building is the Musée de Bretagne, which traces the history of Brittany from prehistoric times.

Quimper
Quimper is more Breton than Rennes. The Musée Breton is here, completely refurbished. The pleasant old quarter centres on a square dominated by the twin spire of the cathedral, St-Corentin. Here is an architectural curiosity: the 15th-century nave is accidentally out of alignment with the 13th-century choir.

Quimper's Musée des Beaux-Arts, totally renovated to include audio-visual presentations, is well provided with 17th-century Flemish paintings. In the same era, Quimper itself began the production of the glazed pottery for which it is still famous. Factories and ceramic artists' workshops welcome visitors.

Legacy of D-Day

Normandy is a land of apples and cider, of spacious sands, of lovely inland *bocage* country with hedges and tree-lined fields, but behind the peaceful present-day scenes the region hides a past once devastated by the D-Day landings in June 1944, when the huge invasion force of Operation Overlord stormed the German defences.

3 DAYS • 456KM • 283 MILES

[i] *Place St Pierre, Caen*

▶ *Leave Caen on the D513 as for Cabourg. Go left on the D37, then take the D514 as for Ouistreham to Pegasus Bridge.*

❶ **Pegasus Bridge,**
Normandy

In the eastern sector of the D-Day landings, the years of planning and training came down to one amazingly audacious feat. Just after midnight on the morning of 6 June 1944, three gliders with no room for a conventional approach suddenly crash-landed beside this ugly but vital little tilting bridge on the Caen–Ouistreham canal. British troops poured out and after four minutes' fierce fighting secured the bridge. They held it until reinforcements arrived, most decisively the Commandos led by Lord Lovat, who reached here exactly two-and-a-half minutes behind schedule after fighting their way inland from Sword Beach.

Three columns in the scrubland southeast of the bridge show where the gliders landed. On the west side, a museum tells the story of that dramatic engagement. In November 1993 the original Pegasus Bridge was removed to be replaced by a wider, stronger bridge more appropriate to modern traffic.

▶ *Take the D35 to Douvres then follow the 'Bayeux' signs. Go right on the D79 to Courseulles-sur-Mer, then right on the D12 and follow signs to Arromanches-les-Bains.*

❷ **Arromanches,** Normandy

Without massive supplies, the D-Day landings could not have developed into an advance across the whole of France. Arromanches was the scene of one of the greatest engineering feats of the war – the building, from thousands of tons of prefabricated parts shipped across the Channel, of Port Winston, the giant Mulberry (artificial) harbour. It threw a 5.7km (3½-mile) breakwater round the sea approaches to Arromanches, from which pontoon bridges reached to the shore, and was operational within 12 days.

Today, Arromanches is a busy but unremarkable little resort on a bay between all but vertical cliffs. A viewpoint on the eastern cliff overlooks the many sections of the artificial harbour which remain offshore. On the seafront, the lively and well-presented Musée du Débarquement illustrates, with working models, films and photographs the creation and operation of 'the key to the liberation of France'.

[i] *Rue du Maréchal Joffre*

BACK TO NATURE

In the busy resort of Courseulles, part of Juno Beach on D-Day, the Maison de la Mer features aquariums with seahorses and conger eels, and a splendid display of shells.

▶ *Leave Arromanches-les-Bains for Bayeux on the D516.*

❸ **Bayeux,** Normandy

Most of the fine historic buildings here, recently restored, survived the 1944 campaign. You can stroll through old streets and over narrow bridges, admiring the gleaming stonework of the mills on the

The Maison Gondrée café, Pegasus Bridge

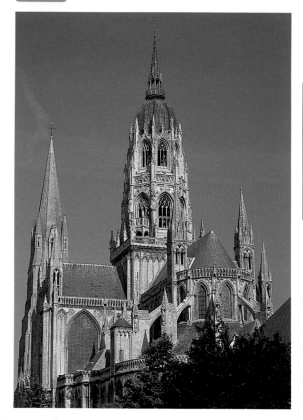

Omaha – housed in a prefabricated wartime building bizarrely described in some French guidebooks as a ship – at the village of Vierville.

FOR HISTORY BUFFS

Turn right off the D514 after Omaha Beach for Pointe du Hoc, to learn about the desperate struggle of the American Rangers to scale the cliffs on D-Day. Later, the landings were re-staged here for the film *The Longest Day*.

▶ *Continue on the D514 then go right on the N13 as for Cherbourg and continue to Valognes.*

5 Valognes, Normandy
In its 17th- to 19th-century heyday, Valognes was 'the Versailles of Normandy'. Aristocratic families owned town houses here, and there was a high-flying social life. The bombardments of 1944 wrecked the centre, which has been rebuilt, and also destroyed part of the Church of St Malo. Now a modern reinforced concrete nave and tower stand beside the 14th-century chancel.

However, several of Valogne's mansions survived. The elegant 18th-century Hôtel de Beaumont is open to visitors. The Hôtel de Thieuville houses the Musée de l'Eau de Vie et des Vieux Métiers, whose two main subjects are brandy

River Aure. On the ring road, the Musée de la Bataille de Normandie is 'guarded' by British, American and German tanks. Everything in Bayeux, however, pales in importance beside the priceless 11th-century tapestry, displayed in the Centre Guillaume le Conquérant, with its lively scenes of the Norman Conquest of England. Weavers and lace-makers still have studios in the town.

Alongside the cathedral, the Musée Baron Gérard shows paintings, lacework and ceramics. It opens from a little courtyard shaded by the famous 'liberty tree', planted according to the Revolutionary calendar (France's official calendar from 1793–1805) on 10 Germinal of the year V – otherwise 30 March, 1797.

Bayeux's splendid Norman Gothic Cathedral of Notre Dame

▶ *Leave Bayeux on the D6 to Port-en-Bessin-Huppain. Go left on the D514 for Plage d'Omaha.*

4 Plage d'Omaha,
Normandy
Most side roads to the right of the D514 here reach memorials and above, the Americans' principal D-Day landing beach, although signs for the Plage d'Omaha lead to a holiday camp area. Look for Wn 62, a high-set German strongpoint above the shoreline. There are American monuments here as well as explanations of the D-Day action and the fearsome German defences.

The American military cemetery for the men lost during the landings is close by, and there is an Exposition

FOR HISTORY BUFFS

Ste-Mère-Église near Utah Beach was the first French town liberated on D-Day. A museum to the 82nd US Airborne Division describes the action and how it is commemorated, and explains why the figure of a paratrooper hangs from the church tower every summer.

i Pont St Jean

and leatherwork. An annexe has displays on the French Revolution with some unusual themes, such as the role of scientists in Revolutionary times.

Close at hand the Musée du Cidre, once a dyer's workshop, then a barracks and then a smithy, concentrates on apples and cider-making.

[i] *Place du Château*

▶ *Leave Valognes for Barneville-Carteret on the D902.*

▶ *Leave Barneville as for La Haye-du-Puits on the* **D903**, *then keep right on the* **D650**. *Go straight on along the* **D20**, *to Bréhal, then right on the* **D971** *and into Granville.*

7 Granville, Normandy
Like Monaco, Granville expanded from a fortified town on a promontory rock. Originally, thanks to the contortions of history, it was fortified by the English against the French! The story of the town is illustrated in the Musée du

6 Barneville-Carteret,
Normandy
These two little towns, administratively linked together, form a family holiday resort with excellent sands, a spectacular rocky headland and a very sheltered tidal river harbour. This is a pleasant walking and watersports area, and summer ferries sail to the Channel Islands. Make for the lighthouse on Cap de Carteret, a wonderful viewpoint towards Jersey, Sark, Herm and, on the northern horizon, Alderney.

Take care at any family bathing parties. Every year people ignore the notices warning that, while the town beaches have a lifeguard service, the quieter one north of the Cap

does not. There, it is all too easy for youngsters to be taken well out of their depth.

[i] *Place Flandre-Dunkerque, Carteret; Rue des Églises, Barneville*

RECOMMENDED WALKS

At Barneville-Carteret, start from either of the beaches flanking the Cap de Carteret along the exhilarating Sentier des Douaniers (the Excisemen's Path), which contours the lichen-clad cliffs and passes the site of an 18th-century coastal gun battery.

The beach at Barneville-Carteret, north of Cap de Carteret

Vieux Granville, just inside the preserved drawbridge gateway of the Haute Ville (High Town).

The 15th-century Notre Dame Church stands among the alleyways of the High Town; a good aquarium here includes shell and mineral collections; and there is a very attractive path along the cliffs below the lighthouse. Views open up of the low-lying Chausey archipelago. Ferries sail to La Grande Île, with its château built by motor magnate Louis Renault.

On no account miss Granville's Jardin Public. Its lush lawns, pine trees and beautifully laid-out flower beds

surround the pink-and-white villa once owned by couturier Christian Dior. In early August, a 'Pardon of the Sea' melds religion with spectacle.

i *Cours Jonville*

▶ *Leave Granville for Villedieu-les-Poêles on the D924.*

8 Villedieu-les-Poêles, Normandy

If every place-name tells a story, how to explain Villedieu-les-Poêles – 'God's Town of the Pots and Frying-pans'? The Knights of Malta (a military religious order) established here in the 16th century, called the place Villedieu, and it became a famous centre of craftsmen and metalworkers.

That great tradition continues. Here you can watch hand-beaten copper being worked at the Atelier du Cuivre and pewterware at the Maison de l'Étain. At the extremes of Villedieu's historic product range, the Fonderie des Cloches is a bell-foundry open to visitors, and the Maison de la Dentellerie displays the lacework for which the women of the town were well known all over northern France.

i *Place des Costils*

▶ *Leave Villedieu-les-Poêles on the N175 as for St Hilaire. Go right on the D924 and D999, then left on the D33 and continue through Mortain. Turn left on the D907, go through Domfront-centre then follow 'Bagnoles-de-l'Orne' signs along the D908 and right on the D335.*

9 Bagnoles-de-l'Orne, Normandy

Retaining its old prominence as the most popular spa town in the west of France, Bagnoles, with the linked Tessé la Madeleine, lies among woodlands rising from the banks of the La Vée river. People come here for bath cures and to 'take the waters', but Bagnoles also offers excellent sporting facilities: golf, tennis, swimming, horse riding, fishing and archery.

Wooded walks extend through the parks of the spa buildings and the château at Tessé. One fine viewpoint path leads to the Roc du Chien (the Dog's Rock) above the narrow river valley where the spa itself is located.

Bagnoles' casino backs on to a very pleasant lake where pedaloes can be hired. Close to the lake there are several restaurants specialising in the substantial Normandy cuisine.

The château at Bagnoles-de-l'Orne adds to the attractions of this famous spa town

FOR CHILDREN

On the way from Villedieu-les-Poêles to Bagnoles-de-l'Orne, turn off the D33 for Le Village Enchanté, a beautiful estate where fairy-tale tableaux are laid out in the woodland.

SPECIAL TO...

At Bagnoles-de-l'Orne is the Musée des Sapeurs-Pompiers, which shows off France's finest collection of horse-drawn and hand-pumped fire engines. Look for La Distinguée, which operated as long ago as pre-Revolutionary times. Normandy is famous for its apples and pears. The region's rich tradition in apple- and pear-growing, and the making of cider, are all explained in the Maison de la Pomme et de la Poire. Reached by turning right after Barenton on the D335, it has indoor displays as well as a walk through an orchard specially planted with many varieties of apple and pear trees.

i Place de la République

▶ *Leave Bagnoles-de-l'Orne for St-Michel-des-Andaines on the D386. Go left and right on the D53 and continue to Flers. Go right as for Caen along the D962, then take the D562 to Clécy and turn off for Clécy-centre.*

10 **Clécy,** Normandy
The River Orne at Clécy makes a dramatic curve below the densely wooded cliffs of La Suisse Normande (Norman Switzerland). Clécy is the main resort in this district whose name should not lead you to expect a Swiss-like landscape of lakes and mountains; but it is one of the most beautiful parts of inland Normandy nevertheless. In the pleasant town centre with its 18th-century houses, look for the Musée Hardy which displays the work of a local artist. An exhilarating walk climbs to the magnificent viewpoint of the Pain du Sucre (the Sugarloaf), high on the cliffs overlooking the Orne. The 16th-century Manoir de Placy houses the Musée des Antiquités Normandes, with a miniature railway and a train museum in the grounds.

FOR CHILDREN

In Clécy, 20-minute programmes at the Musée du Chemin de Fer Miniature show off more than 180 locomotives operating on the biggest model railway layout in Europe.

Bridge over the River Orne in the resort of Clécy

i Place d l'Église

▶ *Leave Clécy on the D133c, then go left as for St-Rémy. Just over the brow of a hill, go sharp right and follow Routes des Crêtes to St-Omer. Avoid St-Rémy itself. In St-Omer turn right as for Pont-d'Ouilly. Ignore the 'La Suisse Normande' turning. Go left at a stop sign to Bretteville and follow the D23. In Bretteville turn left on the D132, left at a give way sign, then return to Caen on the D562.*

SCENIC ROUTES

While many places on this tour offer beautiful coastal views, the inland roads generally beat the ones near the coast for scenery. The D33, after Villedieu-les-Poêles, runs through gorgeous Normandy countryside.
High above Clécy in the valley of the Orne, the Route des Crêtes sums up, without reaching any Alpine levels, the appeal of the Suisse Normande.

Green &
Pleasant Normandy

West of the cross-Channel port and fishing town of Dieppe, the white cliffs and deep valleys which slice into them are hidden from the main roads, but this tour twists along the coast to some very attractive holiday resorts whose sweeping curves border the Forêt de Brotonne and the Marais Vernier.

3 DAYS • 434KM • 270 MILES

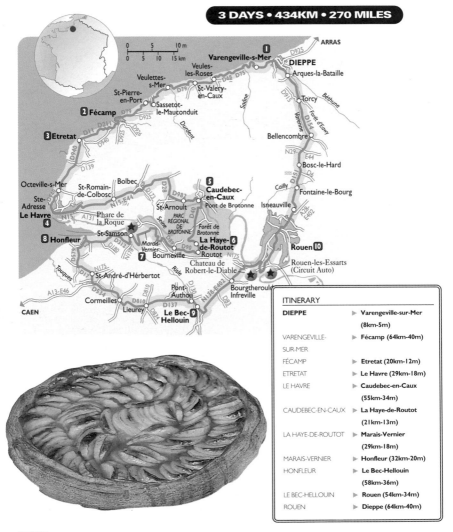

ITINERARY

DIEPPE	▶ **Varengeville-sur-Mer (8km-5m)**
VARENGEVILLE-SUR-MER	▶ **Fécamp (64km-40m)**
FÉCAMP	▶ **Etretat (20km-12m)**
ETRETAT	▶ **Le Havre (29km-18m)**
LE HAVRE	▶ **Caudebec-en-Caux (55km-34m)**
CAUDEBEC-EN-CAUX	▶ **La Haye-de-Routot (21km-13m)**
LA HAYE-DE-ROUTOT	▶ **Marais-Vernier (29km-18m)**
MARAIS-VERNIER	▶ **Honfleur (32km-20m)**
HONFLEUR	▶ **Le Bec-Hellouin (58km-36m)**
LE BEC-HELLOUIN	▶ **Rouen (54km-34m)**
ROUEN	▶ **Dieppe (64km-40m)**

i *Pont Jehan Ango, Dieppe*

▶ *Leave Dieppe on the D75 to Varengeville-sur-Mer.*

❶ Varengeville-sur-Mer, Normandy

You might be deep in the heart of an English county here, with villas and cottages in discreetly private grounds, wooded and grass-banked lanes, and half-timbered farms fitted like jigsaw pieces in between. There is a wonderful English-style landscape garden at the Parc Floral des Moutiers, the garden of the house called Bois des Moutiers created by the architect Sir Edwin Lutyens and landscape gardener Gertrude Jekyll. Up on the farmland plateau, the Manoir d'Ango is a Renaissance manor house with a beautiful dovecote.

At the foot of the Petit Ailly gorge you can wander along the stony shore under the towering cliffs. The artist Georges Braque, a founder of Cubism, is buried beside Varengeville's parish church, for which he designed one of the stained-glass windows.

▶ *Continue on the D75, then go into St-Aubin and follow signs to St-Valery-en-Caux, leaving it on the D925. Turn right to Veulettes-sur-Mer on the D79 then follow the signs to Fécamp.*

❷ Fécamp, Normandy

A fishing, freight and pleasure port at a dip in the cliffs, Fécamp has a shingle-bank beach and some remarkable places to visit. The Palais Bénédictine is the home of the liqueur of the same name, a distillation first carried out by monks of the Benedictine order, of 27 aromatic plants and spices whose precise recipe is a very closely guarded secret. There is a museum in the palace – a glorious 19th-century architectural confection of Gothic and Renaissance styles – which traces the history of Benedictine and also displays items of reli-

The painter Georges Braque (1882–1963) is buried in the churchyard at Varengeville-sur-Mer

gious art, furnishings and, in the Gothic hall, a magnificent oak and chestnut ceiling built by Fécamp shipwrights. The early Gothic abbey church, La Trinité, is enormous, its nave one of the longest in France.

As well as a fine art museum, the town also has the Musée des Terre-Neuves. While going back to the Vikings, who colonised this coast, it concentrates on the years when the local fishing fleet used to spend months among the great cod banks of Newfoundland.

i *Rue Alexandre le Grand*

▶ *Leave Fécamp on the D940 as for Etretat, then go right on the D211 through Yport and follow the D11 to Etretat.*

Malraux, shows works by Renoir, Pissarro, Sisley and Dufy among others. The Musée de l'Ancien Havre illustrates the history of the town. Perhaps the best view of Le Havre is from the high-set fort at Ste-Adresse, a suburb to the northwest, which housed the Belgian government in exile during World War I.

i   *Place de l'Hôtel de Ville*

FOR HISTORY BUFFS

In June 1940, while most of the British troops in France were being evacuated from Dunkirque, the 51st Highland Division was ordered to pull back to Le Havre. In this sacrificial manoeuvre, which helped to divert 10 German divisions, the Highlanders fought until their ammunition was exhausted, and thousands had to surrender at St-Valéry-en-Caux. A granite memorial on a hillside at St-Valéry commemorates the event, and the town is twinned with Inverness, the Highland capital.

▶ *Leave Le Havre on the N15 as for Rouen. Turn right for Trouville on the D40, then go straight on along the D29 and D28. Follow the D28 left as for Anquetierville, but bear right to avoid the village. Turn left at the T-junction for Caudebec-en-Caux.*

🟦 Etretat, Normandy

Nowhere on this coast matches Etretat for location. It lies behind a beach at the foot of a wooded valley. To north and south rise tall white cliffs with weathered natural arches and a great isolated needle rock a little way off shore.

Paths climb to the cliffs called Falaise d'Amont north of the town and the Falaise d'Aval to the south. Amont probably has the finer overall view, as well as a seafarers' chapel with fish carved in the stonework, and a museum to the aviators Nungesser and Coli, whose plane was last seen over Etretat before disappearing during the first attempt in 1927 to fly the Atlantic from east to west. There is also a dramatic memorial to them, with a mosaic tricolour of France.

i   *Place Maurice-Guillard*

▶ *Leave Etretat on the D940 to Le Havre.*

Guy de Maupassant compared the Falaise d'Aval to 'a carved elephant dipping its trunk in the sea'

FOR CHILDREN

By the beach at Etretat, look for the playground with games, a roller-skating rink, a model boat pond and an aquarium.

🟦 Le Havre, Normandy

Parts of Le Havre look curiously all of a piece with their postwar reinforced concrete buildings. The explanation for this is that the town was reduced to rubble in 1944, and had to be largely rebuilt after World War II.

Now it is once again a major freight and ferry port – the second busiest in France, occupying not only the traditional harbour area but also miles of riverside along the Seine. You can take a harbour cruise.

A splendid fine arts museum, Musée des Beaux-Arts André-

🟦 Caudebec-en-Caux, Normandy

Just downstream from the Pont de Brotonne suspension bridge which soars over the Seine, Caudebec is ideally situated to show off the commercial life of the river, to and from the container port at Rouen. The Musée de la Marine de Seine covers the history of river boats and river traffic.

Look for the remarkable Church of Notre Dame in 15th- and 16th-century Flamboyant Gothic style. It has a lovely fretted roof and a west frontage like lacework in stone, with 300 now heavily weathered figures of saints, prophets, musicians and gentlefolk of the town.

A stunning memorial beside the main road commemorates the Caudebec-built Latham seaplane which was lost in 1928 during a rescue mission in the Arctic. Roald Amundsen, discoverer of the South Pole, was one of the crew.

> [i] *Quai Guilbaud*

> ► *Leave Caudebec-en-Caux on the **D982** then turn left to cross the Pont de Brotonne. Go right on the **D65**, left on the **D40**, then bear left to La Haye-de-Routot.*

6 La Haye-de-Routot,
Normandy
This fascinating village lies in farmland on the edge of the Fôret de Brotonne. La Haye's Four à Pain is a restored 19th-century brick-built bakehouse, run as a working museum. The Musée du Sabotier is a work-shop museum devoted to clogs (*sabots*). In early summer, look for the 15m (50-foot) pyramid of wood which, on the morning of 16 July, is set alight to create the Feu de St Clair, an old pagan ritual taken over by the

Christian church. Opposite the Four à Pain, a half-timbered cottage features a wall-niche model of the Feu de St Clair.

From the Café des Ifs (Yew-tree Café), marked walking routes radiate through the village and the forest.

> ► *Leave La Haye for Routot. Go left, then right, at stops signs, then continue through Bourneville as for Quillebeuf-sur-Seine. Go left on the **D95** to Ste-Opportune and straight on at crossroads following the 'Réserve de Faune' sign. Hairpin right at the T-junction. Turn left at the 3.5t sign, then left at the T-junction. Follow Honfleur signs uphill to the view indicator.*

7 Marais-Vernier,
Normandy
Bounded by an amphitheatre of wooded hills, this area was once marshland flooded by the Seine (*marais* means marsh). After vague earlier reclamation efforts, it was at the beginning of the 17th century that Dutch workers dug channels to drain the southern part of the marsh. They are still recalled in the name of the Digue des Hollandais (the Dutchmen's Dyke) alongside the D103.

North of that road, the work was tackled only in 1947.

Now the Marais-Vernier is mostly lush grazing land for Camargue horses and Highland cattle. Some pockets of boggy ground remain, and there are central scrubby woodlands. In spring, pink and white blossom embellishes the surrounding farmland. La Grande Mare is the lake to which most of the drainage water flows on its way eventually to the Seine.

BACK TO NATURE

Where the main route turns sharp right after Ste-Opportune, bear left and after about 0.8km (½-mile) watch for the 'Reserve de Faune' car park. A steeply stepped view-ing tower overlooks the nature reserve around the Grande Mare. You will often see mal-lards, coots, grebes, teal, pochard and tufted duck on the lake itself or in the reed beds and drainage channels round it. Grey herons and Cetti's warblers are present, but more secretive.

Fifteenth-century Notre-Dame Church at Caudebec-en-Caux

▶ *After the view indicator, go right on the D100 to St-Samson then left past the church on the D39. Bear right to the give-way sign then left at the T-junction on the N178. Go first right and follow the signs to Honfleur.*

8 Honfleur, Normandy

To all its other attractions, Honfleur adds the lovely old slate-roofed houses overlooking the sheltered harbour of the Vieux Bassin and, near by, some splendid survivals like the Grenier à Sel (salt stores) in the Rue de la Ville.

Erik Satie, the composer, was born in this fishing town. So was the artist Eugène Boudin, still admired for his skyscapes and his ability to 'paint the wind'. His work is featured in the museum which bears his name. Another museum has 12 rooms richly furnished in traditional Norman style and offers visits to the old town prison. The Musée de la Marine is lavishly stocked with ship models and other memorabilia of the sea.

Honfleur commemorates Samuel de Champlain. It was from here, on eight great voyages between 1603 and 1620, that he explored Canada, claimed it for France and founded the city of Quebec.

ⓘ *Place Boudin*

▶ *Leave Honfleur by the Rue de la République as for Pont-l'Evêque, then go left as for Tancarville on the D17. Turn right on to the N175 then left on the D534 to Cormeilles. Leave Cormeilles on the D810, continue into Lieurey and follow the D137 to Pont-Authou. Go right on the D130 then left on the D39 to Le Bec-Hellouin.*

9 Le Bec-Hellouin, Normandy

This is a lovely hillside village, massed with flowers, including rosebeds by the timbered houses on the square. Many old buildings survive here, from the tiny red-tiled wash-house by a fast-flowing stream to the stalwart ruins of what was once a powerful abbey dating back to 1040. It has a great reputation as a centre of theological learning, and three of its 'sons' became archbishops of Canterbury – Lanfranc in 1070, Anselm in 1093 and Theobald in 1138. A motor museum occupies the parkland of the old abbey church. It displays luxury, sports

The calm of Honfleur harbour belies the town's turbulent past

and racing cars from 1920 onwards, including seven Bugattis.

16th centuries – contributed to the appearance of the cathedral in its doorways, towers, tombs, side chapels and stained-glass windows. From a distance, though, the most remarkable feature of the building is the tall, slim, tapering steeple added in the 19th century. Built entirely of fretted cast iron, it arrows towards the sky. There are museums here devoted to wrought ironwork (Musée Le-Seq-des-Tournelles), and the novelist Gustave Flaubert (in the suburb of Croisset). And

▶ Continue on the **D39** then go left on the **N138**. At the stop sign, go straight ahead on the **D3** as for Rouen, through Moulineaux. Turn right at traffic lights as for Elbeuf, and right over the level crossing. Go sharp left on the **N238** and follow the signs to Rouen.

10 Rouen, Normandy
The glory of the historic capital of Normandy is the magnificent Gothic Cathedral of Notre-Dame in the midst of a splendid 'old town' carefully restored after the devastation of World War II. Rouen's tourist office, for instance, occupies a very attractive Renaissance building, once the headquarters of the tax collector.

Architects and artists of many different eras – mainly 13th to

there is also a wax museum devoted to Jeanne d'Arc (Joan of Arc). After Rouen was lost to the English in the Hundred Years' War, it was here than Joan was brought as a prisoner and subjected to a shameful trial. Its aftermath was even more despicable when, her life having been previously spared, she was burned at the stake in the old marketplace. She was canonised in 1920. The Musée des Beaux-Arts has a good collection of 17th- to 20th-century French paintings.

ℹ️ *Place de la Cathédrale*

▶ *Leave Rouen on the **N28** then go left on the **D928**, left on the **D151** to Bellencombre and left again on the **D154** to Dieppe.*

Richard the Lionheart's tomb in Rouen Cathedral

The Emerald
Country

Starting from Rennes, the capital of Brittany, this tour is drawn briefly into Normandy to visit Mont-St-Michel on its fortified tidal island. Along the Brittany coastline there are headlands offering magnificent views, then it's inland to historic towns such as Vitré, Fougères and Dinan, and St-Malo, on the coast.

3 DAYS • 392KM • 243 MILES

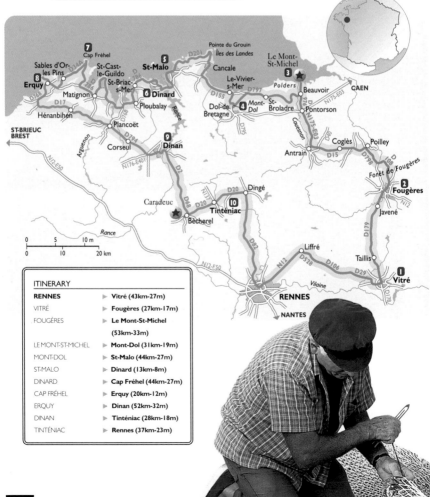

i *Quai Chateaubriand, Rennes*

▶ *Leave Rennes as for Fougères on the N12. Go right on the D528 to Liffré and in the town centre turn right for Vitré via La Bouëxière. Enter Vitré on the D857.*

FOR HISTORY BUFFS

The Musée Automobile de Bretagne on the N12 after Rennes, tells the story of the French motor industry through such fine exhibits as a 1904 Renault with a basketwork canister for the passengers' canes and parasols. Veteran posters and accessories are also on display.

---

❶ Vitré, Brittany

In the days when Brittany was separate from France, Vitré was a frontier fortress. Its triangular-plan castle, high above the River Vilaine, houses the town museum in three of its towers. A fourth provides an all-encompassing viewpoint. Many medieval and Renaissance buildings are still in use. The Centre Social, for instance, occupies a splendid 16th-century mansion with elaborate windows, doors and rooflines. Beautifully restored, the Rue de la Beaudrairie was the leather-workers' quarter.

Walks lead down into the pleasant valley of the Vilaine. On the southern outskirts, in the unlikely setting of an industrial estate, look for the Musée de l'Abeille Vivante (Museum of the Living Bee). Here you can see not only displays on all aspects of bee-keeping but also five colonies working in glass-sided hives.

i *Place St Yves*

▶ *Leave Vitré for 'Fougères par Taillis' on the D179.*

❷ Fougères, Brittany

The most important feature of this second medieval fortress town is the huge and superb castle on a peninsula site all but encircled by the Nançon river. But delay going to the castle itself until you have looked at it from the attractive Jardin Public in the high town. Its situation and layout are seen to best effect from the garden (despite the background scar of a modern quarry). Below the castle, the low town retains many fine buildings, such as the Flamboyant Gothic Church of St-Sulpice and the 17th-century houses round the Place du Marchaix. In the high town, one 16th-century house is now the Musée Emmanuel de la Villéon, devoted to the locally-born artist who was one of the last Impressionists.

i *Place Aristide-Briand*

RECOMMENDED WALKS

Ask at the tourist office at Rennes or Fougères for the leaflet showing the footpaths in the Forêt de Fougères. One, which crosses the route at the Carrefour du Père Tacot, wanders through the beechwoods, passes a line of druids' stones and follows the shore of a recreational lake.

Traditional-style half-timbered houses in Rennes

ⓘ *Corps de Garde des Bourgeois*

▶ *Return to Beauvoir. Turn right for Les Polders, over the bridge and immediately left. Turn left at the first stop sign and right at the second stop sign. Go right on the D797 through St-Broladre, left on the D82 then right on the V5 to the village of Mont-Dol. Watch for a right turn before the Hôtel du Tertre up a steep and narrow road to Sommet du Mont-Dol.*

FOR CHILDREN

On the way back from Le Mont-St-Michel, call in at the Reptilarium in Beauvoir and let the children see the great crocodiles, iguanas, lizards, pythons and boa-constrictors.

---

❹ Mont-Dol, Brittany

From this hilltop with its marvellous 360-degree view, the first thing to notice is the great area of rich, reclaimed marsh-land of the 'polders' – as in the Netherlands – that you crossed after Beauvoir. Beyond them, across the bay, lies Mont-St-Michel.

A good display map shows the features of Mont-Dol itself – which include the scenes of the legendary struggle between St Michael and the Devil. There is also a chapel, an old seaward signalling tower, two 19th-century windmills and other features that add interest to a stroll among the pines, gorse and rock outcrops of a very popular excursion site.

▶ *Return from the summit. Go right to pass the Hôtel du Tertre. Leave Mont-Dol village on the D123. Turn right on the D155 and follow the signs towards Cancale on the D76. Go right on the VC15 signed 'Cancale le Port'. Leave Cancale following 'St-Malo par la Côte' and 'Pointe du Grouin' signs along the D201. Go straight on along*

▶ *Leave Fougères as for St-Hilaire on the D177. Immediately after leaving Fougères bear right along a 'route forestière'. Go left at Carrefour du Père Tacot then straight on across the main road. At Carrefour des Serfilières bear left, taking the fourth exit. Turn right at the stop sign (this is the D108) to Parigné. Leave Parigné on the D108 as for Mellé. At the crossroads go straight on, avoiding the right turn to Mellé. Go right at the stop sign along the D798. Turn left on the D15 through Coglès, left briefly on the D296 then right on the D15 again. In Antrain, turn right at the stop sign to Pontorson and continue via Beauvoir to Le Mont-St-Michel.*

❸ Le Mont-St-Michel,
Normandy

From whatever angle, and from however far away, a first sight of this isolated tidal rock is a stunning experience. It rises from

Fougères Castle – a fine example of medieval military architecture

rampart walls and a clustered village to a magnificent abbey whose highest steeple spears the sky. Reached by a causeway once served by an engaging steam tramway, Mont-St-Michel lies among the mazy channels of a vast encircling bay. The lowest towers and medieval sea-wall protect a village of lanes and stairways, where the Musée Grevin tells the story of the abbey and the island community in a series of tableaux, and the Archéoscope elaborates it with sound and lighting effects. More prosaically, the Musée de la Mer places the island in its marine and tidal context.

Crowning the granite summit, the abbey dedicated to the Archangel Michael is a triumph of Romanesque and then Gothic design. Finest of all the architecture are the 13th-century buildings which include the refectory and cloisters.

*the **C6** to Pointe du Grouin
then return to the **D201** for
St-Malo.*

8 St-Malo, Brittany

An extensive area of sheltered
harbours continues the long
maritime tradition of a town
which was the historic base for
privateers, explorers and the
16th-century Newfoundland
fishing fleets. The heart of St-
Malo is the granite-built district
known as Intra Muros, inside
the coastal rampart walls. It is
almost entirely a reconstruction
from the rubble of World War II.
Look here for the historical
Musée de la Ville in the 15th-
century castle whose great keep
and towers command impressive views of the harbour. Quic-
en-Groigne is a waxwork
museum recalling famous St-
Malo characters and events.
There is a well-stocked aquarium as well as a museum of
dolls and old-time toys.

Ferries sail to destinations
along the coast, and there is a
hydrofoil service to Jersey. But
the Château de Solidor recalls
much grander voyages: it houses
displays on the Cape Horners.

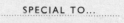

[i] *Esplanade St-Vincent*

▶ *Leave St-Malo as for Dinard.
Go right on the **D114** and
right on the **D266** into
Dinard.*

St Malo was named after a Welsh
monk called Maclow

TOUR

3

The Emerald Country

⑥ Dinard, Brittany

To a beautiful seafront of bays, promontories, sandy beaches and offshore rocky islets, Dinard adds hotels, restaurants, a casino, a golf club, an equestrian centre and other sporting facilities to maintain its reputation as the premier resort of Brittany's Emerald Coast. The weather is mild, some of the vegetation Mediterranean along the footpaths which wander by the coast.

Fine villas stand in lovely wooded grounds, many of them dating from the turn of the century when British high society favoured Dinard – Edward VII and George V are remembered in street names today.

Dinard attracts many musical, film and artistic events. Every summer evening at dusk there is a *son et lumière* presentation on the seafront Promenade du Clair de Lune.

[i] *Boulevard Féart*

▶ *Leave Dinard on the D786 through St-Briac-sur-Mer and continue as for St-Brieuc. After Port-à-la-Duc turn right to Cap Fréhel on the D16.*

⑦ Cap Fréhel, Brittany

In the 1920s a company tried to sell off building plots on this dramatic cliff-ringed headland. Fortunately, the misbegotten scheme failed. From the approach road, you may think that the cape ends at the lighthouse – completed in 1847, immense care having been paid to the design and the masonry work (visits can be arranged most afternoons) – and the 18th-century fortification known as the Tour Vauban. In fact, Fréhel extends much further out to sea.

A stroll around the cape, whose majestic rock stacks are a nature reserve, opens up views into precipitous wave-lashed inlets as well as southeastwards to the spectacularly located Fort la Latte, a medieval fortress situated on a headland some 4km (2½ miles) away.

[i] *Tour Vauban*

BACK TO NATURE

Cap Fréhel and its offshore rock stacks are busy with gulls, fulmars, cormorants and guillemots, for whom this is France's premier nesting area. In summer the approach to the cape is purple with heather and gold with the flowers of gorse and bird's-foot trefoil.

FOR CHILDREN

Sables-d'Or-les-Pins, after Cap Fréhel, caters well for children, with sandy beaches, pony rides, 'bouncy castles' and pedal cars for hire. Look for the little battery-powered electric cars. Kids love to drive these 'grown-up' vehicles on their own.

▶ *Return from Cap Fréhel and turn right on the D34a as for St-Brieuc. Rejoin the D786 for Erquy.*

⑧ Erquy, Brittany

Built round a west-facing bay well sheltered from the northerly wind, Erquy is a pleasant and unpretentious little resort with no trace of obtrusive modern building. The bay is busy with courses in canoeing and windsurfing, and there is a local shellfish fleet.

Take the road to the Cap d'Erquy and you will climb to an exhilarating headland where the heath and low-lying scrub are criss-crossed by wandering footpaths. There are cliff edges to be carefully explored, views to the broken water over dangerous offshore reefs, and a splendid if unexpected east-

The medieval town of Dinan on the River Rance, where boats depart for St-Malo and Dinard

facing beach. There are also ditches and other signs of prehistoric fortifications dated as early as 4,500 years ago.

[i] *Boulevard de la Mer*

▶ *Leave Erquy on the **D786** as for St-Brieuc, then go left for Dinan via Plancoët. Enter Dinan on the **N176**.*

9 Dinan, Brittany

Since its appearance in the Bayeux Tapestry, in the 11th century, Dinan has had a clear line of history, each era marked by its own architectural styles in ramparts, towers, gateways and attractive houses. Streets in the old town bear the names of medieval trade guilds. The castle is a fortress of mellow stonework whose unusual 14th-century oval keep houses the local museum. You can admire Dinan from the upper viewing gallery of the 15th-century belfry, the Tour de l'Horloge

(Clock Tower). Another good viewpoint, although disappointing as an actual garden, is the Jardin Anglais (English Garden). It overlooks the valley of the Rance, in which enticing footpaths lead under the stately viaduct over which you approached the town, towards the downstream quays.

In the Church of St Saveur is buried the heart of Bertrand du Guesclin, who fought in single combat in the Place du Champ Clos in 1359 to free his brother from his English captors.

[i] *Rue de l'Horloge*

▶ *Leave Dinan from Lanvallay and turn right through Évran on the **D2**, which becomes the **D68** as for Bécherel. In La Barre turn left for Tinténiac on the **D20**.*

10 Tinténiac, Brittany

The church here, with its cupolas and sturdy but ornate

stonework, looks slightly puzzling. In fact it is a complete turn-of-the-century rebuilding of an old ecclesiastical site, and well worth a visit.

Tinténiac lies on the Canal d'Ille et Rance. At the Quai de la Donac, a redundant grain store is now the Musée de l'Outil et des Métiers (Museum of Tools and Trades), displaying tools and machinery from half-forgotten rural trades.

East of Tinténiac, the Musée International de la Faune is a spacious zoo park which also features a scented rose garden and a well-equipped children's playground.

FOR HISTORY BUFFS

Before Tinténiac, turn right in La Barre, through Bécherel to the Parc de Caradeuc and its château. The 18th-century lawyer Caradeuc de la Chalotais was devoted to the independence of the Breton parliament. Louis XV imprisoned him without trial. A message he smuggled out of jail, written with a toothpick in ink made from soot, vinegar and sugar, caused a sensation.

▶ *Continue on the **D20** to Dingé. Watch for a right turn on the **D82** before the Confiserie/Épicerie shop. Return to Rennes.*

SCENIC ROUTES

Approaching Vitré, the D22 runs through a pleasant rural landscape, which continues along the D179 to Fougères, with long eastern views. Even at times of hectic traffic, the approach to stately Mont-St-Michel has a magic all its own.

The coastal stretch of the D155 looks over salt marshes and oyster beds to the rocky islets off Cancale. A succession of cliffs and sandy bays follows the D34a after Cap Fréhel.

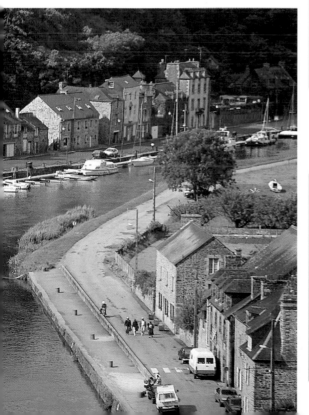

The Celtic
Connection

Quimper is the capital of old Cornouaille. This is Celtic country, as you will see from the place-names. The Breton language is still spoken by more than half a million people, giving western Brittany the position in France which Wales occupies in the UK.

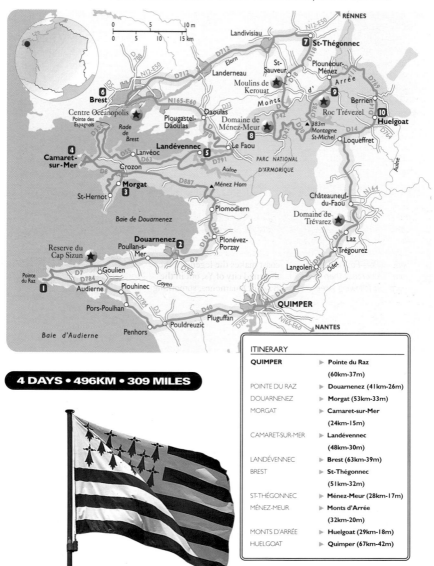

4 DAYS • 496KM • 309 MILES

ITINERARY		
QUIMPER	▶	**Pointe du Raz**
		(60km-37m)
POINTE DU RAZ	▶	**Douarnenez (41km-26m)**
DOUARNENEZ	▶	**Morgat (53km-33m)**
MORGAT	▶	**Camaret-sur-Mer**
		(24km-15m)
CAMARET-SUR-MER	▶	**Landévennec**
		(48km-30m)
LANDÉVENNEC	▶	**Brest (63km-39m)**
BREST	▶	**St-Thégonnec**
		(51km-32m)
ST-THÉGONNEC	▶	**Ménez-Meur (28km-17m)**
MÉNEZ-MEUR	▶	**Monts d'Arrée**
		(32km-20m)
MONTS D'ARRÉE	▶	**Huelgoat (29km-18m)**
HUELGOAT	▶	**Quimper (67km-42m)**

1 *Place de lu Résistance,
Quimper*

▶ *Leave Quimper on the **D785**
as for Pont l'Abbé, then
through Pluguffan and follow
the **D40** through Pouldreuzic
to Penhors. Bear right as for
Plozévet, then left, and follow
signs to Pors-Poulhan. Climb
from the harbour, then turn
sharp left following 'Allée
Couverte' sign. Turn left at two
stop signs. In Audierne, look
for 'Pointe du Raz' signs and
take the **D784** to Pointe du
Raz.*

0 Pointe du Raz, Brittany
One of Brittany's classic headlands plays host to a commercial
square of souvenir shops and
cafés. A wasteland of bare, trod-
den earth and rock leads
beyond the coastguard station to
the actual point, and then the
atmosphere changes. No care-
less exploitation can damage the
magnificent seaward views.
Pointe du Raz looks over a
savage strait where jagged
rocks, the last topped with a
lighthouse, march towards the
weird outline of the Île-de-Sein
– something like a Pacific atoll

moved to the windswept
Atlantic edge. Guides escort
parties of visitors round the cliff
paths, and with or without them
it is easy to appreciate why the
statue near the point is to *Notre-
Dame des Naufragés* – Our Lady
of the Shipwrecked. Knowing
that Sein was once the mainland
coast makes the legend of the
drowned city of Ys, out in the
Bay of Douarnenez, something
to ponder.

FOR HISTORY BUFFS

The Alée Couverte, at Pors-
Poulhan, is a reconstructed
burial chamber. Great rock
slabs form the walls and
others are laid across them
as the roof.

▶ *Return from Pointe du Raz
and turn left for Douarnenez
par le CD7 on the **V8** and
D7. On the approach to
Douarnenez, follow 'Autres
Directions' and 'Toutes
Directions' signs at round-
abouts, then turn left on
the **D765** and left to
Centre-Ville.*

Pointe du Raz, Cap Sizun – a
sanctuary for seabirds

BACK TO NATURE

Turn left off the D7 for the
Réserve Ornithologique on the
seabird cliffs of Cap Sizun. This
was the first bird reserve in
France with a definite
educational programme. The
movements and associations of
whole gull colonies are
followed by computer

2 Douarnenez, Brittany
Douarnenez is the fifth busiest
fishing port in France. The
narrow river inlet of Port-Rhu
slices deep into Douarnenez,
but the main harbour of
Rosmeur is on the east side of
the peninsula which it helps to
form. There are early morning
fish auctions here, and cruise
boats visit the cliffs, inlets and
grottoes of the bay. Town
beaches are scattered in some
unexpected locations, and a
good coastal walk leads from
Rosmeur along the Sentier des
Plomarc'hs. Le Port-Musée
opened in 1993. A tidal wall has

been built to dam a basin 2km long at Port Rhu. Visitors can explore dozens of boats and admire craftsmen rebuilding a 19th-century clipper. This floating museum is unique in France.

i Rue du Docteur Mével

▶ *Leave Douarnenez as for Brest on the **D7**, then turn left*

South of Morgat, just before the village of St-Hernot, the interesting Maison des Minéraux houses a fascinating array of crystals, fossils and semi-precious stones such as agates and amethysts from all over Brittany, in their natural state as well as cut and polished. Make sure you see the fluorescent cabinet where many of them gleam in exotic colours.

Vauban, the great 17th-century military architect, fortified Camaret. The local history museum in the Tour Vauban recalls events such as the British and Dutch landing of 1694, which was furiously and famously repulsed.

The prehistoric standing stones of Lagatjar retain their strict straight-line alignment and, to the south, the Pointe de

*on the **D107** to Plonévez-Porzay. Watch for the left turn on to the **D63**, then take the **D47** through Plomodiern and left to Ste-Marie. Turn left on the **D887**, right to the Ménez-Hom summit and return to the **D887**. Follow 'Morgat' signs through Crozon, watching for an unexpected left turn. In Morgat, follow 'Maison des Minéraux' signs towards St-Hernot.*

❸ Morgat, Brittany

This resort on the sheltered side of Douarnenez Bay is well equipped for watersports and enjoys good, extensive beaches with coastal promenades. There are daily summer cruises to the marine caverns of La Chambre du Diable (the Devil's Chamber), La Cheminée des Cormorans (the Cormorants' Chimney) and the loveliest, l'Autel (Altar Grotto).

i Boulevard de la Plage

▶ *After the Maison des Minéraux, bear right as for Kerdreux then almost immediately right at crossroads. Go straight on at the stop sign, follow 'Crozon' signs, then turn right at a T-junction (**D308**) into Crozon. At the roundabout, take the third exit along the **D8** to Camaret-sur-Mer.*

❹ Camaret-sur-Mer, Brittany

Set on a stunning peninsula, Camaret is a resort surrounded by beaches facing in different directions. A substantial crayfish fleet is based here, and some discarded fishing boats are beached as rotting hulks. Lobster is also fished locally, so the seafood restaurants, naturally, are well and freshly stocked.

Camaret-sur-Mer's beach is strewn with shipwrecks

Penhir is a majestic clifftop viewpoint with dramatic natural rock formations.

i Quai Kléber

BACK TO NATURE

Well out of reach of any road approach, the dramatic rock stacks of the Tas des Pois – the Pile of Peas – can be visited on the *Sirène IV*, which sails from Camaret. Their cliffs teem with gulls, fulmars, cormorants, guillemots and storm petrels.

▶ *Leave Camaret-sur-Mer on the **D355** to Pointe des Espagnols and through Roscanvel. At a roundabout take the **D55** to Lanvéoc,* *then the **D63** as for Brest. At the brow of a hill at Maison Blanche, watch for a left turn at crossroads. Turn right at the crossroads at a stop sign. At the give-way sign, turn left on the **D60** to Landévennec.*

5 **Landévennec,** Brittany
Occupying an attractive peninsula where the estuaries of the Aulne and the Faou combine, Landévennec is a village in which a glance down almost any lane offers a view of the water. Brittany's oldest abbey was founded here in 485 by the Welsh missionary St Gwennolé. It crumbled away after the Revolution. The ruins of the final Romanesque buildings are approached by a palm-tree avenue. Exhibitions explain the history of the abbey itself, and also how Brittany rose from the wreckage of the Roman Empire, colonised in Gwennolé's time by Celts driven from Britain by the Anglo-Saxon invasions.

▶ *Return along the **D60** to the **D791** and turn left. In Le Faou go left as for Hanvec, over a bridge and left – at first along the riverside – through Lanvoy. Turn left at a T-junction and through Daoulas on the **D770**. Follow signs for Brest on the **N165**.*

6 **Brest,** Brittany
For almost 2,000 years, the sea has been Brest's delight and its despair. From Roman times its great roadstead – perhaps the most beautiful in Europe, with its bays, peninsulas and feeder rivers – has been a naval base. Such places are vulnerable in time of conflict. Brest came out of World War II shattered by bombing raids. Even the street plan was redrawn, let alone the buildings. This remains the home of many capital ships. Only French citizens, though, may visit the base itself. Foreigners can take advantage of harbour cruises, and the Musée de la Marine, repository of Brest's tumultuous history,

housed in the medieval castle, is open to all. Excellent parks include the Vallon du Stangalard, with its lawns, lakes, tree-shaded walks and Conservatoire Botanique, preserving hundreds of endangered plant species.

One of Brest's newest attractions is Océanopolis, a fascinating complex of aquariums (the largest in Europe), marine exhibitions and pictures beamed from weather satellites in space.

Only the ruins of the Abbey of St Gwennolé testify to Landévennec's monastic beginnings

[i] *Place de la Liberté*

▶ *Leave Brest for Landerneau on the **D712**. Follow the 'Centre Ville' sign at a roundabout in Landerneau. Continue to Landivisiau, still on the **D712**, then as for Morlaix on to the **N12**. Take the exit for St-Thégonnec.*

7 **St-Thégonnec,** Brittany

In their parish closes, Breton villages vied for glory with their neighbours. At St-Thégonnec, the 16th- to 18th-century masonry work of the church is far more elaborate than is justified by the status of the little place. The churchyard gateway and the funeral chapel are similarly ornate, and the calvary of 1610, its clustered figures telling the story of the Passion, was one of the last in the exuberant Breton style. Inside the church, look for the intricately carved pulpit of 1683.

i *Rue de la Gare*

RECOMMENDED WALKS

The Pont Hir walk at St-Thégonnec follows a waymarked route across rural landscapes to an eerie tunnel taking the River Coatoulsac'h through a railway embankment. Another feature of the walk is a wood where you may easily surprise roe deer.

SPECIAL TO...

At the stop sign after Croas-Cabellec, turn left for the restored hamlet of Les Moulins-de-Kerouat, with its two antique watermills. Lessons are sometimes given on how to bake your own country-style bread. There is also the miller's home with its traditional furniture and an exhibition relating the history of the village through the lives of five generations of millers.

▶ *Leave St-Thégonnec as for Sizun on the* **D118**, *then the* **D18**. *After St-Sauveur, carry straight on at the crossroads at Croas-Cabellec, following '5 Sizun' sign. After a double-bend sign, take the first left, then go straight on at the stop sign as for Goas ar Vern. Follow the 'Barrage du Drennec' sign, then continue to St-Cadou. Turn right on the*

The numerous statuettes on St-Thégonnec's elegant 1610 calvary depict the Passion

D30, left on the **D130** *as for St-Eloy, and watch for a left turn to Ménez-Meur.*

8 **Ménez-Meur,** Brittany

The wooded surroundings of this estate conceal a series of open grazing areas where you can admire red, Sika and fallow deer, wild boars, several breeds of horses, and specialities such as Highland cattle and Swaledale sheep.

Ménez-Meur is approached along a beautiful avenue, where interlocking trees arch over from mossy walls. There are three waymarked trails with animal, forest and general countryside themes, and the estate is famous for its displays, fairs and festivals celebrating the sturdy Breton horse.

▶ *Continue to St-Rivoal on the* **D30**, *then turn left on the* **D785**.

9 **Monts d'Arrée,** Brittany

After Ferme St-Michel, now a showplace for modern Breton artists and craftworkers, the D785 runs along the upper reaches of the Monts d'Arrée,

where the Parc National d'Armorique opens out in a world of moorland summits. Mont St-Michel is one of the highest points, at 383m (1,256 feet). From it, a superb all-round view gives a slightly perplexing impression of a completely circular horizon. Roc Trévezel, further along the road, is a viewpoint granite tor.

RECOMMENDED WALKS

Ferme St-Michel is an access point to the footpaths shown in the Yeun Elez leaflet published by the Parc d'Armorique. One of them climbs the open moorland to Mont-St-Michel and circles back by the lovely countryside around St-Rivoal.

▶ Continue on the D785 to Plounéour-Ménez. Turn right on the D111, right on the D769 and follow signs to Huelgoat, turning right on the D14 in Berrien.

10 Huelgoat, Brittany
Built beside a peaceful lake, this is an inland resort with two contrasting characters. The town is bright and open, with lakeside walks, pedalo hire and fishing. Go to the bridge over the lake's outflow and you look immediately into a more dramatic world. From a chaos of jumbled rocks, footpaths wander through the most beautiful forest in Brittany. Beech, oak and conifers clothe the landscape of leafy glades, tumbling streams and mysterious Celtic stones, where the legends of King Arthur, Merlin and the Druids survive.

SPECIAL TO...

The Moulin du Chaos, in Huelgoat, is an old mill housing exhibits of archaeology, geology, flora and fauna.

Great moss-covered boulders litter the streams and tumbled hills in Huelgoat Forest

i   Place Aristide-Briand

FOR HISTORY BUFFS

On the return route to Quimper, the Maison des Pilhaouerien in Loqueffret recalls the 'rag and bone' families who, until the 1950s, toured the district with their donkey carts. After Châteauneuf-du-Faou, the rose castle in the beautiful park of Trévarez was one of the last built in France. During World War II it was a rest centre for the German Navy, until gutted in an RAF bombing raid. History, art and floral exhibitions are held here.

▶ Leave Huelgoat for Loqueffret on the D14. Turn sharp left on the D36 through Châteauneuf-du-Faou. Follow 'Domaine de Trévarez' signs, then continue on the D36 to Trégourez. Turn right on the D51 and return to Quimper.

SCENIC ROUTES

The Ménez-Hom road, the D83, climbs to one of the finest viewpoints in Brittany. After Camaret, the D355 rounds a peninsula with a beautiful outlook over the roadstead of Brest. Later, look for the view from the suspension bridge that takes the D791 over the River Aulne. Around St-Rivoal, the D342 is a lane set in wooded combes.

THE LOIRE & CENTRAL FRANCE

As it sweeps from the mountain country of the Central, by the Valley of the Loire and the Cognac vineyards, to the coastline and islands around La Rochelle, this area illustrates the great variety of landscape in France.

Not far from the industrial city of Clermont-Ferrand you drive through a country of ancient volcanoes, with high cattle pastures closed till the clearance of winter snows. In the valleys of the Loire and its principal tributaries you will encounter many of France's most magnificent castles. The 'conspicuous consumption' they represented was one of the elements which brought about the French Revolution. Fortunately, the major castles such as Chenonceau and Blois survive.

At high levels you will find windy, upland grazings and conifer plantings, and there is a chance of snow flurries even in late spring. Lower down lie arable and pastoral farms, but the finest ground, especially near Tours and along the valley of the River Charente, is reserved for vineyards. This is the country of Pays Nantais, Vouvray, Rosé d'Anjou, Cognac and Côtes d'Auvergne wines.

The two islands of Ré and Oléron are microcosmic worlds of their own. Rimmed by beautiful beaches and holiday resorts, with fine climates tempered by the Atlantic breezes, they have a strong off-season life. Farms, vines and oyster beds all play their part, and the little towns enjoy intriguing histories. Ré, for instance, was the last place on metropolitan French soil seen by criminals shipped to Devil's Island.

As in most of France, the road network is extensive. In some places, for instance approaching Angoulême on the La Rochelle tour in the attractive valley of the Charente, you should keep a close watch on the route instructions.

Recently, ferries to the major islands have been replaced. The drive to Ré is notable for the splendidly proportioned toll bridge from the mainland. This is how an island should be approached, on a dramatic, high-level curve.

Clermont-Ferrand

A great industrial centre in the heart of France, Clermont-Ferrand is the world headquarters of the Michelin tyre company. The city is dominated by its Gothic cathedral, but not far from it there stands another church of equal if not greater architectural merit, Notre-Dame-du-Port. The Musée des Beaux-Arts is housed in a wonderful old restored building. The Musée Bargoin recalls the victory of Vercingetorix and the Gauls over the legions of Julius Caesar, on the plateau of Gergovia near by.

Limoges

Limoges is the city of porcelain. Its Musée National Adrien-Dubouché shows porcelain in all its colour, elegance and stages of preparation. Enamelware is one of the specialities of the Musée Municipal. As in Clermont-Ferrand, there are attractive individual houses, churches and public buildings in Limoges, as well as gardens around the old Roman arena and overlooking the River Vézère.

La Rochelle

La Rochelle carefully guards its waterfront. Le Gabut is an engaging modern harbourside development whose colour-washed wooden buildings, with stairs and gangways, have a maritime air. The older houses have an agreeably regular appearance, forced on the builders by strict town-planning laws.

Museums here include one of mechanical toys, another of model ships, planes and railways, a third devoted to a century and a half of yacht racing. The maritime collection occupies a sturdy harbour-entrance tower, and there is a weathership museum and a major modern aquarium.

Nantes

Very much a river city, Nantes includes two channels of the Loire, three of its tributaries and, for good measure, a canal. The city centre has undergone a major face-lift and has an efficient modern tram newtork. Look for the moated castle of the dukes of Brittany, the cathedral, begun in 1434, the old quarters and the half-dozen parks, includ-

ing a riverside Japanese garden. A planetarium complements the nearby museum devoted to the life and works of the science fiction pioneer Jules Verne.

Tours

If you want to hear perfect spoken French, go to Tours. The capital of Touraine is spacious and unhurried, with elegant public buildings and a beautiful cathedral. There are promenades on rivers – the Loire and the Cher. The Château-Royal houses historical museums. The Musée des Beaux-Arts is in an archbishops' old palace. Archaeology, and Renaissance and medieval art are found in the Musée Archéologique in the superb 16th-century mansion called the Hôtel Gouin. Other museums and studios cover the wines of Touraine, dolls, gemstones and enamelwork, military transport, the story of journeymen-craftsmen and the handloom weaving of silk.

Opposite: Fontenay-le-Comte, an old market town on the Vendée
Below: Tours has managed to preserve (with much restoration) its historic heart

Land of Quiet
Volcanoes

Clermont-Ferrand has the advantage of backing immediately on to hill country, and these are no ordinary hills. They are the relics of huge volcanic convulsions thousands of years ago. Now green and wooded, they provide space in the valleys for holiday resorts, including spas whose thermal waters were famous in Roman times. The area's 20 mineral springs supply the nation with bottled water.

3 DAYS • 335KM • 209 MILES

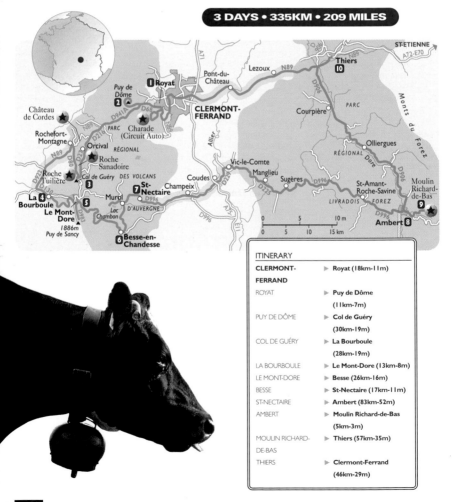

ITINERARY	
CLERMONT-FERRAND	▶ **Royat (18km-11m)**
ROYAT	▶ **Puy de Dôme (11km-7m)**
PUY DE DÔME	▶ **Col de Guéry (30km-19m)**
COL DE GUÉRY	▶ **La Bourboule (28km-19m)**
LA BOURBOULE	▶ **Le Mont-Dore (13km-8m)**
LE MONT-DORE	▶ **Besse (26km-16m)**
BESSE	▶ **St-Nectaire (17km-11m)**
ST-NECTAIRE	▶ **Ambert (83km-52m)**
AMBERT	▶ **Moulin Richard-de-Bas (5km-3m)**
MOULIN RICHARD-DE-BAS	▶ **Thiers (57km-35m)**
THIERS	▶ **Clermont-Ferrand (46km-29m)**

[i] *Boulevard Gergovia, Clermont-Ferrand*

▶ *Leave Clermont-Ferrand on the N89 as for Tulle. Go right on the D767 then right on the D941c to Royat.*

1 Royat, Auvergne

Not in the least overshadowed by its great industrial neighbour Clermont-Ferrand, Royat is a perfect example of a French spa which has moved with the times. Since Roman times, people have drunk the mineral waters and relaxed in thermal baths here for 2,000 years, but its development as a fashionable spa dates from the 19th century. Today everything is up to date, with attractive modern buildings. To the traditional 'cures' Royat has added keep-fit regimes and courses for anyone who wants to give up smoking.

Its central area is crammed into a narrow river valley where there is still room for parks and open spaces as well as for the Etablissement Thermal (Thermal Establishment) and the inevitable casino. Among the alleyways of the upper town, look for the Maison du Passé (House of the Past), the museum of old Royat, and for the Taillerie, where rock crystals and gemstones are cut and polished.

[i] *Place Allard*

SPECIAL TO...

Turn left off the D941c to follow the D5 to the motor racing circuit of Charade. It hosts important national races, but lost Grand Prix status some years ago. Jim Clark won the first French Grand Prix run on the circuit in 1965.

▶ *Leave Royat on the D68. Go left on the D941a and immediately right on the D68. Go straight on to join the toll road to the summit of Puy de Dôme. Check for 'ouvert' sign.*

2 Puy de Dôme, Auvergne

The toll road to this volcanic summit spirals upwards at an average gradient of 12 per cent (1 in 8.3). It reaches a high-level world apart – Puy de Dôme is a glorious viewpoint, a spectacular hang-gliders' launch area, the site of a Roman temple, dedicated to Mercury and an exhilarating walkers' hill. You may be lucky enough to see colourful hot-air balloons wafting across the lovely Auvergne countryside. The modern world, in the form of an observatory, television mast and souvenir shop, is also present on top. Access to the Puy de Dôme is a fascinating story and many old illustrations are displayed locally. The first car reached the summit in 1913, but in those days the usual way up was by a steam train. The toll road opened only in 1926. On the summit look for

Imposing Puy de Dôme, the highest peak (1,416m/4,645 feet) in an extinct volcanic chain

the statue of Eugène Renaux. In 1911 his biplane landed safely on the plateau at the end of a prize-winning flight from Paris. The elegant lava and wood buildings covered with copper roofs house a reception and information centre.

SPECIAL TO...

Just before the junction with the D941a, the Village Auvergnat is a recently built centre where many of the specialities of the region are on sale, including honey, jams, liqueurs, the well-known local cheese and Côtes d'Auvergne wines.

FOR CHILDREN

Before the Puy de Dôme toll road, the Zoo des Dômes includes an imaginative children's playground. The 'mini-plane' roundabout introduces youngsters to the thrills of hang-gliding without actually launching them into the air.

BACK TO NATURE

At 1,465m (4,085 feet) the Puy de Dôme is the highest of 80 extinct volcanoes in the district. It dominates a characteristic volcanic landscape. Some hills retain their hollow crater shapes; others are the old volcanic cores. Flowers and butterflies are abundant, and look for red kites and honey buzzards in the skies above.

▶ *Return to the* **D941a** *and turn right. Go straight ahead on the* **D216** *then on the* **D27** *and on the* **D983**. *Stop at a major car park immediately before the junction with the* **D80**.

3 Col de Guéry, Auvergne

This is one of the most dramatic viewpoints in the Auvergne, looking down the precipitous valley between La Roche Tuilière and La Roche Sanadoire.

These two huge rock towers rise from a wooded crater and are the remains of a volcanic eruption which occurred something like two millions years ago. Like the Puy de Dôme, they are included in the biggest regional nature park in France, the Parc des Volcans d'Auvergne (Regional Nature Park of Auvergne Volcanoes).

Tuilière, as you will see close up later from the D80, was the vent of the volcano, whose lava spewed out from the earth's molten core and cooled into the tall, brittle columns exposed today. Sanadoire was part of the cone. But the landscape was shaped by more than just volcanic activity: the valley between the rock towers was ground out by a retreating Ice Age glacier.

▶ *Turn right on the* **D80** *to Rochefort-Montagne, then turn left and follow the* **N89** *and* **D922** *to La Bourboule.*

4 La Bourboule, Auvergne

Two thermal establishments continue the spa traditions of this little valley town where tree-lined streets follow the banks of the upper Dordogne. The mineral waters here contain arsenic – in medicinal, not murderous proportions. La Bourboule is very well supplied with sports facilities, and has many attractions for children, including a model train museum and another devoted to fairy-tales.

The Parc Fenestre is a pleasant wooded area with pathways, a lake and a narrow-gauge railway. It also houses the town station for the cable-car system to the Plateau de Charlannes. At 1,250m (4,100 feet), Charlannes is a place of wide-ranging views, and a ski resort in winter. For a more intimate view of La Bourboule itself, walk up to the granite boulder called Le Rocher des Fées (the Fairies' Rock) which rises some 50m (165 feet) over the town to the northwest.

ⓘ *Place de l'Hôtel de Ville*

The pretty spa of La Bourboule is also a thriving winter resort

but a forest clearing reached by
a funicular railway (built in
1898 and now a historic monument) and then a final climb on
foot. The superlative high-spot
of Le Mont-Dore is up the
D983 as it climbs a steeply
wooded valley to the ski runs
and chairlifts on the alpine
meadows below the Puy de
Sancy. Be ready for a drop in
temperature. Take a cable-car
and then walk to the summit at
1,885m (6,180 feet), to admire
the colossal views from the
highest point in the Auvergne.

6 Besse-en-Chandesse,
Auvergne
This is an engaging little town
which has preserved, in narrow

▶ *Leave La Bourboule on the
D130 to Le Mont-Dore.*

5 Le Mont-Dore, Auvergne
Upstream from La Bourboule,
here is another spa resort. Le
Mont-Dore is well known for
activities as diverse as fishing,
mountaineering and amateur
classical music. Instrumentalists
and singers from all over France
gather here to practise, rehearse
and perform in concert. The
Promenade des Artistes is a
pleasant walk on the woodland
ridge overlooking the town.
There are higher attractions
here, too: the Salon du
Capuchin for instance, is not
some elegant town-centre hall,

i **Place de l'Hôtel de Ville**

▶ *Return on the **D983** from the
Puy de Sancy, then right on
the road signed 'Besse par
Col-Croix St Robert'. Check
'ouvert' sign. Follow the **D36**
to Besse-en-Chandesse.*

The pleasant little village of Orcival
nestles among the hills on the
banks of the Sioulet

streets and tiny squares, many
old houses from the 15th and
16th centuries. Some have
connecting doors which allow
the townspeople – walking
through their neighbours'
homes – to reach the church in
winter while avoiding the chill
open air. The Auvergne has
snowy winters, and Besse has
created a satellite ski resort
called Super-Besse. One fascinating place to visit in the old
town is a ski museum, the first
in France. Here, Pierre-André
Chauvet has assembled a

remarkable collection of skiing memorabilia. There are skis and bindings ancient and modern, of many different styles, from France, Switzerland, Norway, Sweden and the Austro-Hungarian empire. Illustrations cover curiosities such as historic Russian army snowploughs, and early events of the pioneering ski club of Besse, founded in 1902.

i *Place Docteur-Piper*

▶ *Leave Besse on the **D5** to Murol then go right on the **D996** to St-Nectaire.*

7 St-Nectaire, Auvergne

One of the most exuberant of the typical Romanesque churches of the Auvergne is the one in this village split into upper and lower parts in the winding and wooded valley of the Courançon. A hundred and more ornamented pillars surround the nave and the choir.

The Maison du St-Nectaire allows you the chance to sample the local cheese – St-Nectaire gave its name to a round, nutty-flavoured cheese made in many parts of the Auvergne – as well as the wines and bayberry liqueur special to the district.

St-Nectaire is another spa. There are modern thermal baths, but at the Cornadore grotto you can see the naturally warm water welling up. Try the mineral waters at a little pavilion in the parkland at Les Thermes.

i *Les Thermes*

▶ *Continue on the **D996** to Champeix. Follow signs to Coudes and Vic-le-Comte, then continue on the **D225** and **D996** (sometimes signed **N496**) to Ambert.*

FOR HISTORY BUFFS

A Scottish-Auvergne connection exists in the 16th-century Sainte-Chapelle at Vic-le-Comte, built for Jean (or John) Stuart, a descendant of the Scottish royal family and regent of Scotland during James V's minority. He was Duke of Albany and Comte d'Auvergne. The chapel features an unexpectedly light interior and a splendid balustraded gallery with statues of the Apostles. There are also remains of the castle of the Comtes d'Auvergne.

The Puy de Sancy, at 1,886m (6,185 feet), is the highest peak in the Massif Central

8 Ambert, Auvergne

Two notable buildings here are the granite church of St John and the curious town hall. Begun in 1471 in Flamboyant Gothic style, and decorated by a master mason obviously enjoying himself, St-Jean Church has later additions such as a frisky little Renaissance belfry. Look for the carved coat of arms of Ambert's old trade guilds – saddlers, shoemakers and the rest – and for the optical illusion which makes the interior seem longer than it really is.

The Hôtel de Ville (town hall) is entirely circular and arcaded all the way round. It was built in 1820 as the grain market. In the industrial area, a splendid museum of steam and traction engines, road rollers, tractors and mobile distillation plants is known, thanks to the French passion for acronyms, as AGRIVAP.

In the centre of town a museum of a different kind is devoted to the 'divine cheese' Fourme d'Ambert. Tasting sessions follow the guided tour.

i *Place de l'Hôtel de Ville*

▶ *Leave Ambert on the **D57** for Moulin Richard-de-Bas.*

9 **Moulin Richard-de-Bas,** Auvergne

Traditional papermaking is one of the most fascinating industrial processes. This restored 14th-century mill in the valley of the River Laga, which still turns its waterwheel, tells the story of papermaking from ancient Egyptian papyrus via the strict rules of the craft laid down by the Chinese in about 14th-century mill in the valley AD105, to the Arabs' discovery of its secrets from Chinese soldiers captured in the defence of Samarkand in 751, and on beyond the invention of mechanical printing.

All the traditional processes of crushing linen into the basic pulp, the smoothing, drying and pressing are displayed. There are early manuscripts on show, a gorgeous 18th-century atlas, a mid-19th-century printing press, parchments, vellums and thousands of watermarks.

Richard-de-Bas also produces papers of the highest quality. One speciality, made when the petals of cornflowers and marigolds from the mill's own gardens are mixed with the pulp, is flowered paper, where each sheet is individually patterned.

▶ *Return to Ambert and take the **D906** then the **N89** to Thiers.*

10 **Thiers,** Auvergne

France's 'capital of cutlery' is an attractive town with its red roofs rising on a hillside from a bend on the River Durolle. Many fine medieval and later half-timbered houses survive along the steep streets of the old quarter.

The museum and workshop of La Maison de Couteliers display an astonishing variety of knives, scissors, table settings and hallmarks. There are workshops all over the town where modern craftsmen and designers keep up the ancient tradition. Down on the Durolle, several little waterfalls used to provide power for the cutlery factories. Look for the Creux d'Enfer, much less forbidding than its name – the 'Drop to Hell' – suggests.

i *Place du Pirou*

A papermaker at work in Moulin Richard-de-Bas

▶ *Return from Thiers on the **N89** and continue to Clermont-Ferrand.*

TOUR
6

Heartland
of France

Porcelain from Limoges and tapestries from Aubusson are two of the main features of this tour, where historic towns are matched by fine recreational facilities, especially on and around two beautiful wooded reservoirs. Limoges, the starting point, has been an industrial centre for centuries and is still expanding.

3/4 DAYS • 411KM • 255 MILES

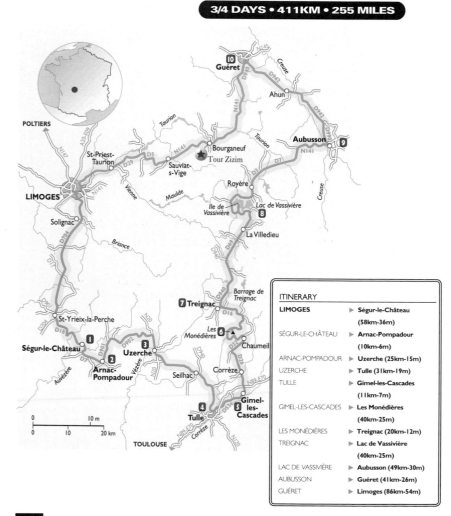

ITINERARY		
LIMOGES	▶	**Ségur-le-Château** (58km-36m)
SÉGUR-LE-CHÂTEAU	▶	**Arnac-Pompadour** (10km-6m)
ARNAC-POMPADOUR	▶	**Uzerche** (25km-15m)
UZERCHE	▶	**Tulle** (31km-19m)
TULLE	▶	**Gimel-les-Cascades** (11km-7m)
GIMEL-LES-CASCADES	▶	**Les Monédières** (40km-25m)
LES MONÉDIÈRES	▶	**Treignac** (20km-12m)
TREIGNAC	▶	**Lac de Vassivière** (40km-25m)
LAC DE VASSIVIÈRE	▶	**Aubusson** (49km-30m)
AUBUSSON	▶	**Guéret** (41km-26m)
GUÉRET	▶	**Limoges** (86km-54m)

i *Boulevard Fleurus, Limoges*

▶ *Leave Limoges on the D704
to St-Yrieix-la-Perche, then
take the D18, which becomes
the D6, to Ségur-le-Château.*

❶ Ségur-le-Château,
Limousin

You may be mystified by the
number of rivers at Ségur. In
fact, they are all the Auvézère,
which double loops through a
narrow, winding valley. The tiny
medieval town has long since
lost its influential position, but
once-aristocratic mansions still
fight off the years. Riverside
mills remain in place, the ruined
12th-century castle broods
absent-mindedly on its hilltop,
and in summer the 15th-century
Tour St Laurent shows off
embroidery, lace, dolls and other
souvenirs of days gone by.

RECOMMENDED WALKS

Clearly waymarked from the
D6 through Ségur-le-Château,
four numbered pathways
explore a beautiful countryside
of modest hills and woodlands.
The 'rivers and streams' walk
wanders along the banks of the
Auvézère, and there are fine
views down to the river from
the low ridges which follow its
winding course.

SPECIAL TO...

Ségur-le-Château is noted for
the craft of working with
chestnut wood. By the
riverside here look for the little hut with a display illustrating the work of the *feuillardiers*
– the woodcutters who
supplied the chestnut stakes
for the plants in the Périgord
vineyards. Dozens of
craftsmen in the district still
work with chestnut wood.

FOR HISTORY BUFFS

Turn right at the entrance to
St-Yrieix on the way from
Limoges to Ségur-le-Château,
for the unobtrusive but well-
stocked Musée de la Porcelaine
at the Les Palloux china factory. Limoges, Meissen, Delft,
Chinese and Japanese figures,
vases and dinner services are
all on display. It was the kaolin
deposits of St-Yrieix which
launched the porcelain industry
at Limoges.
On the return route to
Limoges, La Tour de Zizim in
Bourganeuf was the home (or,
in some versions of the story,
the prison) of an exiled 15th-
century Ottoman prince who
equipped it with Turkish baths
and even a harem. It is now a
museum with less glamorous
exhibits.

The tiny medieval town of
Ségur-le-Château

❷ Arnac-Pompadour,
Limousin

In the 18th century this was the
estate of the Marquise de
Pompadour. Since 1872 it has
been the home of the French
National Stud Farm, devoted
principally to the breeding of
Anglo-Arab horses. The stal-
lions are stabled in the Puy
Marmont; La Jumenterie de la
Rivière is the home of the
mares and their foals. Flat and
cross-country races, show-jumping and carriage-driving events
are held regularly.

i *Château de Pompadour*

▶ *Leave Arnac-Pompadour on
the D901 to Lubersac, then
follow the D902 and turn
right on the N20 to Uzerche.*

▶ *Continue on the D6, then the
D7 to Arnac-Pompadour.*

3 Uzerche, Limousin
Historic gateways and fine old houses with towers, turrets, carved lintels, ornamented windows and heraldic designs are all preserved here. Uzerche stands on a peninsula ridge bounded on three sides by the River Vézère, and there are attractive views from the high-set Esplanade de la Lunade. Behind the esplanade, the Romanesque Church of St-Pierre features an eerily impressive crypt built around 1030.

[i] *Place de la Lunarde*

▶ *Leave Uzerche on the N20, then immediately take the N120 to Tulle.*

4 Tulle, Limousin
You may find this a place of odd contrasts. The pleasant approach road swinging down wooded valleys arrives at a town whose modern parts are dull; but it has a fascinating old quarter crossed by lanes and stairways, and there is a bustle around its riverside quays. Tulle gave its name to a fine-woven silk, but one of its main

industries now is armaments.

There is some fine modern stained glass in the 12th-century cathedral, and the Musée de la Cloître, built round the arcades and gardens of a dignified old Benedictine monastery, illustrates local history in a quiet and peaceful setting. Paintings, sculptures, porcelain and archaeological finds share a building with historic firearms.

You will need a strong stomach to look over some of the illustrations in the Musée de la Résistance et de la Déportation, which recalls the grim days of World War II when many local men were deported, never to be heard of again.

[i] *Quai Baluze*

▶ *Leave Tulle as for Clermont-Ferrand. After a hairpin climb out of the built-up area, go straight on under a bridge, following the D9 then the D53e to Gimel-les-Cascades.*

5 Gimel-les-Cascades, Limousin
On the approach to Gimel, try to catch a glimpse of the dash-

ing waterfalls of the Montane which gave the village its name. From Gimel itself there is a dramatic outlook down a steeply wooded ravine. Footpaths wander past the spray-soaked triple falls. Although nowadays it is off the main roads, a hint of Gimel's previous religious importance is given by the great treasure of its parish church – a 12th-century gold and bejewelled reliquary of St Stephen. The saint's stoning to death is one of the scenes picked out in fine enamel and precious stones.

▶ *Leave Gimel-les-Cascades following the 'Tulle 13' sign. Turn right following the 'Etang de Ruffaud' signs, then follow 'Gare de Corrèze' and 'vers RN 89' signs. Cross the N89 and continue on the D26 through Corrèze. Go right on the D32 to Chaumeil, left on the D121, right on the D128 as for Lestards, then take a side road right to Les Monédières.*

Uzerche, the 'Pearl of Limousin', stands on a spur above the Vézère

6 Les Monédières, Limousin
At about 911m (2,990 feet) above sea-level, the summit here is a magnificent all-round viewpoint. Many of the faraway hills are *puys* – the remains of extinct volcanoes. The hilltop is a favourite launching-place for hang-gliders.

▶ Return to the **D128** and turn right following 'Chaumeil' sign. Go left on the **D32** to Lestards then left on the **D16** to Treignac.

Lac de Vassivière offers many facilities for sports

7 Treignac, Limousin
Roofs are slaty-grey here, a sign that this is a different part of the country from the warmer villages visited before Les Monédières. There is a fine view of the town from a viewpoint tower in the centre, but Treignac demands closer investigation before it reveals its old buildings in medieval and Renaissance styles. They descend to the Vézère river, which is crossed by a 15th-century bridge. A museum exhibits historic furnishings, craft and farm tools, weaving equipment and local ironwork. The restored parish church displays locally-worked stained glass and there is a simple little chapel, reached by a walk past the Stations of the Cross, which offers a good view westwards through a woodland clearing.

▶ Leave Treignac on the **D940** as for Eymoutiers. Turn right on the **D132e** which becomes the **D69**, signed 'Lac

---

RECOMMENDED WALKS

Treignac offers high- and low-level paths, some to hilltop viewpoints. Best of these is the walk past the local hospital, by wooded lanes and an open hillside, to the poised granite boulder called La Pierre des Druides (the Druids' Stone).

BACK TO NATURE

In the winding gorge of the Vézère just below Treignac, the Rocher des Folles is a series of granite pillars on the edge of a weathered cliff.

---

de Vassivière'. Go right on the **D992** to La Villedieu, where you should watch for a left turn on the **D34**. Go straight on avoiding a '19t' sign, left at a Stop sign as for Beaumont, then follow signs 'Ile de Vassivière'.

try workshops and studios are open to visitors. They work on a full range of designs, from copies of the style of Louis XIV's reign to something suitable for France's TGV superexpress trains.

ⓘ *Rue Vieille*

▶ *Leave Aubusson on the **D990** and turn left on to the **D942** to Guéret.*

🔟 Guéret, Limousin

You may be tempted to skip through Guéret, but its museum deserves a visit. Occupying an 18th-century mansion surrounded by pleasant formal gardens, it has valuable collections of Aubusson and other tapestries; ceramics from France, the Netherlands and Ming dynasty china; and a wonderful display of religious art, especially in enamel-work, dating from the 12th century.

ⓘ *Avenue Charles de Gaulle*

▶ *Leave Guéret on the **D940** then follow 'Limoges' signs through Pontarion and take the **N141**. Go through Bourganeuf and continue before turning right on the **D5** as for Ambazac then watch for a junction where you should bear left uphill on the **D29** at the 'Limoges 27' sign. Return to Limoges.*

🔟 Lac de Vassivière, Limousin

The route here stops before a bridge across to the main island in an extensive and well-wooded reservoir. The lake offers sports and leisure activities of many kinds. It has a 45km (28-mile) shoreline.

Aubusson's museum proudly displays the town's heritage

Visitors are welcome to walk to the island, where there are woodland paths, outdoor sculpture displays and a castle.

▶ *Retrace your route and turn right on the **D222** as for Peyrat-le-Château. Turn right at the stop sign to Royère. Go left on the **D3**, watch for a right turn signed 'Aubusson 24' and continue to Aubusson.*

🔟 Aubusson, Limousin

At heart Aubusson is a dignified old town with many discreetly restored buildings. Most of all, though, it is the capital of French tapestry, introduced here in the 14th century by Flemish weavers.

La Maison du Vieux Tapissier displays hundreds of examples of tapestry work, from classical works of the 17th century to dazzling ultra-modern abstracts. Several tapes-

---

FOR CHILDREN

There are sandy beaches at the wooded Barrage de Treignac reservoir, formed by a dam on the Vézère. It is ideal for fishing, swimming and sunbathing parties. Swimming from the main beach, beside the D940, is supervised in summer.

Further on, the Lac de Vassivière offers tuition in sailing, windsurfing and horse and pony rides. This beautiful reservoir is a noted recreational area, and there are easy walks, suitable for children, in the forest which surrounds it.

SCENIC ROUTES

From St-Yrieix to Ségur-le-Château the D18 and D6 run through pleasant undulating country of low hills and little valleys, and woodlands interspersed with grazing land. The N120 sweeps down wooded valleys to Tulle, the D9 to Gimel is a fine winding road with views to the tumbling waterfalls, and after Gimel there are attractive roadside fishing lakes. West of Chameil, alpine-like country rises to conifer-clad summits.

Of Rivers
& Islands

The arms of La Rochelle feature a full-rigged ship with cannons at the ports. That mixture of war and sea dominates the history of the coast and islands here. Inland, this is the country of the Cognac vineyards, and in the gentle Marais Poitevin you will be tempted to explore the canals of what was once the Gulf of Poitou.

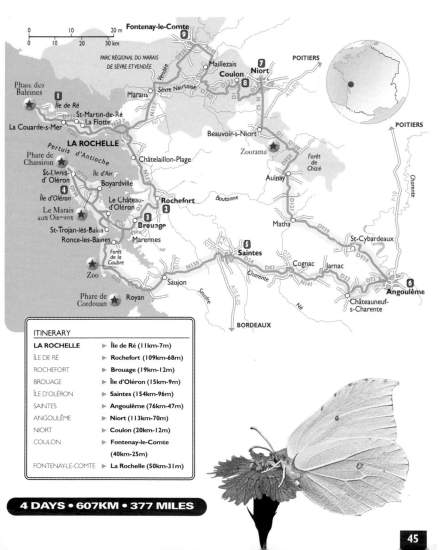

ITINERARY

LA ROCHELLE	▶ **Île de Ré** (11km-7m)
ÎLE DE RÉ	▶ **Rochefort** (109km-68m)
ROCHEFORT	▶ **Brouage** (19km-12m)
BROUAGE	▶ **Île d'Oléron** (15km-9m)
ÎLE D'OLÉRON	▶ **Saintes** (154km-96m)
SAINTES	▶ **Angoulême** (76km-47m)
ANGOULÊME	▶ **Niort** (113km-70m)
NIORT	▶ **Coulon** (20km-12m)
COULON	▶ **Fontenay-le-Comte** (40km-25m)
FONTENAY-LE-COMTE	▶ **La Rochelle** (50km-31m)

4 DAYS • 607KM • 377 MILES

[i] *Place de la Petite Sirène, La Rochelle*

▶ *Leave La Rochelle over the toll bridge to Île de Ré. Take the 'Itinéraire Nord', visiting La Flotte and St-Martin-de-Ré on the way to Phare des Baleines. Return by the D201 via Le Bois-Plage, then right on the D735 back over the toll bridge.*

❶ Île de Ré, Poitou-Charente
Linked to the mainland by a modern bridge, here is an island – 28km (17 miles) long and 3–5km (2–3 miles) wide – of holiday beaches. The old fishing and trading port of La Flotte once shipped salt and brandy to America. St-Martin-de-Ré, the principal town, has unexpected rampart walls, a town centre virtually on an island, a local museum (Musée Naval et E-Cognac) and a citadel where visitors are welcome to admire the outer defences and the old quay. The inner part is a state prison. At the northern point of the island you can visit the Phare des Baleines, a lighthouse named after the whales that used to be seen offshore. A little marine museum stands near by.

[i] *Quai de Sénac in La Flotte and Avenue Victor Bouthillier in St-Martin-de-Ré*

FOR CHILDREN

There is plenty for children at L'Arche de Noé (Noah's Ark) before the Phare des Baleines on Île de Ré.

St-Martin-de-Ré, the principal town of Île de Ré

FOR HISTORY BUFFS

Until 1938, prisoners shipped to Devil's Island, the infamous penal colony in French Guinea, left from the citadel at St-Martin-de-Ré. There is still a prison here.

▶ *Follow the D735 as for La Rochelle, on to the dual-carriageway numbered N237 then N137, and continue to Rochefort.*

❷ Rochefort, Poitou-Charente
You may wonder, entering it through unremarkable suburbs, if Rochefort is worth a visit, but this is a special town. In 1666 thousands of workers, under the orders of Louis XIV's chief minister Jean Baptiste Colbert, built a huge arsenal and naval shipyard here. There are guided tours of the beautiful mansard-roofed Corderie Royale, with its 372m (1,220-foot) hall where the ropes were twisted. Museums in Rochefort cover art and history, and its background as a military port. The unobtrusive but exotically furnished Maison de Loti, house of Pierre Loti (1850–1923), who mixed two careers, as a marine officer and a novelist of the sea, stands in a quiet side street.

[i] *Avenue Sadi Carnot*

▶ *Leave Rochefort on the D733 as for Royan, then go right on the D238e to Soubise and left on the D3 signed 'Hiers-Brouage'.*

❸ Brouage, Poitou-Charente
Away from main roads, this fine little fortified town is now also away from the sea and today it stands half deserted among the salt marshes. The retreat of the waters ruined its position as a busy trading port. From the ramparts, the French tricolour and the maple leaf of Canada fly side by side. Samuel de Champlain, the founder of

Quebec, was born here in 1567
There is a comprehensive exhibition in the church on the founding of what was at first 'New France'.

i Porte Royale

▶ *Continue on the D3, turn right at the traffic lights over the toll bridge on to Île d'Oléron. Bear right on the D734 through Le Château-d'Oléron. Go right in Dolus on to the D126 through Les Allards and Boyardville, then via Foulerot, Port du Douhet, La Brée and St-Denis to the Phare de Chassiron. Return to St-Denis, then take the D734 to Dolus and follow 'Le Viaduc' signs back over the toll bridge.*

FOR HISTORY BUFFS

Reached by ferry from Boyardville on the Île-d'Oléron, the Napoleonic museum on the little island of Aix, Maison de l'Empereur, recalls how Napoleon spent his last night on French soil before surrendering to the British ship *Bellerophon*.

4 Île d'Oléron, Poitou-Charente
Larger than Ré (30km/18 miles long and 6km/3½ miles wide), this is another holiday island of villages, picturesque harbours, vineyards, woodlands and fine sandy beaches

Look for the grassy site of the 12th-century fortress which gave the island's main town of Le Château-d'Oléron its name, the river resort of Boyardville with its pinewood dunes and beach, and the lighthouse tower of the Phare de Chassiron, where the waves are seen breaking over offshore reefs and shallows.

RECOMMENDED WALKS

Go north through Boyardville on the Île d'Oléron to the Forêt des Saumonards, where you can follow any number of pinewood paths behind the sand dunes. In the channel between Oléron and Aix, look for the isolated rock prison of Fort Boyard, for a time in the 19th century a French equivalent of Alcatraz.

The fortified town of Brouage was once an important port

i Place de la République, Château-d'Oléron.

BACK TO NATURE

On the Île d'Oléron, turn left in Les Allards for the extensive nature reserve of pools, canals and woodland at the Marais des Oiseaux. Wildfowl, waders, storks and birds of prey are all featured.

FOR CHILDREN

Before you leave Île d'Oléron, turn right for St-Trojan-les-Bains and the narrow-gauge railway which potters for 6km (3½ miles) through pinewoods.

▶ *Follow the D26 off the island then turn right at the 'La Tremblade' sign. Go right opposite Camping les Pins, and right at the T-junction over another toll bridge. Go right on the D25 to Royan, then take the N150 to Saintes.*

L'Arc de Germanicus, Saintes' Roman triumphal arch

▶ Leave Angoulême on the **D939** to Matha. In the town centre, turn right to Aulnay, following the **D121**. After Aulnay, go right on the **D950** left on the **D109** and join the **D1** through Chizé. Turn right on the **N150** to Niort.

RECOMMENDED WALKS

Turn right off the D939 on the way between Angoulême and Niort, at St-Cybardeaux, for the informal paths which penetrate a hilltop woodland and reveal the unexpected sight of a Gallo-Roman theatre with tiers of stone-blocked seats facing what was once the stage.

---

5 Saintes, Poitou-Charente

Back from the resorts and islands of the coast, this is a handsome district capital. There is a good regional museum here, others concentrating on fine arts, folklore and archaeology. Roman remains include a triumphal arch. Saintes lies astride the River Charente, and cruise-boats sail from its garden-backed quays.

ⓘ *Cours National*

SPECIAL TO...

At Cognac and Jarnac on the route between Saintes and Angoulême, are world-famous cognac houses such as Hennessy, Martell, Rémy Martin and Courvoisier and Hine.

▶ Leave Saintes on the **D24**, which becomes the **D83**. Go
right on the **N141** and right on the **D83** to Cognac. Take the **N141** through Jarnac, then turn right on the **D22**. After Vibrac watch for a left turn – away from Châteauneuf-sur-Charente – to St-Simieux. Go right through Sireuil, left on the **D53**, right on the **D84**, left on the **D41** and right on the **D72** to Angoulême.

6 Angoulême, Poitou-Charente

This is a busy industrial town, but its old upper town is worth a visit. The chief glories of the old town are its imposing hilltop location, the views from the wooded paths round its ramparts, and the glorious façade of its subtly-lit cathedral (much restored in the 19th century). There are museums, exuberant Renaissance buildings, and rare active survivors of the papermills which once made Angoulême's fortune.

ⓘ *Place St-Pierre*

---

7 Niort, Poitou-Charente

Niort, on the River Sèvres, is a working town with various industries. The riverside has walks and footbridges, gardens and vestiges of old mill streams. Past and present town halls are richly ornamented, and there is much fine Renaissance design. Customers bustle around the glass-and-wrought-ironwork market hall. The multi-towered castle or donjon may have been built by the 12th-century English Kings Henry II and Richard the Lionheart.

ⓘ *Rue Ernest-Pérochon*

▶ Leave Niort on the **N11**. Turn right on the **D3**, then right on the **D1** to Coulon.

8 Coulon, Poitou-Charente

In the heart of one of the most appealing landscapes in France – the farms, market gardens, woodlands and waterway maze of the long-drained Marais Poitevin – Coulon is an attractive village where punts are available for hire, and escorted cruises also start, on some of the 40,000km (25,000 miles) of water channels. Not all, of course, are navigable, but they are an enchanting haven. Some picnic sites, reachable by water, are remote from any road. Coulon's museum tells the story of the marshes, and the aquarium displays all the fish species of this 'Green Venice'.

 *Place Église*

BACK TO NATURE

Turn left off D1 after Chizé for Zoorama, a park and study centre concentrating on European animals such as wildcat, lynx, bison, deer and tortoise.

▶ *Leave Coulon on the D123 as for Le Vanneau, then go right on the D102, which becomes the D104 through Damvix. Go straight on at the give way sign, then right on the D15 through Maillezais. Go left on the N148 to Fontenay-le-Comte.*

9 **Fontenay-le-Comte,**
Loire Valley West
There are no fishing-smacks now, sailing under the Pont des Sardines (Sardine Bridge) at Fontenay, but the riverside is a pleasant recreational area with footpaths and little gardens. Fontenay preserves its historic buildings – even the tourist office was once a toll-house for the port. The Église Notre-Dame is an impressive Gothic church with a beautiful walnut pulpit and, high on an outer wall, a gilded Madonna. Beside it there is a regional museum. The Château de Terre-Neuve is a splendid 16th-century castle whose richly ornamented fireplaces feature alchemists' symbols and griffins.

During the Renaissance, the town became the home of poets and writers, including Rabelais, who was educated in a convent here.

i *Quay Poëy d'Avant*

SPECIAL TO...

At Ré and Oléron are the oysterbeds which cover great areas and are a vital part of the local economy. You can join a tour of the beds from La Flotte on Ré, and there is an oyster museum at St-Trojan on Oléron.

▶ *Leave Fontenay on the D938ter for La Rochelle.*

SCENIC ROUTES

Once off Oléron, the route follows a minor road towards the next toll bridge, with attractive views of the strait between the island and the mainland. Then the D25 to Royan runs through the undulating pine-clad sand dunes of the Forêt de la Coubre. From Saintes to Cognac, the D24 follows the River Charente through a pleasant countryside of farms, vineyards and woodlands. Beyond Jarnac, still in the Charente valley, there is a succession of quiet villages off the usual tourist trail.

The Marais Poitevin is an understated landscape, but it is particularly attractive where the route winds alongside the Sèvre Niortaise west of Coulon, and again on the approach to Damvix.

The charming canalside village of Coulon is typical of the marsh villages of the Marais Poitevin

The Western
Loire Valley

Starting in Nantes, this tour soon leaves all Breton influences behind as it heads for the valleys of the Loire and the Sarthe. You will find some of France's finest *son et lumière* presentations here, one of the world's most famous motor-racing circuits, and the Pays Nantais and Anjou are packed with vineyards.

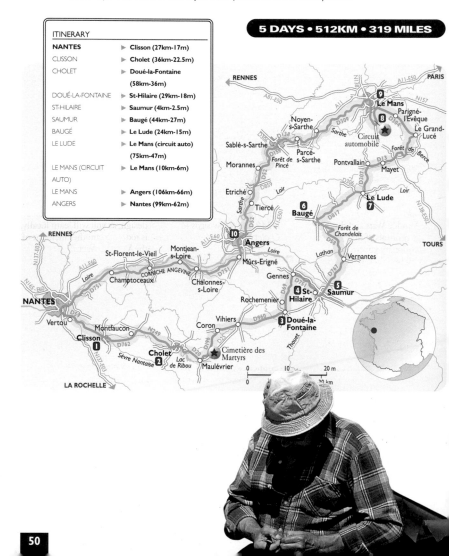

5 DAYS • 512KM • 319 MILES

ITINERARY	
NANTES	▶ **Clisson (27km–17m)**
CLISSON	▶ **Cholet (36km–22.5m)**
CHOLET	▶ **Doué-la-Fontaine**
	(58km–36m)
DOUÉ-LA-FONTAINE	▶ **St-Hilaire (29km–18m)**
ST-HILAIRE	▶ **Saumur (4km–2.5m)**
SAUMUR	▶ **Baugé (44km–27m)**
BAUGÉ	▶ **Le Lude (24km–15m)**
LE LUDE	▶ **Le Mans (circuit auto)**
	(75km–47m)
LE MANS (CIRCUIT	▶ **Le Mans (10km–6m)**
AUTO)	
LE MANS	▶ **Angers (106km–66m)**
ANGERS	▶ **Nantes (99km–62m)**

ℹ️ *Place du Commerce, Nantes*

▶ *Leave Nantes for Clisson on the **D59** through St-Fiacre. In Gorges go left of the **D113** then take the **D59** again into Clisson.*

❶ Clisson, Loire Valley West
The Vendée Wars and the savage reprisals of the Revolutionary government army all but obliterated this little riverside town. Then it was completely rebuilt, but not as it had been before. Present-day Clisson is mostly a tribute to Palladian Italy, with colonnades, loggias and belltowers of a style seen nowhere else in western France.

Look for the stabilised but unfurnished ruin of the 13th- to 15th-century castle, the 15th-century market hall, the two medieval bridges contrasting with the soaring 19th-century road viaduct, and Italianate creations such as the Temple d'Amitié and the Church of Notre-Dame.

There are beautiful walks in the valleys of the Sèvre Nantaise and the Moine. Local wines may be tasted. But

Clisson itself is the great attraction, especially as an Italianate skyline to a leafy riverside view.

ℹ️ *Place de la Trinité*

▶ *Leave Clisson on the **N149**. Turn left as for Beaupréau on the **D762** then go along the **N249** and follow signs to Cholet.*

❷ Cholet, Loire Valley West
The Musée des Guerres de Vendée, here in a town where only 20 buildings were left standing in their brutal aftermath, is the place to learn about the Vendée Wars of 1793–96. It explains how the Vendée rising against the Revolutionary government's policies of mass conscription and the overthrow of all previous loyalties, was at first successful, then viciously crushed.

Other exhibitions are at the Musée des Arts, the Musée Paysan with its old-style dairy and country house interiors in the leisure park by the Ribou lake, and the Maison des Sciences, Lettres et Arts whose many attractions include a planetarium.

Clisson's impressive ruined 13th-to 15th-century castle sits atop a rocky outcrop

This is a famous textile town with many splendid modern buildings. Its trademark is the red-and-white handkerchief – the *mouchoir de Cholet* – whose design, as you will learn locally, is rooted in another incident of the Vendée Wars.

ℹ️ *Place de Rougé*

▶ *Leave Cholet on the **D20** as for Poitiers. In Maulévrier turn left and right as for Vihiers, then left on the **D196** through Chanteloup to Coron. Go right on the **D960** to Doué-la-Fontaine.*

SPECIAL TO...

In Maulévrier, after Cholet, go straight on past the turn as for Vihiers to visit the Parc Oriental. Created early this century, abandoned in 1940 and completely restored in 1987, this is probably Europe's finest Japanese garden.

i *Place du Champ de Foire*

FOR HISTORY BUFFS

In a forest clearing beside the D196 after Maulévrier (on the way from Cholet to Doué-la-Fontaine), the chapel at the Cimetière des Martyrs commemorates victims of the Revolutionary fury in the Vendée Wars. Virtually alone in France, the Vendée region saw little to celebrate at the bicentennary of the Revolution in 1989.

---

3 Doué-la-Fontaine, Loire Valley West

If you arrived in the middle of Doué without paying attention to its outskirts, you might shrug it off as an ordinary little town. It is far from that. The zoo, adapted from the cliffs, caverns and ditches of an old quarry site, houses lions, tigers, lemurs, birds of prey, deer, emus, rarities such as snow panthers, and 15 separate monkey enclosures. Its Naturoscope explains the problems of threatened species and the destruction of their habitats.

The Musée des Vieux Commerces features seven old-style shops and a rose-water distillery, in part-restored 18th-century stables. The Maison Carolingienne is the substantial ruin of a fortress built before 1050.

Nobody is certain about the origins of Doué's arena, Roman in style but much later in date. However, there is no doubt about the Moulin Cartier. Built in 1910, it was the last windmill raised in Anjou.

BACK TO NATURE

Doué-la-Fontaine is France's great rose-growing centre. The Jardin des Roses displays dozens of different varieties, coloured crimson, scarlet and yellow – *Caroline de Monaco*, *Sarabande* and *Moulin Rouge* among them. Every July, an exhibition of 100,000 roses is held in the arena.

▶ Leave Doué on the **D69** to Gennes. Go right as for Saumur on the **D751** through La Mimerolle and into St-Hilaire.

FOR HISTORY BUFFS

After Doué-la-Fontaine, turn left off the D69 for Rochemenier and its strange troglodytic farms. You can visit furnished underground dwelling houses – with their cowsheds, barns, wine-cellars and even a chapel – still inhabited early this century.

---

4 St-Hilaire, Loire Valley West

Just before this village suburb of Saumur, the Musée du Champignon, in a cave system cut into the roadside cliffs, is more than simply an exhibition about mushrooms and how they are grown. The underground galleries were dug in medieval times, part of a network of more than 480km (300 miles) throughout the district, which produces 75 per cent of France's cultivated mushrooms. Turn right in St-Hilaire for the École National d'Équitation. This is France's national riding academy, excellently housed and staffed. In the practice arena, in front of high wall mirrors, you may see members of the academy's Cadre Noire put their horses through the intricate, disciplined and stylish movements for which they are famous all over Europe. They also perform summer season shows.

▶ Continue on the **D751** into Saumur.

5 Saumur, Loire Valley West

Straddling the Loire, this very appealing town is passionate about horses and the cavalry, wines, museums and exuberant outdoor displays. The Château de Saumur, overlooking the river, houses three separate collections. The Musée des Arts

Décoratifs concentrates on the decorative arts – ceramics, enamelware, carvings in wood and alabaster. Another, Musée du Cheval, celebrates centuries of horsemanship; the third, Musée de la Figurine-Jouet has more than 20,000 models and figurines.

The cavalry has two separate exhibitions, one recalling its mounted days, the other taking the story to more recent times with a comprehensive display of tanks and armoured cars.

Second only to Champagne, Saumur is famous for its sparkling wines. Several firms welcome visitors to their cellars. Notre-Dame de Nantilly, dating from the 12th-century, houses a valuable collection of medieval and Renaissance tapestries. And the old quarter of Saumur with its restored 17th-century houses adds to the attractions of a justifiably self-confident town.

i *Place de la Bilange*

▶ *Leave Saumur on the N147 as for Le Mans. At the round-*

SPECIAL TO…

In Saumur, numerous wine cellars offer tastings of the region's wines.

about take the second exit to Vernantes on the D767. In Vernantes, turn sharp left at the traffic lights as for Baugé, then right on the D58 as for Baugé through Mouliherne. In Le Guédéniau go right in the D186 as for Lasse. Turn left following 'Les Caves de Chanzelles' sign. At the round-about in the forest take the fifth exit for Baugé. Rejoin the D58 and continue to Baugé.

6 Baugé, Loire Valley West
Plenty of space has been left around Baugé's 15th-century castle, originally a hunting lodge of Good King René, Duke of Anjou. Holding displays of weapons, coins and ceramics,

The château at Saumur has been dubbed 'the castle of love'

it stands before public gardens dipping to an attractive river-side. The Convent of La Girouardière houses a venerated relic – a jewelled cross believed to contain a piece of the True Cross brought to France by a crusader knight. Its unusual design was adopted as the Cross of Lorraine. Look also for Baugé's charming 17th-century Hospice-St-Joseph (pharmacy) with its beautiful array of apothecaries' jars.

Sometimes an unfamiliar language may be seen or spoken here, describing Baugé, for instance, as 'bela kaj malmova urbeto': the Château de Grésillon, on your exit route from 'this fine old town', is an international Esperanto centre.

i *Place de l'Europe*

BACK TO NATURE

Before Baugé, pause in the Forêt de Chandelais. Three-quarters of its trees are oak, most of the rest beech. Roe deer, wild boars and foxes live in the forest, and the beechwoods are alive with birdsong, including the liquid, fluty song of the golden oriole.

▶ *Leave Baugé on the D817, which becomes the D305, then go right on the D306 to Le Lude.*

7 Le Lude, Loire Valley West
Pride of this little town is the richly furnished château, rebuilt in Renaissance style after an English garrison was driven out – with heavy damage to the fabric – in 1427. Its situation is most attractive, above balustraded gardens rising from the River Loir, whose waters eventually feed the larger Loire. One of France's most dramatic *son et lumière* presentations takes place here. It recalls five centuries of events and person-alities, from the English occupa-tion to the Second Empire. This outstanding show is enhanced

by fountains and a lively fire-work display reflected in the river. In the town itself, La Sentinelle is an unusual museum with a huge collection of military uniforms and flags from all over the world.

[i] *Place Nicolay*

▶ *Leave Le Lude on the D307 to Pontvallain. Go right on the D13 through Mayet and across the N138 to Le Grand-Lucé. Turn left at the give way sign and left on the D304 as for Le Mans. Go under the bridge, then left following the 'Angers' sign, under another bridge and follow the 'Tours' signs along the N138. Go right at the roundabout on the D140 as for Arnage, then right on the D139 to the grandstands of the racing circuit.*

RECOMMENDED WALKS

At the first right-hand bend after crossing the N138 between Le Lude and Le Grand-Lucé, bear left and fol-low signs to the Fontaine de la Coubre. A map opposite this woodland pool shows the way-marked footpaths in the Forêt de Bercé. They explore the beautiful deciduous woodland split by murmuring streams in the unexploited part of the for-est, and the conifer plantations beyond. As the Musée du Bois in Jupilles shows, this was once a great centre for ships' timbers and, later, wooden clogs. When you continue from Fontaine de la Coubre, turn right at the first crossroads then left to rejoin the D13 through Jupilles.

at over 320kph (200mph).

There is a smaller but linked Bugatti Circuit. The two tracks play host to five major car and motor-cycle events, plus a 24-hour truck race! You can watch test sessions from the main grandstands, which are infor-mally open on non-competition days.

An excellent motor museum also recalls that this was where Wilbur Wright, over from the United States, made the first powered flight in Europe in 1908.

[i] *Acceuil Reception*

▶ *Continue on the D139 into Le Mans.*

9 Le Mans, Loire Valley West
Apart from some handsome churches, the busy, modern town offers little to the visitor,

8 Le Mans Circuit, Loire Valley West
Prosaically, they may be the N138, D140 and D139, but these roads are also part of the great motor-racing circuit where the Le Mans 24-Hour Race is held every June.

The N138 is the Mulsanne Straight, along which Jaguars, Porsches and Mercedes howl

Fascinating exhibits in Le Mans' automobile museum

but Le Mans has strong links with the Plantagenets. Henry II of England, for instance, was born here. Long before his time there was a Gallo-Roman settle-ment on the great rock-ridge in the heart of the modern sprawl. The old walled town – Vieux

Mans – retains its high-level medieval street plan. Split by the rue Wilbur Wright, which lies at the foot of a ravine cut through the heart of the rock, it features finely detailed Renaissance houses and later town mansions, leading to the majestic Cathédrale St Julien.

i Rue de l'Étoile

▶ *Leave Le Mans on the D309 as for Sablé. In Parcé cross the river then go first right at the crossroads, left to Solesmes then continue to Sablé-sur-Sarthe. Go straight across the D306 for Centre-Ville. At the roundabout take the last exit, then a side road right for Pincé. This is the D159. Bear right on the C15 for 'Pincé par la Forêt'. Rejoin the D159 then follow the D18 and D52 through Morannes. Continue through Etriché and Tiercé. Go straight on along the N160 then right on the N23 to Angers.*

10 Angers, Loire Valley West
Here in the heart of Anjou lies a university town of parks, gardens and colourful floral decorations, with a grand Plantagenet castle rising in towers of banded stonework, and a cathedral, Cathédrale Saint Maurice, best approached by the Montée St-Maurice, a stairway climbing from the River Maine.

The longest tapestry in France, *La Tenture de l'Apocalypse*, completed in the late 14th century to show the Apocalypse, is on display in the castle. Angers is a tapestry town. Many others, ancient and modern, are on show in the castle itself and in individual museums and galleries.

Fine Renaissance buildings survive, both around the cathedral and elsewhere. River cruises follow the Maine, and for the adventurous there are hot-air balloon flights to waft you high above the castles, vineyards and villages of Anjou.

i Place Kennedy

▶ *Leave Angers through Les-Ponts-de-Cé on the N160. In Mûrs-Érigné, turn right to go through Chalonnes-sur-Loire and Champtoceaux on the D751 and return on the N249 to Nantes.*

Detail of Catedrale St-Maurice's tympanum above the 12th-century west front door in Angers

FOR CHILDREN

On the return route to Nantes, turn left instead of right in Mûrs-Érigné to visit the Aquarium Tropical. It shows a brilliantly coloured collection of exotic fish from Asia, Africa and America swimming in tanks which have unexpected décors, such as the Grand Canyon or craters of the moon.

SCENIC ROUTES

From Nantes to Clisson the route runs through the attractive Muscadet vineyards. Around the D13, the Forêt de Bercé is one of the most beautiful areas in the district. The D751 after Angers runs along the lovely Corniche Angevine above the Loire. The Layon vineyards are impressive, but the route is at its best near the 'panorama' viewpoint at La Haie Longue ('the long hedge'). A roadside memorial commemorates the pioneer aviator René Gasnier, whose first flights were from the level fields across the river.

SPECIAL TO...

Angers is the home of Cointreau, which has been produced here since 1849. Guided one-hour tours of the distillery (La Distillerie Cointreau) show off the processes, production methods and famous advertising posters of this much-exported liqueur, but the recipe remains a secret.

Through
Château Country

Some of the most elegant castles in Europe are within easy reach of Tours, in and around the valley of the Loire. Vineyards abound in Touraine, 'the garden of France'. Although this route starts and finishes beside the Loire, it also goes into the lonely area of pools, farms and woodlands known as the Sologne.

3/4 DAYS • 428KM • 267 MILES

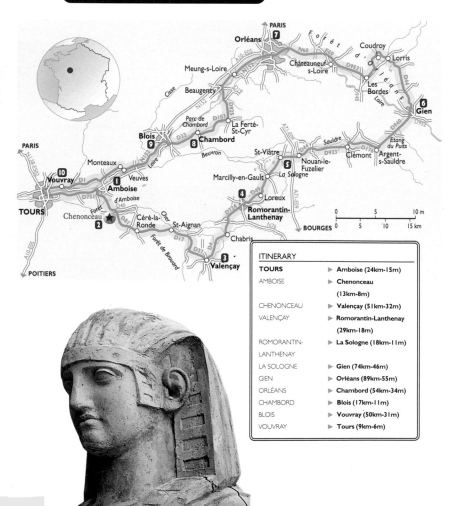

ITINERARY		
TOURS	▶	**Amboise (24km-15m)**
AMBOISE	▶	**Chenonceau (13km-8m)**
CHENONCEAU	▶	**Valençay (51km-32m)**
VALENÇAY	▶	**Romorantin-Lanthenay (29km-18m)**
ROMORANTIN-LANTHENAY	▶	**La Sologne (18km-11m)**
LA SOLOGNE	▶	**Gien (74km-46m)**
GIEN	▶	**Orléans (89km-55m)**
ORLÉANS	▶	**Chambord (54km-34m)**
CHAMBORD	▶	**Blois (17km-11m)**
BLOIS	▶	**Vouvray (50km-31m)**
VOUVRAY	▶	**Tours (9km-6m)**

ⓘ *Boulevard Heurteloup, Tours*

▶ *Leave Tours on the D751 to Amboise.*

❶ Amboise, Loire Valley Central

You will enter Amboise along a classic plane-tree avenue, with the Loire out of sight beyond the riverside embankment. The château's massive walls tower over the town centre streets. This impressive building is only a fifth of the size it was during its 16th-century heyday. A *son et lumière* presentation brings to life François I's glittering court of those days. In the Musée de la Poste, model coaches, postilions' liveries, records, engravings and other relics tell the story of the mail service by land, sea and air.

On the climb out of Amboise, pause at the exotic 18th-century pagoda of Chanteloup (all that remains of a château there). The topmost gallery of this 44m (144-foot) hillside tower is a splendid viewpoint over the Loire.

ⓘ *Quai Général de Gaulle*

SPECIAL TO...

In Amboise, be sure to visit the brick and stone house called Le Clos Lucé, home till his death, in 1519, of Leonardo da Vinci. The great artist and engineer was installed here by his patron François I, King of France, who was to buy the *Mona Lisa* and *Virgin on the Rocks* after Leonardo's death. Here Leonardo worked on astonishing engineering drawings. Forty of these, featuring machines resembling an aeroplane, a helicopter and an army tank, have been turned into an amazing display of three-dimensional models such as Leonardo himself never saw in his lifetime.

▶ *After the pagoda turn left then right as for Chenonceaux on the D81. Go left on the*

D40, then right to Château de Chenonceau.

❷ Chenonceau, Loire Valley Central

Lacking the final 'x' of the similarly named little town near by, with its ivied houses and old coaching inns, this 16th-century riverside castle was one of the most striking architectural exercises of its day. The bridge which linked it to the south bank of the Cher was adapted as a gallery of two storeys and attic-level rooms, with the River Cher flowing through the arches underneath. Extending for almost 61m (200 feet) across the river, this is still the most noteworthy feature of a richly furnished castle. Chenonceau stands surrounded by water channels. The woodland grounds include formal riverside gardens, and a waxworks museum recalls the personalities involved in its lively story. There are excellent *son et lumière* shows.

▶ *Continue on the D40. In Chisseaux, go straight on the D80 to Francueil, take the D81 to Céré-la-Ronde, then the C5 and D90 to St-Aignan. Go left on the D675, right on the D17, right for Valençay on the D33, left on the D37 in Villentrois and right on the D956 into Valençay.*

❸ Valençay, Loire Valley Central

The great 16th-century castle here was owned by several famous financiers. A half-inter-

Basilique St-Martin's Tour Charlemagne, in Tours

est in the vast 19,000-hectare (47,000-acre) estate was briefly held by the Scotsman John Law, who introduced the system of credit. In 1719–20 he dominated the French banking system, until his enterprises collapsed in insolvencies and rancour.

Later, Valençay became the residence of Talleyrand, Napoleon's foreign minister, whose diplomats and dignitaries were extravagantly entertained. From 1808 to 1813 Ferdinand VII of Spain was held in virtual house arrest here, which is why the town's Hôtel d'Espagne is so named. A *son et lumière* show brings these varied characters back to life.

The castle is still lavishly furnished. Fallow deer graze in a sunken park, and you will hear peacocks' screams echoing through the grounds. Do not be put off by the ramshackle

---

FOR CHILDREN

On the way to Valençay turn right on the D657 in St-Aignan to the Zoo Parc de Beauval. Originally a bird garden, Beauval has expanded to house a splendid collection of lions and tigers, panthers, pumas and jaguars.

---

appearance of the separate motor museum, whose exhibits include a spidery Bedelia cyclecar of 1914, a lovely little 1930 Amilcar sports model and an Alpine-Renault of 1971.

[i] *Avenue de la Résistance*

▶ *Leave Valençay on the* **D4** *through Chabris, then continue straight ahead on the* **D128**. *Cross the* **N76** *and follow the signs to Romorantin-Lanthenay.*

4 Romorantin-Lanthenay, Loire Valley Central

In this 'capital' of the Sologne district, the River Sauldre splits into several channels. From the main-road bridge there is a most beautiful view downstream to the ivy-covered walls and colourful flower boxes of the restored watermills.

The town centre includes several attractive buildings, notably the ancient-timbered Carroir d'Orée which houses an archaeological museum. In the elegant Hôtel de Ville (town hall), the second floor is devoted to a museum about the rural life and traditions of the Sologne.

Matra, the aerospace company, has a factory here. The town's Musée de la Course Automobile is of far higher qual-

Valençay château is a fine example of classic Renaissance architecture

ity than you might expect, because it houses historic Matra competition cars, such as a Le Mans 24-Hour Race winner and Jackie Stewart's Formula One Matra-Ford V8.

[i] *Place de la Paix*

▶ *Leave Romorantin-Lanthenay for Loreux on the* **D49** *and continue to Marcilly-en-Gault. Turn left at the T-junction there and first right for St-Viâtre, still on the* **D49**.

5 La Sologne, Loire Valley Central

At St-Viâtre you are well into the Sologne, a huge tract of more than half a million hectares (nearly 2,000 square miles). It is an all but level countryside of heath and woodland, widely separated arable and livestock farms, red-tiled brick houses and hundreds of lonely pools. In this slightly mysterious landscape, whose people are regarded in other parts of France as clannish and self-contained, only the trees create any kind of horizon.

The Sologne is also a land of hunters, wild-fowlers and fishermen. Until the second half of the 19th century much of it was unhealthily covered by even greater areas of stagnant water. Extensive drainage schemes and tree-planting created the landscape of today.

▶ Leave St-Viâtre on the **D49**, then avoid the left turn for Lamotte-Beuvron and go straight ahead on the **D93** to Nouan-le-Fuzelier. Go left as for Orléans, then right as for Chaon on the **D122** and left on the **D44**. Go right on the **D923** as for Aubigny to Clémont. Turn left at the cross-roads on the **D7**, then follow signs to Étang du Puits. Continue to the **D948**, turn right for Argent-sur-Sauldre then left on the **D940** to Gien.

achieved in brickwork. Its dedication to St Joan is appropriate. It was here in 1429 that she first made contact with the Dauphin's army and began her mission to liberate France.

[i] Rue Anne de Beaujeu

▶ Leave Gien for Lorris on the **D44**. Continue as for Bellegarde. Immediately after the 'La Chaussée' sign take the first left. Go right on the **V3** into Coudroy. Turn left at the stop sign, through Vieilles-Maisons-sur-Joudry and left on the **D88**. Bend right then left, and watch for a right turn at the crossroads along a gravel forest road, passing the '3t' sign. Bear left at a junction

of forest roads, left after a 50m warning sign for give way ahead, and turn right along the tarred road (this is the **D961**). Turn right on the **D952** and follow the **N60** and the **N152** to Orléans.

FOR CHILDREN

The kids will have plenty of opportunity to work off some energy at the Étang du Puits, before you reach Gien. This wooded recreational lake offers sandy beaches, rowing boat and pedalo hire, pony rides and a little children's playground. Sailing dinghies and windsurfers hurtle around.

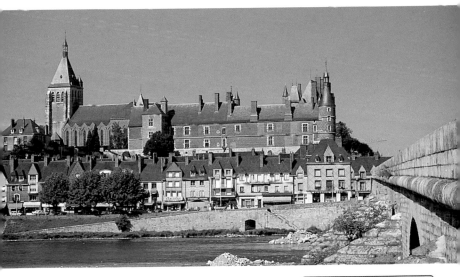

6 Gien, Loire Valley Central
From a leafy promenade by the Loire, the hillside in this town, famous for its faïenceware, rises to a little plateau shared by the 15th-century castle and the modern church, both of brick rather than stone. The castle houses the Musée International de la Chasse, with displays on every imaginable aspect of hunting.

Replacing a building wrecked in World War II, the church shows inside and out, what decorative effects can be

Gien has been meticulously restored since World War II

RECOMMENDED WALKS

Pause for a few minutes at Coudroy, after leaving Gien. Here, there is a short footpath which follows the bank of the Orléans Canal. Only fishermen now come to this 300-year-old waterway, long since closed to navigation.

FOR HISTORY BUFFS

In Lorris, after leaving Gien, turn left on the D961 to find the Musée de la Résistance et de la Déportation.
Set in well-tended gardens, it tells the story of the Resistance movement in World War II through displays of documents, photographs, maps and weapons, and newspapers of the clandestine press.

[i] *Place Albert 1er*

▶ *Leave Orléans on the N152 as for Blois, avoiding the autoroute. Continue through Meung-sur-Loire to Beaugency. Go left on the D925 as for Limoges, crossing the river bridge. Continue straight over the D951 and on to La Ferté-St-Cyr. Go right on the D103 to Crouy, left on the D33 and continue through the Parc de Chambord to Chambord.*

SPECIAL TO...

At Beaugency, between Orléans and Chambord, follow signs to the Musée Dunois. In a 15th-century castle, the arts and traditions of the district round Orléans are preserved. Each of its rooms has a special theme such as furniture, toys or costumes.

FOR HISTORY BUFFS

On the way from Orléans to Chambord, turn left in Meung-sur-Loire for the château and its grim medieval dungeons. They feature a torture chamber and a hideous underground oubliette where prisoners generally died in an agony of starvation or disease. One famous prisoner in the 15th century was the vagabond poet François Villon.

---

7 Orléans, Loire Valley Central

Every spring, Orléans organises a festival celebrating Joan of Arc's intervention – not at all appreciated by the French official army commanders – which raised the English siege of the city in 1429. Visit the Maison Jeanne d'Arc for the whole dramatic story. Her equestrian statue stands in the Place du Martroi.

The Musée des Beaux-Arts houses a valuable collection of French and Italian paintings. Now used for civic receptions, the luxuriously furnished 16th-century Hôtel Groslot is open to visitors. The Musée Historique et Archéologique (local history and archaeology) is housed in the Renaissance surroundings of the Hôtel Cabu.

Cathédrale Sainte-Croix dominates the townscape above

Orléans' splendid neo-Gothic Cathédrale Sainte-Croix

the Loire. Look inside for its stained-glass windows telling the story of Joan of Arc, its beautifully carved choir stalls and its 32 18th-century medallions illustrating the life of Christ.

BACK TO NATURE

In Orléans, the magnificent floral park called La Source takes it name from a curious natural feature. Officially, the River Loiret rises here. In fact, its waters are diverted from the Loire almost 30km (19 miles) upstream. They disappear underground for all that distance before welling up again in the park.

---

8 Chambord, Loire Valley Central

The Renaissance château of Chambord is the biggest of all the castles of the Loire. Begun as the favourite hunting lodge of François I, it has no fewer than 440 rooms, and stands in the midst of a 5,443-hectare (13,450-acre) estate circled by a 32km (20-mile) wall.

Most of the forested estate is a hunting reserve, but parts of it are open to visitors. Chambord is beautifully furnished, with fine paintings and tapestries. It houses an exhibition on hunting, and another on its own history. A viewing terrace stands high among the intricate rooftop decorations.

BACK TO NATURE

Turn left off the D33 in the Parc de Chambord for a high-level 'hide', from which you can watch a herd of red deer in a grazing enclosure in the forest.

▶ Continue on the *D33*. After Nanteuil go under the bridge through St-Gervais-la-Forêt and right on the *D956* to Blois.

9 Blois, Loire Valley Central
A gorgeous open-air staircase built for François I (and possibly designed by Leonardo da Vinci) is only one of the architectural delights of the hilltop castle here. The same king commissioned the decorated façade which overlooks the lovely little garden in the Place Victor-Hugo.

Archaeological and fine arts museums are housed in the castle and there is a gallery

devoted to Robert Houdin, the great 19th-century conjuror from whom the escapologist Houdini took his stage name. In the town, a street, a stairway and a statue commemorate Denis Papin, an early steam-engine pioneer.

Attractive old buildings include the half-timbered Maison des Acrobates with its carvings of jugglers and tumblers. Tours can be arranged of the famous Chocolaterie Poulain, the chocolate factory founded in Blois in 1848. Bicycles can be hired from the railway station and several shops in town.

i Avenue Laigret

RECOMMENDED WALKS

Ask at one of the tourist offices about walks around the Val de Cisse. Monteaux, between Blois and Vouvray, is a good centre for them. Using minor road and field tracks, you can wander through farms, woods and vineyards on a fresh, airy plateau above the valley of the Loire.

▶ Leave Blois on the *N152* as for Tours. In Veuves, turn right on the *D65* to Monteaux. Bear left for Cangey along the *D58* which becomes the *D1*. Continue through Limeray. Keep left in Pocé-sur-Cisse as for Amboise then go right following the 'Vouvray' sign. Turn left on the *D46* and continue to Vouvray.

10 Vouvray, Loire Valley Central
There hardly seem to be enough vineyards around Vouvray to justify its reputation as a white wine village, but most are on the upland plateau hidden by limestone cliffs. You can buy wine at several caves, some of them dug into the limestone. The Écomusée explains the cultivation of vines, shows old-style crafts including the sewing of the local embroidered bonnets, and describes the impact on the countryside of the TGV superexpress railway lines.

i Rue Gambetta

▶ Leave Vouvray on the *N152* and return to Tours.

Royal Blois: a former capital of France and famous for its château

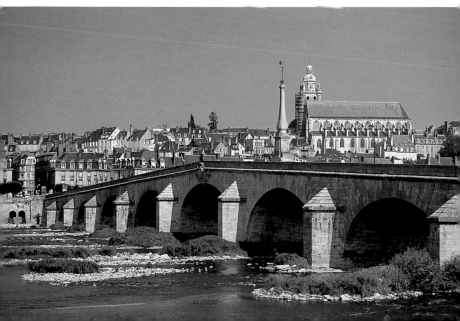

THE DORDOGNE &
SOUTHWEST FRANCE

Here is another region which shows the remarkable variety of France. On the coast there are uninterrupted expanses of surf-washed beaches. Behind them stretch vast areas planted with pines. The Pyrenean foothills offer bracing spa resorts where walks by mountain streams and wildflower meadows are the order of the day. In the valleys of the Dordogne and the Vézère you will find the greatest cluster of prehistoric sites in Europe, many of them troglodytic dwellings quarried thousands of years ago.

Lourdes attracts millions of pilgrims and visitors every year. Smaller numbers make the journey to the glorious hilltop church in St-Bertrand-de-Comminges. You can visit weird underground caverns, one group bizarrely reached, not by going deep into the bowels of the earth, but by heading uphill in a cable car, and you can find out about traditional rural crafts and ways of life in display areas large and small.

Oysters are a major crop where the Bordeaux route reaches the coast. Inland, connoisseurs of wine and brandy can lose themselves among the vineyards of Armagnac, Bergerac, Barsac, Graves and Sauternes.

West and south of Bordeaux there are few natural obstacles to divert the roads from long, flat straights through the forests. Winding river valleys are the norm for Périgueux. The Pau tour, as it climbs into the Pyrenees, is for pass-stormers.

Some of France's most glorious towns and villages are here. Rocamadour is one of the most stunningly located places in Europe, but there are also Domme and Sarlat and Labastide-d'Armagnac to cherish.

Wildlife parks include bird reserves, zoos for endangered species and an atmospheric place devoted to the ancient worship of the bear. You can find out in museums and exhibitions about tobacco, seaplanes, prehistoric art, clockwork figures and hussars.

Bordeaux

Bordeaux is the capital of Aquitaine and of wine, the heart of a region of world-renowned vineyards. It was one of the first cities in France to pedestrianise its shopping streets, and a pioneer in computerised traffic management. Among its elegant public buildings, look for the river façade of the 18th-century Place de la Bourse and the sumptuous Grand-Théâtre of the same era. There are bustling covered markets, craft shops and studios of every kind. Museums and galleries take in painting and decorative arts, the history of the region of Aquitaine, vintage printing presses, natural history collections with magnificent crystal displays, the customs service, military history and the Resistance movement. Cruise boats sail down the Garonne and their joint estuary, the Gironde. A recently introduced touring opportunity is a helicopter jaunt over your own selection of Bordeaux vineyards.

Périgueux

Périgueux is a handsome town whose beautiful old quarter, where the merchants and craftsmen used to live, includes many fine Renaissance and medieval buildings. The perhaps over-restored cathedral, Saint-Front, is a fascinating sight, all domes and cupolas, giving Périgueux an almost Ottoman-Empire skyline.

The Musée du Périgord in Cours Tourny has expanded well beyond its original brief to exhibit the results of excavated Roman sites. The Musée Militaire shows uniforms and weapons from several centuries, and tells the story of the district's war-ravaged past. There are pleasant gardens, and squares with pollarded trees. You can stroll along the rue des Gladiateurs to the site of the Roman arena. This is a cool place in

summer, planted with shrubs and trees, its fragmentary Roman archways within sight and sound of a modern mosaic-tiled fountain.

Pau

In the 19th century, the British invaded Pau, but not with any martial intent. Three Scots laid out a golf course for the British colony. At the turn of the century and through the 1920s, Pau was one of the great British resorts of Europe. There was American influence, too. Orville and Wilbur Wright set up the world's first aviation school here. The town has lovely parks and gardens. Find the boulevard des

Opposite: vineyard in Bordeaux
Above: the opulent, fertile valley of the Dordogne at Périgueux

Pyrénées and you will see not only a fine promenade, but also a glorious southern mountain horizon. A rebuilt funicular railway climbs from a lower avenue.

Some of the finest state rooms in France are in the majestic, if much restored, château, which houses a rich collection of tapestries. On one weekend in June, Pau echoes to the scream of high-pitched engines. There is a famous racing circuit here, including public roads and driveways to the leafy Parc Beaumont.

Coast, Dunes
& Forests

South of Bordeaux, the flatness of the Landes region is disguised by two notable features. Along the coast there are long fine-sand beaches backed by substantial dunes, while inland lies a huge forest area with carefully watered croplands in extensive clearings.

4 DAYS • 486KM • 301 MILES

ITINERARY		
BORDEAUX	▶	**Gujan-Mestras** (47km-29m)
GUJAN-MESTRAS	▶	**Arcachon** (13km-8m)
ARCACHON	▶	**Biscarrosse** (42km-26m)
BISCARROSSE	▶	**Mimizan** (38km-24m)
MIMIZAN	▶	**Sabres** (47km-29m)
SABRES	▶	**Mont-de-Marsan** (81km-50m)
MONT-DE-MARSAN	▶	**Labastide-d'Armagnac** (29km-18m)
LABASTIDE-D'ARMAGNAC	▶	**Barbotan-les-Thermes** (16km-10m)
BARBOTAN-LES-THERMES	▶	**Nérac** (42km-26m)
NÉRAC	▶	Sauternes (82km-51m)
SAUTERNES	▶	Bordeaux (49km-30m)

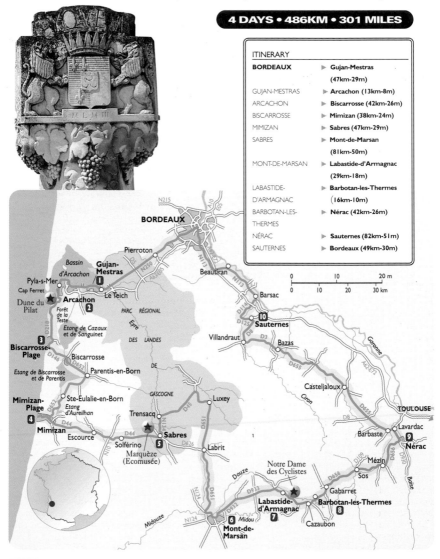

▶ *Leave Bordeaux on the* **N250**. *Go straight ahead on the* **D650** *through Le Teich to Gujan-Mestras.*

BACK TO NATURE

Turn right in Le Teich, on the way to Gujan-Mestras, at the 'Parc Ornithologique' sign. The bird reserve here in the scrubland delta by the Bassin d'Arcachon is especially strong in wildfowl, but you should also look for whiskered terns, black-winged stilts, herons, storks and little egrets, as well as numerous dragonflies.

---

❶ Gujan-Mestras, Aquitaine
The two parts of this strung-out cluster of villages on the southern side of the great Bassin d'Arcachon could hardly be more oddly matched. Take any of the streets with 'port' signs, to the right of the main road, and you enter the almost timeless world of the oyster farmer. The ports are seven rectangular inlets of the bay, lined by identical wooden workshop cabins.

Outside lies the paraphernalia of oyster cultivation – boat tackle, mounds of emptied shells and piles of sharpened wooden stakes to be driven into the bed of the bay where the oysters grow.

Elsewhere, Gujan-Mestras is a modern holiday resort. Turn left for the 'Parc Aquatique' (water park) called Aquacity. The pools, slides, wave machine and water chutes of Aquacity share the large leisure area at La Hume with a flimsy-looking 'rustic' village where some 50 serious craftworkers settle every summer. There is also a well-stocked museum of ship models and ship design.

⌐i⌐ *Avenue de Lattre de Tassigny*

FOR CHILDREN

Street signs in Gujan-Mestras are decorated with ladybirds – *coccinelles*. This is a link with La Coccinelle animal park at La Hume. Here, children are offered 'a nothing like and surprising walk' among domestic and farm animals, with pony rides, trampolines, swings and toboggans as a bonus.

Arcachon's modern yacht marina provides a safe haven

▶ *Continue on the* **D650** *to Arcachon.*

❷ Arcachon, Aquitaine
Although the oysters of the Bassin d'Arcachon have been celebrated since the 16th century, the town itself is a resort created in the railway age. Arcachon has a well-equipped yacht haven and fishing port. A high-set figure of Christ blesses the harbour. Walk to the end of the breakwater and you will see not only the far-out oyster beds but also a stone anchor sailors' memorial. The aquarium and museum specialise in the creatures of the bay and the open sea. You can sail to the oyster beds, to the Île aux Oiseaux (Bird's Island) in the bay, and across the mouth of the bay to the peninsula resort of Cap Ferret. Back from the waterfront the town has lively shopping and café areas, and it is generously supplied with woods and parkland. Arcachon's status as the most stylish resort on the Côte d'Argent ('silver coast') is well deserved.

⌐i⌐ *Place Roosevelt*

BACK TO NATURE

South of Arcachon, the Dune du Pilat is the greatest sand dune in Europe, more than 106m (350 feet) high and extending for nearly 3km (1¾ miles). You will not be able to see its imperceptible wind-driven inland movement, but take the long stairway to the summit for a beautiful view of pine forests and the sea. Heathland in the area supports Dartford warblers, red-backed shrikes and wrynecks, as well as plenty of insect life.

RECOMMENDED WALKS

After the Dune du Pilat south of Arcachon, the D218 runs through the pinewoods, scrub and sandhills of the Forêt de la Teste. Park here, and you will find many informal footpaths off to the right, leading to beaches lapped by the Atlantic breakers.

▶ *Leave Arcachon on the D218 to Pyla-sur-Mer and past the Dune du Pilat to Biscarrosse.*

❸ Biscarrosse, Aquitaine

A pinewood resort with bungalows, hotels and a few colour-washed apartment blocks, Biscarrosse-Plage has a not-yet-finished air, added to by the fact that sand blows around its streets. But there is a splendid beach here, backed by dunes, with white-topped breakers creaming in. The older part of the settlement, Biscarrosse-Bourg or Biscarrosse-Ville, is separated from the beach resort by a full 9.6km (6 miles) of open road. This is a handsome place. Its church stands among bright and well-watered gardens dotted with birch trees.

On the southwestern edge of town lies an attractive lake rimmed by low wooded hills. This is a good sailing and angling centre, and it was briefly, between the wars, the French base of a flying-boat service from New York. The Musée de l'Hydraviation, on the road to the lake, recalls those flying-boat days, and there is a Musée de la Nature.

ⓘ *Avenue Plage*

▶ *Leave Biscarrosse on the D652 through Parentis-en-Born to St-Eulalie, then take the D87 to Mimizan.*

FOR HISTORY BUFFS

Parentis-en-Born, on the way from Biscarrosse to Mimizan, is a place with a rustic appearance and a pleasant lakeside. Incongruously, since 1954, oil has been pumped from the lake bed and from offshore deposits. The Musée du Pétrole tells the story of this local industry.

❹ Mimizan, Aquitaine

This is another split-personality town, approached along the shore of the Étang d'Aureilhan, where Winston Churchill was often a guest of the Duke of Westminster on an estate there. He left several paintings of local scenes. Mimizan divides at the Papeteries de Gascogne, a huge papermill which wafts an unmistakable smell along the prevailing wind. The holiday resort is very modern, with fine beaches ideal for surfing. You can explore the forest to the south, on foot or along the cycle tracks.

The inland part of Mimizan is built round a largely derelict

Mimizan's fine sandy beach lies to the west of the town

11th-century Benedictine abbey. The little town museum faces it. In summer the riverside bull-ring promotes *courses landaises*, acrobatic affairs, similar to the Provençal form of bullfighting in which the bulls are unharmed. Stilt-walking is another speciality.

ⅈ *Avenue Martin*

▶ *Leave Mimizan on the D44 to Sabres.*

> ### FOR HISTORY BUFFS
>
> On the D44 before Sabres, the village of Solférino recalls a battlefield in Italy. The estate here, owned by Napoleon III, was given the name after his successful part in the battle against Austria in 1859. A museum holds mementoes of his Second Empire.

5 Sabres, Aquitaine
A pleasant if unremarkable road-junction village, with its half-timbered houses and old church, Sabres still has a station on the railway built in 1890 to link it with Mimizan. The line is now used to take visitors to the remotely located Écomusée at Marquèze, 5km (3 miles) to the northwest.

This splendid place is part of the Parc Régional des Landes de Gascogne. Displays make it clear how the great forests used to support little local industries such as iron and glass works, brick and tile kilns. Then, in the second half of the 19th century, the government decided to manage the pine forests on a virtually industrial scale.

Marquèze, based on a large forest clearing, shows you both how the timber resources have been exploited and what kinds of activity were discarded – charcoal-burning, water-mills, sheep-farming and the cultivation of fruit trees. Traditional buildings, many of them raised on stilts, have been painstakingly reconstructed here.

▶ *Leave Sabres on the N134 as for Bordeaux. In Trensacq turn right on the D45. Turn right on the D651 through Luxey, then continue to Mont-de-Marsan.*

> ### FOR CHILDREN
>
> On the way to Mont-de-Marsan, to keep the children occupied on the drive across the flat forest and farmland after Trensacq, ask them to count how many bends there are in the 18km (11 miles) of the D45.

> ### SPECIAL TO...
>
> On the way to Mont-de-Marsan, turn left in Luxey following the 'Écomusée' sign, and park beside the church. The nearby museum deals with the uses of resin from the vast pine forests of the Landes.

The Ecomusée at Marquèze is an open-air museum documenting the life of the Landes region

6 Mont-de-Marsan,
Aquitaine
You will not be long in Mont-de-Marsan before realising that this is a place of some consequence. Its elegant 19th-century public buildings, immaculately kept, stand among modern equivalents, which are imaginative in design, but do not clash. In fact, Mont-de-Marsan is an important government centre.

It stands where the Rivers Midou and Douze merge into the waggishly named Midouze. The Parc Jean Rameau is an attractive woodland area, with many flowering shrubs, overlooking the Douze.

A pair of restored 14th-century buildings house the museum and the art gallery. The Church of Ste Madeleine is worth visiting for its marble-work and elegant ornamented ceiling.

Like Mimizan, Mont-de-Marsan is a centre for *courses landaises*, but the great sporting enthusiasm is for horse-racing. The impressive race-course plays host to a dozen meetings every year.

i *Place Leclerc*

▶ Leave Mont-de-Marsan on the **D932** as for Roquefort. Bear right on the **D933** to St-Justin, then right on the **D626** to Labastide-d'Armagnac.

costume museum. There is also a display of Armagnac brandy. Away from the square, a 17th-century chapel houses an exhibition of the *bastides*, the historic fortified villages.

Beyond Labastide, turn right on the C1 for Château Garreau. At the end of a dusty gravel road between its ridgetop vineyards, the estate's Musée du Vigneron has exhibits on old distillery techniques and equipment, and on the rural life of Armagnac.

i *Place Royal*

SPECIAL TO...

About 2.4km (1½ miles) beyond Labastide-d'Armagnac, look for the isolated 11th-century church called Notre-Dame des Cyclistes. Since 1959 this historic building has been a cyclists' sanctuary, with old machines and the jerseys of famous race-winners on display.
Close at hand, the Maison des Cyclistes houses a museum of more bicycle types.

7 Labastide-d'Armagnac, Aquitaine

Almost miraculously, the arcaded square here, Place Royale, has survived with little alteration since 1291. Three sides are still taken up by arches and cool, covered walkways. The fourth features the 15th-century church. Some guide-books give Labastide a cursory mention, but go to the flowery Place Royale and you will find an architectural gem of effortless charm.

The tourist office, in one of the arcades, leads to a little

RECOMMENDED WALKS

Ask at the tourist office in Labastide-d'Armagnac for the map of the waymarked walks southwest of the little town. They climb gently into a lush landscape of woodlands, farms and Armagnac vineyards.

▶ Continue on the **D626** to Cazaubon and turn left on the **D656** to Barbotan-les-Thermes.

Cool, shady arches in the Place Royale, Labastide-d'Armagnac

8 Barbotan-les-Thermes, Aquitaine

Unlike the spa towns of some other countries, those in France have not mouldered away. Barbotan, whose thermal baths were probably known to the Romans, has been completely refurbished. Brightly decorated hotels, shops, cafés and restaurants line the busy and effectively pedestrianised main street. Sparkling new buildings house the baths which attract an increasing number of *curistes* (cure-seekers) – more than 20,000 of them every year.

There are attractive gardens, pleasant walks and an opportunity to admire relics of the past, such as the 12th-century church whose clocktower is built above one of the medieval town gateways.

Just outside Barbotan is the Lac de l'Uby. This well-equipped leisure area offers sailing, tennis and mini-golf facilities as well as a sandy beach, pony rides, pedalo hire and a children's play park.

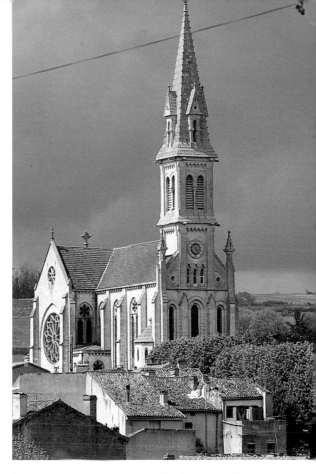

The Church of St Nicholas in the town of Nérac

i Maison du Curiste

▶ Continue on the **D656** through Gabarret to Nérac.

Nérac, Aquitaine

Only one wing remains, high above the River Baïse, of Nérac's lovely Renaissance château. Climb the stairs to the elegant, open, first-floor gallery, and you will find a museum of archaeology and history. Close by, the Church of St Nicholas has a severe frontage but some good 18th-century stained glass. There are grand views across the river to Petit Nérac, a hillside quarter of fine old buildings with dark red roofs. Its church spire soars in glorious silhouette against the sky.

River boats run cruises on the Baïse. Upstream, the Promenade de la Garenne offers you a stroll through a pleasant woodland park with fountains and an open-air theatre.

▶ Leave Nérac on the **D930** to Lavardac, then go left to Casteljaloux and follow signs to Bazas. Continue to Villandraut. Turn right on the **D8** through Nouillan and Brouquet, then left on the **D125** to Sauternes.

Sauternes, Aquitaine

Arriving at Sauternes, the centre of one of the most famous white wine districts, you will come to the Place de l'Église, which would be the heart of the village if there were a village for it to be the heart of. Only a handful of buildings surround the square, one of them where the local wine producers offer their wares. There is also a map showing the locations of the eight vineyards which regularly welcome visitors.

Not included in this display is the aristocratic 16th- and 17th-century Château Yquem. Its Château Yquem wine, with the superlative classification of *Premier Grand Cru Classé*, was the first to be produced from grapes affected with the 'noble rot' provoked by the misty mornings and warm afternoons of autumn.

▶ Continue on the **D125** as for Budos, then go right on the **D114**. Follow this road over the autoroute to the **N113**. Turn left there through Barsac and return to Bordeaux, avoiding the autoroute.

SCENIC ROUTES

Heading south for Biscarrosse-Plage, the D218 runs through the attractive pine and sandhill country of the Forêt de la Teste.
Later, the D146 continues in similar country over a low winding pass among the pinewood dunes.
Around Luxey, the D651 leads across a lovely quiet countryside of forests and farms, with characteristic timber-framed houses and attractive villages drowsing in the summer sun.
Immediately after Sauternes, the D125 opens up a delicious little landscape of undulating vineyards in the valley of the River Ciron.

Journey into
Prehistory

Although there are remains of old Roman buildings in the heart of Périgueux, this tour, featuring two of France's loveliest rivers, the Dordogne and the Vézère, takes you much further back into the history of man. Here, limestone provides the huge cliffs, the amazing caves and underground rivers, and the golden building stone of beautiful towns like Sarlat and Domme.

4 DAYS • 383KM • 238 MILES

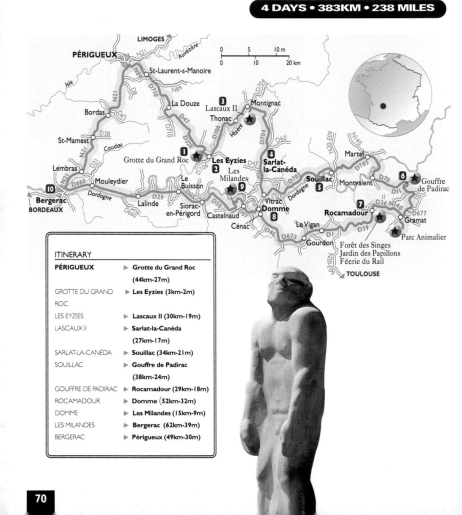

ITINERARY

ⓘ *Place Francheville, Périgueux*

▶ *Leave Périgueux on the **N89** as for Brive. Go right on the **D710**, left on the **D45** then right on the **D47** to Grotte du Grand Roc.*

SCENIC ROUTES

The approach to the Grotto du Grand Roc on the D47 introduces the stunning limestone cliffs which characterise this tour.

---

❶ Grotte du Grand Roc, Aquitaine
The great natural limestone wall here, facing the Vézère, with its overhangs forming the pitched roof lines of some bizarrely located houses, is honeycombed with ancient dwellings and caverns. In the Grotte du Grand Roc you will find an underground wonderland whose cave floors and hanging gardens of fretted limestone look like a spiky coral reef (wire grills protect some of the formations). In the same magnificent cliff, the prehistoric rock shelters of Laugerie Haute

and Laugerie Basse, which yielded countless objects left behind by their Ice Age inhabitants, are open to visitors.

Less forbidding than its name, the Gorge d'Enfer (Gorge of Hell) is set in a little wooded, grassy side valley whose caves display 25,000-year-old wall carvings. There is also an animal reserve, a fishing lake and a picnic site. Further on, the Musée de Spéléologie, entered by a stairway up a colossal overhanging cliff, illustrates the daring work of the modern cave explorers.

▶ *Continue on the **D47** into Les Eyzies.*

❷ Les Eyzies, Aquitaine
If the Vézère is the 'valley of mankind', the village of Les Eyzies, spectacularly located between a northern limestone cliff and the river, is at the heart of the greatest concentration of prehistoric sites. The Musée National de la Préhistoire, built into the cliff face, is devoted in particular to the palaeolithic era, starting perhaps 2½–3 million years ago with the first traces of primitive man. Near by, the Abri Pataud is a cliff shelter of

more than 20,000 years ago. As a complete contrast, Les Eyzies also offers a botanical garden of medicinal plants; other displays here explain the culture of the crayfish and the bee.

ⓘ *Place de la Mairie*

▶ *Leave Les Eyzies on the **D706** to Montignac. Turn right on the **D704**, then right again for Lascaux II.*

❸ Lascaux II, Aquitaine
Discovered in 1940, the caves at Lascaux are decorated with the most celebrated prehistoric paintings in the world – lively representations of bulls, deer and horses created nearly 18,000 years ago. The caves have had to be closed to the public to prevent deterioration of the original paintings, but painstakingly exact replicas are on display at the neighbouring site called Lascaux II. A visit here cures visitors of any notion that our ancestors of 800 generations ago were nothing more than primitive louts. Much older than Lascaux, the nearby cave

Périgueux has a rich historical mixture of architectural styles

Replicas of Lascaux' original cave paintings on show at Lascaux II

site of Régourdou is also open to visitors. The brown bears in its park match displays in the museum there about the prehistoric cult of the bear.

[i] *Place Léo-Magne, Montignac*

FOR HISTORY BUFFS

Off the **D706**, after Les Eyzies, several sites illustrate the everyday life of our very remote ancestors. Préhisto-Parc features outdoor tableaux of Neanderthal and Cro-Magnon (a type of 'modern' man), hunting expeditions and household scenes of 15,000 years ago. La Roque-St-Christophe is an amazing troglodytic fortress town, lived in from prehistoric days to the 18th century, with five great terraces overlooking the River Vézère. At Le Thot, a modern museum and gallery explain the environment and art of prehistoric times. In the parkland, present-day animals such as red and fallow deer, bison, tarpan and Przewalkski's horses can be compared with life-size replicas of mammoths and aurochs (an extinct type of ox).

▶ *Return to Montignac and turn right on the **D704** to Sarlat-la-Canéda.*

4 **Sarlat-la-Canéda,**
Aquitaine

The golden stone of Sarlat and the effortless grace of its Gothic and Renaissance buildings make this one of the loveliest towns in the Dordogne region. Even the tourist information office is housed in a 15th-century mansion near the handsome cathedral of the 16th and 17th centuries. Shaded alleys and courtyards in the old town are busy with a craftsmen's market and shops at which every third or fourth seems to specialise in *foie gras*. L'Homo Sapiens is a little museum of archaeological discoveries, prehistoric art forms, stone and flint tools. There is an imaginative Aquarium concentrating on the 30 or more species of fish found in the River Dordogne. On a wooded hillside above the square, pleasant public gardens can be found.

SCENIC ROUTES

The first ridge-top road on the tour is the **D704** to Sarlat, giving wide-ranging views over rolling wooded hills.

---

[i] *Place de la Liberté*

▶ *Leave Sarlat-la-Canéda on the **D46** for Vitrac. In Vitrac-Port watch for a left turn on to the **D703** to Carsac and Souillac. Turn left on to the **N20** in Souillac.*

5 **Souillac,** Midi-Pyrénées

The glory of this busy centre in the Dordogne valley is the restored 12th-century Romanesque church called Abbatiale Sainte Marie, whose red-and-white tiled roofs culminate in a series of cupolas, as in the cathedral at Périgueux. The carvings in the church are particularly fine. Behind the church you may hear the incongruous music of a 1920s jazz band. This is just one of the lifelike exhibits in the Musée de l'Automate. Tableaux of moving life-size figures also include a glamorous lady snake-charmer, a clown and a splendid animated 19th-century Passion Play.

FOR CHILDREN

Quercyland is a fun park on the outskirts of Souillac, where children subdued by all the prehistory can work off some energy.

---

i *Boulevard Louis-Jean Malvy*

▶ *Leave Souillac on the D703 to Martel. Turn right on the N140, left on the D70 then right on the D11 to Miers and left on the D91. Go left on the D60, right at the Y-junction at the stone cross, then right at the T-junction to Gouffre de Padirac.*

SCENIC ROUTES

After Montvalent, on the way from Souillac to Padirac, there is a landscape change as the D70 and D11 run through the parcels of sheep-grazed land on the limestone plateau known as the *causse*.

⑥ Gouffre de Padirac, Midi-Pyrénées

Open since the late 19th century when it was discovered, the Padirac chasm is one of the greatest underground sights in Europe. Lifts and stairways descend to the otherworldly cavern of a subterranean river where, by boat and pathway, you can visit glorious floodlit limestone chambers like the Great Dome Gallery, walls of stalagmites and a petrified waterfall. Cafés and restaurants, a picnic area and a small zoo are clustered above ground.

▶ *Continue on the D90 to Padirac, turn left and follow signs to Gramat. Leave Gramat on the N140 northwards, then turn left on the D36. Turn left on the D32 into Rocamadour.*

⑦ Rocamadour, Midi-Pyrénées

Words and pictures rarely do justice to the reality of Rocamadour, the magnificent fortified pilgrimage town whose historic houses, sanctuary churches, bishops' palace, museums and – at the highest level – skyline castle cascade down a terraced limestone cliff. It became a place of pilgrimage in the 12th century, visited by the great and the good of Christendom. Lifts and staircases, including the long and tiring pilgrims' Holy Way, are threaded through the town. Once you have turned on to the D32 you should pause to admire the stunning situation of the place, from the viewpoint beside the Hotel Belvedere. In Rocamadour itself, the finest view is from the castle ramparts. The D32 road avoids the town centre often crammed with visitors. There are parking places in the valley.

RECOMMENDED WALKS

At busy times, you may appreciate leaving the narrow streets of Rocamadour for a walk, steep in places, based on old sheep tracks in the Alzou Valley. It starts from the bridge on the D32 below the town and heads up-river.

FOR CHILDREN

Just after the Jardin des Papillons on the D36 before Rocamadour, La Féerie du Rail (The Enchanted Railway) is a huge model layout with 60 trains hauling coaches and freight wagons past mountain villages, farms, a castle, a fairground and a windmill, and over a viaduct menaced by the ice cliffs of a glacier.

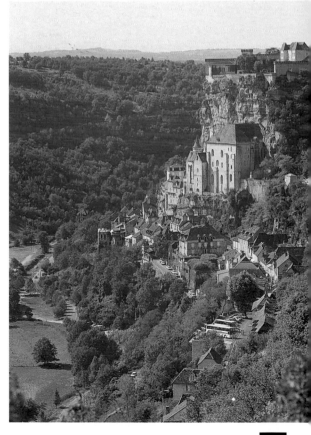

The ancient town of Rocamadour, situated above the Gorge of Alzou

BACK TO NATURE

Turn left in Gramat, then take the **D677** and the **D14** to the Parc Animalier. This zoo houses more than 300 species including bear, chamois, lynx, yak, moufflon, birds of prey and breeds of farm animals 'in peril of extinction', such as Limousin, Gascon and Normandy pigs. To find the park, turn left on the **N140**, then take the **D677** and the **D14**.

On the **D36** approaching Rocamadour there is an impressive Forêt des Singes (Monkey Forest), where macaques (similar to the Barbary apes of Gibraltar) roam freely. You can buy and distribute popcorn, one of the monkeys' favourite snacks. Alongside, the Jardin des Papillons houses free-flying exotic butterflies of many colourful species from Europe, Asia, Africa and the Americas. There are falconry displays at the Rocher des Aigles in Rocamadour.

SCENIC ROUTES

After Rocamadour, the **D32** climbs above a deep canyon with tiers of limestone cliffs. The riverside road from Castelnaud beyond Fayrac opens up a tremendous view to the castle of Beynac, and the **D29** runs past rapids and wooded islets in the Dordogne on the way to Lalinde.

▶ *Continue on the **D32** to Couzou, go right on the **D39** through St Projet, right on the **D1** then join the **D673** to Gourdon. Turn left as for Sarlat then left as for Salviac, leaving Gourdon on the **D763**. Go right on the **D6**, which becomes the **D46** to Cénac. Go right on the **D49** to Domme.*

8 Domme, Aquitaine
This lovely, mellow hilltop town, founded with defensive ramparts and gateways around 1280, provides one of the finest viewpoints in France. The River Dordogne curves below the town, giving way to fields, farmhouses and lines of poplars on the riverside plain.

Limestone cliffs, woods and hill villages march to the horizon. In Domme itself there are beautiful townscape views round every corner. A good museum illustrates local domestic life in the past. Shops sell local honey, jams, truffles and *foie gras*. In the central square, an old covered market hall is now the entrance to a marvellous series of underground caverns with mirror lakes and floodlit limestone columns.

ⓘ *Place de la Halle*

RECOMMENDED WALKS

A leaflet you can collect at Domme shows three waymarked walks, starting from the walled gateway of the Porte des Tours. They descend by shady paths to the River Dordogne and wander through higher farmland.

▶ *Return to Cénac and go straight on along the **D50**, through St-Cybranet, then continue as for Siorac-en-Périgord. In Pont-de-Cause bear right for Castelnaud. In Castelnaud, go straight ahead for Fayrac and Les Milandes. Turn left on the **D53** as for Siorac then after a 'virages' sign watch for a sharp right uphill signed 'Château des Milandes'.*

9 Les Milandes, Aquitaine
Perched on a terrace giving spreading views over the Dordogne valley, the restored 15th-century castle in the attractive and tucked-away hamlet of Les Milandes was owned from

Domme's spectacular hilltop position has made it a coveted prize throughout France's turbulent history

1949 to 1969 by the American singer Josephine Baker, star of the Paris cabarets between the wars. It was here that she founded a philanthropic foundation to look after children from all over the world.

Beyond the castle, the white courtyard of the farm which was also part of Josephine Baker's estate houses a rural museum explaining the improvements in agricultural techniques through the years.

FOR HISTORY BUFFS

On the way from Domme to Les Milandes, on a glorious viewpoint site above the village of the same name, Castelnaud is a restored medieval castle which houses displays on artillery and siege warfare. During much of the Hundred Years' War, the castle was held by the English.

▶ *Continue from the farm museum and bear left as for Veyrines-de-Vergt. Turn right on the D53 then take the D50 to Siorac and the D25 to le Buisson-de-Cadouin. Follow signs to Lalinde, then Bergerac.*

⑩ Bergerac, Aquitaine
A cobbled car park which slopes down towards the River Dordogne is a convenient base for a stroll round the restored old town at the heart of present-day Bergerac. There are narrow lanes of part-timbered houses, and tiny squares, one of them shaded by chestnut trees where a statue of Rostand's hero Cyrano de Bergerac, the 17th-century nobleman and soldier famous for his large nose, stands, nobly cloaked.

The impressive Musée du Tabac in the town hall (Maison Peyrarède) illustrates the discovery of tobacco, its sources, and the local tobacco trade, as well as displaying beautifully worked pipes, cigarette holders, snuffboxes and tobacco jars. Its

Medieval houses grace the revived old town in Bergerac

curious second-floor exit leads back down to street level through the town museum (history and regional ethnography).

Near by, the Musée du Vin et de la Batellerie combines several long-standing Bergerac interests – wine, barrel-making and river traffic. There are also guided visits to the old monastery housing the wine council on which all the Bergerac growers are represented.

[i] *Rue Neuve d'Argenson*

▶ *Leave Bergerac on the N21 and return to Périgueux.*

SPECIAL TO...

Two great gourmet specialities of the Dordogne are truffles and *foie gras*. Truffles are rare edible fungi which grow underground, often in oak woods, and are dug out by truffle-hunting dogs – and even pigs. These trained animals are weaned on truffles from an early age and are trusted not to eat the precious quarry. The production of *pâté de foie gras* – goose or sometimes duck-liver pâté – involves grotesque force-feeding of the birds with huge quantities of maize. The pâté is preserved, often with a minute portion of truffle included, and sold at a luxury price.

Through the
High Pyrenees

This is primarily a summer tour, exploring some of the highest roads in the Pyrenees mountains. The Col du Tourmalet usually opens only after the snows clear in June. The mountain roads are exhilarating in fine weather, hairpinning to great summit viewpoints. There are pleasant resorts in the foothills.

4 DAYS • 392KM • 243 MILES

[i] *Place Royale, Pau*

▶ *Leave Pau on the N117 to Tarbes, avoiding the autoroute.*

❶ Tarbes, Midi-Pyrénées
With centuries of history as a regional capital behind it, Tarbes is a busy, prosperous, confident and go-ahead city. There is a strong summer programme of musical, theatrical, artistic, floral and sporting events.

Just off the town centre, the Jardin Massey is an attractive woodland park with pools, statues, a bandstand, an open-air theatre and peacocks' outlandish cries echoing over the lawns. Be prepared to give way to families of mallards waddling between the ponds and streams. In the heart of the park, the Musée Massey is an elegant 19th-century mansion with a fine collection of French, Flemish and Italian paintings, and a superb display on the hussars, the élite cavalry corps not only of France, but also of countries all over the world.

Although the present-day hussars stationed at Tarbes are mechanised units, the national stud of Anglo-Arab horses

founded in 1806 continues to flourish. The stables are regularly open to visitors, and Tarbes hosts several show-jumping and dressage events during the year.

[i] *Place de Verdun*

> **FOR HISTORY BUFFS**
>
> In Tarbes, the boyhood home of the great World War I commander Marshal Foch is a museum with films and photographs, uniforms and honours, and the moving text of his final order of the day in 1918.

▶ *Leaves Tarbes on the D935 to Bagnères-de-Bigorre.*

❷ Bagnères-de-Bigorre, Midi-Pyrénées
Offering thermal baths, a casino, sports facilities and healthy walks, with industry kept discreetly in the outskirts, Bagnères is a typical southern spa nestling in the forested foothills of the Pyrenees. Occupied in prehistoric times, it was taken over by the Romans, who were the first to build bathhouses over its warm-water

View from the Pic du Midi de Bigorre

springs. Its reputation as a spa increased through the years and came to a peak in the 19th century, as the architecture of the thermal establishments shows. The Musée Bigourdan has local displays, while the Musée Salies is given over mostly to paintings.

Bagnères is well known for its authentic folk-singing concerts. Tennis and the hiring of horses, ponies or all-terrain bicycles can be arranged. As well as fishing, often for rainbow trout, the River Adour running through the town is used for lively white-water canoeing.

[i] *Allées Tournefort*

> **RECOMMENDED WALKS**
>
> On the south side of Bagnères, make for the wooded Parc Thermal de Salut. Pathways zigzag to the crest of a beautiful forested ridge, with views down over the spa town in the valley floor.

▶ *Leave Bagnères-de-Bigorre on the **D938** as for Toulouse. Turn right on the **D26**, then right on the **D929** through Hèches. Watch for a left turn, just as you see the 'Rebouc' sign, down over a level crossing and immediately left, following the **D26** again. In St-Bertrand-de-Comminges, go right at the crossroads, uphill on the **D26**.*

❸ St-Bertrand-de-Comminges, Midi-Pyrénées

Here is a most attractively located village whose red-roofed houses climb a modest ridge between the farmlands of the plain and the wooded Pyrenean foothills.

The village and its unexpectedly majestic cathedral both take their name from a 12th-century bishop buried here. Pilgrims have been coming in great numbers since the Middle Ages. In the 16th century the cathedral interior was remodelled with stunning carved-wood screens around the choir. The splendid organ also dates from that time, and is played at many recitals. Outside, the beautiful arcaded cloisters look incongruously across to the wooded hillsides, which were a refuge for Resistance fighters in World War II.

The village preserves several fine old buildings, such as the 15th-century Maison Bridaut with its stone tower and timber-framed upper storeys. The tourist office gives access to a museum of sculptures and local archaeological finds.

Below the village stands an

St-Bertrand-de-Comminges can trace its history back to 72BC

isolated 12th-century basilica in Italianate surroundings with tall cypress trees. Much of its masonry was taken from the ruins of a Roman settlement.

ⓘ Les Olivetains

▶ *Return downhill then go straight ahead on the **D26** through Valcabrère. Turn right on the **N125** and follow signs to Bagnères-de-Luchon.*

❹ Bagnères-de-Luchon, Midi-Pyrénées

Most elegant and luxurious of the Pyrenean spas, Luchon (as it is generally known) is centred on a lively tree-lined avenue, with pavement cafés leading to the gardens of the thermal establishment. There is a stylish atmosphere both about the town itself and about the way it conducts its business. Walking, rock-climbing, fishing, clay-pigeon shooting, canoeing and rafting, tennis, hang-gliding and horse-riding, archery and golf are all catered for here. Many visitors come to the spa (the largest and most fashionable Pyrenean spa) not because they are unwell, but because they want a 'toning-up'.

The history of the town and district is well illustrated in the Musée du Pays de Luchon. This 18th-century mansion has a dozen exhibition rooms also devoted to the wildlife of the Pyrenees, the development of mountaineering and 2,000 years of *curistes* from the time of notable Romans such as Pompey and Tiberius, who sojourned at the even-then handsomely equipped resort they knew as *Ilixion*.

SPECIAL TO...

You can see the great Basque game *pelota* being played at Luchon. It is a fast and exciting contest, something like squash, with the racket replaced by a curved wickerwork scoop called a *chistera*.

---

i   *Allées d'Étigny*

FOR CHILDREN

The Col de Peyresourde near Luchon is an area where the children can play place-name games. Ask them to find the villages with no consonants in their names, and the one which sounds singularly unhealthy.

RECOMMENDED WALKS

After Luchon, turn left on the D76 towards the Lac d'Oô. From a car park in this green steep-sided Pyrenean glen, it is a straightforward walk up to the lake, fed by a 275m (900-foot) cascade from Lac d'Espingo higher still.

SPECIAL TO...

The passes of Aspin and Tourmalet are classic stretches of the famous Tour de France cycle race. If you are here on the day of the Tour, forget about driving. Park among the thousands of spectators and watch the battle for the coveted 'King of the Mountains' title.

BACK TO NATURE

In summer, the foothills of the Pyrenees are carpeted with wildflowers – aconites, asphodel, Pyrenean lilies and many more. The Office de la Montagne in Luchon organises guided visits to some of the best botanical areas. For ornithologists, the area might afford sightseeing of Alpine choughs, snow finches, golden eagles and griffon vultures.

▶ *Leave Luchon on the D618 over the Col de Peyresourde. In Arreau go right on the D929 then, opposite the Esso station, not before, bear left uphill over the Col d'Aspin on the D918. Turn left in Ste-Marie-de-Campan to follow the D918 to Col du Tourmalet.*

The ski resort of Col du Tourmalet, virtually deserted in summer, livens up in the winter

◾ Col du Tourmalet, Midi-Pyrénées

At an altitude of 2,114m (6,936 feet), this is the highest through-road summit in the French Pyrenees. The road climbs relentlessly under five avalanche shelters to the ski resort – almost a ghost village at the height of summer – of La Mongie. Hairpin bends then take it up the final stretch, overlooked by colossal granite peaks and pinnacles, to the Col. From the top, the view ahead is magnificent, over peaks and ridges ranged to the horizon.

At a neck-craning angle to the north you will see the still higher observatory buildings and soaring television mast on the 2,865m (9,400-foot) summit

of the Pic du Midi. A right turn just after the actual Col leads along the steep and twisting toll road – to be driven cautiously – which climbs towards the summit and its astounding viewpoint.

BACK TO NATURE

From July till September, when the toll road is open, visitors are welcome to find out about extra-terrestrial affairs at the dramatically located Observatoire et Institut de Physique du Globe on the Pic du Midi. It has carried out pioneering work on cosmic rays and the huge, arching solar protuberances, and produced some of the finest-quality photographs ever taken from Earth.

▶ *Immediately after the summit of the Col du Tourmalet, bear left through Barèges to Luz-St-Sauveur. Turn left on to the D921 to Gavarnie.*

6 Gavarnie, Midi-Pyrénées
The narrow road to Gavarnie can be a trial in summer, because it is the busy dead-end approach to one of the most dramatic landscapes in Europe. South of the village lies the sublime Cirque de Gavarnie, a mountain amphitheatre piled with snow, whose rim at over 3,000m (10,000 feet) marks the boundary between France and Spain. Of its many waterfalls, the Grande Cascade, one of Europe's biggest, drops 442m (1,450 feet). You can get really close to the Cirque only on foot or on horseback. A spectacular winding road does, however, climb through wild country from Gavarnie to finish at a border col further west.

Gavarnie itself lies in a fine location with a river crashing through. It has an information centre for the Parc National des Pyrénées (Pyrenees National Park) and, in the heart of a famous climbing area, several monuments to the pioneering mountaineers. Try to be here in the evening after the press of

day visitors has eased. In the mountains, dusk brings a special magic.

i Maison du Parc National

▶ *Return to Luz-St-Sauveur and take the D921 as for Lourdes. Immediately after leaving Soulom, turn left on to the D920 to Cauterets.*

7 Cauterets, Midi-Pyrénées
Situated in a narrow river valley, Cauterets is the remotest of the Pyrenean spas. In medieval times it was believed the waters cured sterility. It has sulphur waters, thermal baths, a casino, unexpectedly handsome town houses and hotels, and well developed winter sports facilities. Victor Hugo and George Sand were among the famous literary figures who came this way and helped to spread its reputation.

There is another information centre here for the Pyrenees National Park, which you can enter by various roads and footpaths. There is also a small museum with seasonal film shows. Waterfalls tumble down near by, especially alongside the road to the Pont d'Espagne.

One of the most engaging features of Cauterets is that,

A variety of excursions into the Pyrenean valleys are possible from Cauterets

although the railway which used to serve it has long since gone, the glorious rustic station, all varnished ornamental wood-work, has been lovingly preserved. Looking at it, you are not quite literally transported back to the 19th century.

i Maison de la Montagne, place Clemenceau

▶ *Return to the D921. Turn left and continue to Lourdes.*

8 Lourdes, Midi-Pyrénées
In 1858, a 14-year-old girl called Bernadette Soubirous, walking by the rocky banks of the river at Lourdes, experienced the first of a long series of visions of the Virgin Mary. During her lifetime, pilgrims in increasing numbers, having heard of these wonders, journeyed to Lourdes. Two splendid basilicas were built beside the original grotto. In 1958, a third underground basilica was opened.

The beautiful riverside parkland where this complex is located attracts millions of visitors every year, many of them seeking cures for ailments or disabilities. The Pavilion Notre-Dame tells the story of St Bernadette and the pilgrimages (Musée Bernadette) and there is also a museum of sacred art (Musée d'Art Sacré du Gemmail). Climbing through woodland, the Chemin du Calvaire passes the 14 Stations of the Cross.

Lourdes itself is often crammed with people and their cars. Overlooking the town from a rocky bluff, the medieval château-fort houses the Musée Pyrénéen, a museum of the arts and traditions of the folk of the foothills. One-tenth scale models show off typical Pyrenean architecture.

Take the funicular railway to the Pic du Jer. It opens up elevated views of the town, the valleys and the mountains.

[i] *Place du Champ Commun*

FOR CHILDREN

Check at the tourist office in Lourdes if there is a meeting at the Model Racing Club 3 Vallées. If you are lucky, the children can watch radio-controlled scale-model cars – competition models, not toys – race on its miniature outdoor circuit.

FOR HISTORY BUFFS

Away from the sanctuary area, Lourdes has two museums devoted to showing how it looked in 1858, the year of Bernadette's first vision. The Musée de Lourdes features shops and street scenes, while the Musée du Petit Lourdes is a miniature stonework reproduction of the original simple village, towered over by its château-fort.

▶ *Leave Lourdes on the **D937**, following 'Bétharram' signs. Go through St-Pé-de-Bigorre, then turn left off the **D937** and left*

again to the Grottes de Bétharram.

9 **Grottes de Bétharram,** Midi-Pyrénées

These underground caverns are explored by remarkably varied forms of transport – cable cars, boats and a little 'train' of towed wagons. There are five different levels of caves and stalagmites, stalactites and curious limestone formations such as the Sphinx Window. You are shown old river levels, and taken for a cruise on a subterranean lake in a cavern 50m (165 feet) high. The fourth and fifth levels are linked by the present river dashing over a series of 80m (260-foot) falls.

▶ *Return to the **D937**, turn left and continue to Pau.*

▶ *Return to the **D937**, turn left and continue to Pau.*

SCENIC ROUTES

After Bagnères-de-Luchon, the D26 is a constantly twisting road round the wooded foothills ending in lovely farming country near St-Bertrand-de-Comminges.
The approach to Luchon takes you through an ever-narrowing wedge of valley towards the Pyrenean mountain wall. While the lower Col d'Aspin has more varied views, the Tourmalet is a classic of granite mountain landscape. From Luz-St-Sauveur, the D921 threads its way through a spectacular gorge to Gavarnie.

The grandeur and opulence of Lourdes' enormous basilica

THE SOUTH OF FRANCE

There is no single theme along the littoral of the south of France, nor even a single name for it. West of Marseille lie the flamingo lagoons, the pools, the rice fields and the summer pastures of the Camargue. East of the city stretches a sublime coast of capes and rocky inlets – the beautiful *calanques*. Beyond the great roadstead of Toulon are the islands off Hyères, including, at Port Cros, an entire island nature reserve.

St-Tropez is ... quintessentially St-Tropez, and you can have a great deal of fun simply people-watching. On a grander scale are the great resorts of the Côte d'Azur – Cannes, Nice, the immensely wealthy and independent principality of Monaco, and Menton.

Behind Nice and Monaco is the *arrière-pays*, the 'back country', the mountain country. Europe's answer to the Grand Canyon lies there.

Back from the Camargue lie Avignon and the haunting remains of the troubadours' court at Les Baux; Arles and St Rémy with their memories of the artist Vincent van Gogh; and the landscapes made famous in the mocking tales of Alphonse Daudet.

On the Cannes and Nice routes, be ready for hairpinned mountain roads, although most have been improved for tourist traffic.

On the coast, try the seafood restaurants serving Mediterranean mullet, bass and cod, and the great bouillabaisse. Be ready for lots of garlic and olive oil. In Nice, the cuisine reflects the Italian past. Vines were planted here by Greek colonists 2,500 years ago. Most of the modern wines are classified as Côtes de Provence, and the most attractive vineyard country is perhaps around Gassin and Ramatuelle on the St-Tropez peninsula. There is also intense cultivation behind the little resort of Cassis.

Should the coast become too crowded and stylish for you, half an hour inland you will find yourself in a dramatically different world of hills and mountains, forests and river valleys, where time slows down in delightful hilltop villages drowsing beneath a dazzling southern sky.

Marseille

Marseille is the greatest port in France, extending west to the faraway oil refineries of the Golfe de Fos. The yacht harbour, right in the heart of the city, makes a pleasant area for a stroll. The story of Marseille from the days of the Ligurians, Greeks and Romans, by way of the Revolution and the patriotic song which came to be called *La Marseillaise*, is told in four separate museums. Other museums cover art, pottery, furniture, tapestries, marine life etc.

There are many substantial churches, parks, gardens and, at La Canebière, a renowned avenue of shops, hotels, restaurants and pavement cafés. A magnificent view opens up from the hilltop Church of Notre-Dame-de-la-Garde. Offshore lies the sea-bound rock of the Château d'If. You can sail here and recall the story of Dumas' Count of Monte Cristo.

Cannes

In Cannes, the great boulevard de la Croisette stretches eastwards from the casino and the Palais des Festivals.

Every May, during the world-famous Cannes Film Festival, the Palais steps are staked out by twitchy television crews. The finest viewpoint is the observatory at Super-Cannes, at 325m (1,065 feet) above sea-level and 2km (1 mile) to the northeast, from which the town is seen in its wider landscape context between the Alps and the sea. Sail to the Îles des Lérins: St-Honorat is a monastery island and on Ste-Marguerite, which offers scented forest walks, was the prison of the real-life Man in the Iron Mask.

Nice

Nice is the capital of the Côte d'Azur. Its Promenade des Anglais recalls the 19th-century British visitors who made its name. The Russian royal family also favoured Nice, and you will see the green and gilded towers of the Orthodox cathedral where they and their court, which transferred here en masse every year, used to worship. There are fine shops, markets (notably the flower market), squares and gardens. Corsica ferries leave from the port. Eastwards, by the Cap de Nice, expensive villas hide

above flowery balustrades. In addition to churches, palaces, museums and galleries, there is the Parc des Miniatures, enjoyed by children, which tells the story of Nice itself. The Musée Terra Amata is an imaginative exhibition based on a prehistoric site, whose story starts 400,000 years ago.

Nîmes

Nîmes found favour with the Romans. Their arena, with space for 21,000 spectators, plays host to concerts and bullfights today. The Maison Carrée is a pillared 1st-century BC temple (one of the best preserved in existence) housing a little museum. Archaeology, history, the planets, fine arts and the story of Nîmes are topics covered in other exhibitions. Below a hillside park lies the grand if somewhat faded Jardin de la Fontaine. Its 18th-century masonry and water channels were built on the site of the Roman baths, providing a cool retreat from the harshness of the Provençal summer sun.

Opposite: the view west from Les Baux-de-Provence
Below: Marseille's harbour

East From Marseille

Starting from Marseille, France's second biggest city, this tour visits fishing villages which now have their own substantial holiday clientele, and larger resorts as different in style as Hyères and St-Tropez. All these places have grown up over the centuries, but Port-Grimaud is a modern development. Inland, the tour follows the high wooded ridges of the Massif des Maures as well as visiting an awesomely remote monastic house and the country of a film-maker who captured the soul of Provence.

4 DAYS • 352KM • 221 MILES

Map showing the route from Marseille with locations including Cassis, Cap Canaille, Bandol, La Ciotat, Sanary-s-Mer, Six-Fours-les-Plages, Toulon, Hyères, Gassin, St-Tropez, Port-Grimaud, Grimaud, Chartreuse de la Verne, Aubagne, Signes, Le Camp du Castellet, OK Corral, Méounes-les-Montrieux, Forcalqueiret, Pierrefeu-du-Var, Cavalaire-s-Mer, Ramatuelle, and the Massif des Maures.

ITINERARY

MARSEILLE	▶ **Cassis** (23km-14m)
CASSIS	▶ **Cap Canaille** (7km-4m)
CAP CANAILLE	▶ **Bandol** (25km-16.5m)
BANDOL	▶ **Toulon** (35km-22m)
TOULON	▶ **Hyères** (25km-16.5m)
HYÈRES	▶ **Gassin** (69km-43m)
GASSIN	▶ **St-Tropez** (18km-11m)
ST-TROPEZ	▶ **Port-Grimaud** (8km-5m)
PORT-GRIMAUD	▶ **Grimaud** (6km-4m)
GRIMAUD	▶ **Chartreuse de la Verne** (24km-15m)
CHARTREUSE DE LA VERNE	▶ **Aubagne** (93km-58m)
AUBAGNE	▶ **Marseille** (19km-12m)

[i] *La Canebière, Marseille*

▶ *Leave Marseille on the D559 to Cassis.*

❶ Cassis, Provence-Alpes

With cream and ochre-washed buildings overlooking the harbour, bars, cafés and seafood restaurants, and convenient beaches, Cassis has the obvious look of a holiday resort. But it is a fishing port too, and boats take visitors to the beautiful *calanques*, the rocky inlets in the roadless coastline to the west.

Cassis has a life and history independent of the summer tourist crush. A ruined castle (not accessible to the public) on a cypress-clad hill watches over it. A modest but informative local museum shows how the settlement dates back to Roman times and before. The town hall is also worth a visit, illustrations show how it was rebuilt from a shambolic ruin in the 1980s.

[i] *Place Baragnon*

▶ *Head out of Cassis on the D559 then right following 'Route des Crêtes' signs on to the D41a and the D141 to Cap Canaille.*

FOR CHILDREN

In Cassis, a pleasant little park by the post office includes a pond with goldfish, mallards and terrapins. There is a scrambling frame which takes the shape of jocular-looking fish with gaping mouths.

SPECIAL TO...

Cassis is noted for the highly regarded white wines which the sheltered climate and fine soil of the hillsides behind the town allow more than a dozen vineyards to produce.
The vines here were wiped out by disease in the 19th century, but the growers have revived the trade by using grafting techniques brought from Texas

---

❷ Cap Canaille, Provence-Alpes

Less a conventional cape than a wall of towering sea-cliffs – at 395m (1,300 feet) Europe's highest cliff – this is one of the most superb viewpoints in France. It looks west to the mazy coastline of the *calanques*, with offshore islands and rock pinnacles seeming to float in the air, like dreamy hills in old Chinese paintings.

▶ *Continue into La Ciotat. Go right at the T-junction on to Avenue Victor Hugo, then left and left again along the seafront, following signs for Bandol.*

RECOMMENDED WALKS

The three magnificent rocky inlets west of Cassis – the *calanques* – and the wooded peninsulas which border them are easily reached by a network of footpaths. Park your car at the far end of the Avenue des Calanques and follow the marked paths to sheltered Port-Miou, the limpid waters and Aleppo pines of Port-Pin and the wild, needle-like rocks of En Vau.

Painters such as Matisse and Dufy enjoyed the Provençal charm of Cassis – and probably its wine, too

3 Bandol, Provence-Alpes
This is Cassis writ large, a resort with a marina, a fishing port and even more seafood restaurants. Boats sail from Bandol on cruises along the coast, but the most popular trip is to Bendor, a rocky island crammed with hotels and restaurants, beaches, sailing, diving and tennis clubs, an art gallery and an exhibition on wines and spirits from nearly 50 countries. It also has a maritime museum, an open-air theatre and a zoo.

☐ *Allées Vivien*

▶ *Continue on the **D559** through Sanary-sur-Mer, then go left on the **D63** and follow signs to Toulon.*

naval museum, the Musée Naval.

Toulon has perhaps the most amazing suburban background of any city in Europe. The hillside districts behind the town centre suddenly rear up in the colossal limestone cliffs of Mont Faron. A one-way road system reaches the summit, the climb being up a steep incline with forbidding drops. As an option, a cablecar runs from Super Toulon. There are wonderful views from Mont Faron, pinewood picnic sites, a children's playground, a zoo and a comprehensive memorial exhibition on the 1944 liberation of Provence.

☐ *Avenue Colbert*

▶ *Leave Toulon on the **N98** to Hyères.*

5 Hyères, Provence-Alpes
Hyères is a town of colourful gardens. This is the oldest of all the modern Riviera resorts, although standing back more than most of them from the sea. The old quarter, reached through its original medieval gateways, is a place of cool narrow streets, historic buildings and an authentic atmosphere of people going about their daily business. Hyères is mature enough not to be any kind of tourist trap.

The museum takes the town's history back to the times of the Greeks and Romans – as *Olbia* it was a Greek colony,

4 Toulon, Provence-Alpes
With its interlocking harbours and a busy dockyard, Toulon is a famous and historic naval port. In World War II, in 1942, much of the French fleet was scuttled here, so that it would not come under German control. There is a great deal of civilian activity too. Ferries sail to Corsica and Sardinia, cargo ships use the freight quays, and smaller boats run scheduled services to the offshore islands as well as making shorter trips round the harbour. There is a well-stocked

FOR HISTORY BUFFS
....

As Captain Bonaparte, Napoleon first made a name for himself at the age of 24, when the Republican army attacked British-held Toulon in 1793.
Under withering enemy fire, his artillery battery bombarded a British strong-point at the fort now named after him, forcing the British ships to withdraw.

Toulon, France's second-largest naval base, is a surprisingly lively place

established by settlers from Marseille. There are some handsome old churches (St Louis associated with King Louis IX who landed at Hyères after crusading, and St Paul with its Romanesque front), and from the castle ruins in a hilltop park a panoramic view is revealed of the inland hills and the sea.

☐ *Rotonde Jean-Salusse*

The cathedral of St Paul dominates the old town of Hyères

BACK TO NATURE

From Hyères-Plage, on the D97 south of town, ferries run to the beautiful nature reserve island of Port Cros. Footpaths explore its bays and forests, and a summer exhibition in the Fort de l'Estissac uses audio-visual programmes and aquariums to explain the sea life of the Mediterranean. There is even an underwater offshore nature trail for swimmers with flippers and masks.

▶ Leave Hyères on the **N98** as for Le Canadel. Watch for a left turn following the **N98** signed 'La Môle'. Turn right on the **D41** as for Bormes then, at a blind bend on a brow, left on the **RF32**, the Routes des Crêtes. Go straight on along this road, always on a tarred surface. Turn right at the Col de Canadel, away from La Môle, then left on the **D559** through La Croix-Valmer. Watch for 'Auberge les Sarments' sign, then immediately bear right off the **D559** to Gassin.

6 Gassin, Provence-Alpes
Sensitively restored in recent years, this hilltop village often attracts cooling breezes on hot summer days. There are lanes and stairways, houses with potted flowers and pocket-handkerchief gardens, a parish church barely illuminated by the modern abstract stained glass in its three tiny original windows, restaurants on a shaded terrace and, above all, views to the delicious miniature landscapes of the St-Tropez peninsula.

▶ Leave Gassin for Ramatuelle, turn left at a stop sign, right at a second stop sign, then left towards the **N98a**. At traffic lights, turn right on that road into St-Tropez.

BACK TO NATURE

On the left after Gassin, the Chemin du Radio Phare passes three old stone windmills on the way to a short circular walk outside the perimeter fence of a radio beacon. This is a splendid viewpoint, but the great attraction is the number and variety of brightly-coloured butterflies which flit around.

7 St-Tropez, Provence-Alpes
Publicity about the personalities – from the writers Guy de Maupassant and Colette to artists Henri Matisse, controversial writer, designer and film director Jean Cocteau and 'sex kitten' actress Brigitte Bardot – who have settled here, has always tended to hide the fact that this red-roofed town clustered beside a bay is an interesting place in its own right.

St-Tropez shops ask high prices, and the resort is full of deeply tanned characters in high summer fashion, who may be wealthy residents or simply mere day-trippers putting on an act – it can be fun to try to classify them. Needless to say, café and nightlife is abundant if you can afford the price and keep the pace.

An old chapel has been turned into a museum – the Musée de l'Annonciade – featuring paintings and sculptures by some of the notable artists who have lived here including Bonnard, Braque, Dufy and Utrillo, while lesser lights try to sell their canvases in an unofficial gallery by the harbour rails. The hexagonal 16th-century citadel is now a naval museum (Musée de la Marine) on several floors, where you can peruse the exhibits (which include a reconstructed Greek galley) to the accompaniment of unearthly cries from the local peacocks.

The fine sandy beaches are 4 to 5km (2½–3 miles) from St-Tropez town, on the far side of the headland on which it stands. They are varied and very popular. Parking can be difficult.

⟦i⟧ *Quai Jean-Jaurès*

▶ *Return along the N98a. At a roundabout join the N98 as for Fréjus, then under the bridge take the right lane for Port-Grimaud and left at the roundabout to the 'Visiteurs' car park.*

8 **Port-Grimaud,** Provence-Alpes

In the 1960s this was simply a wasteland of marsh and gravel pits. Then the architect François Spoerry created a brand-new village on a lagoon by the sea – a kind of Provençal Venice with canals and peninsulas, bridges and water-buses, shops, cafés, restaurants and colour-washed houses, each with its own boat mooring right outside the door. Everything was to be a modern expression of traditional Provençal design. In the wrong hands, Port-Grimaud could have been a tacky disaster. Instead, it is a triumph.

▶ *Return to the roundabout, go over the bridge then turn right at the T-junction. Continue straight on at the next junction then left on the D14 to Grimaud.*

9 **Grimaud,** Provence-Alpes

Further inland, the medieval hillside town which gave Port-Grimaud its name retains many old buildings, notably the houses in the arcaded street of the Knights Templar, and the massive Romanesque church of St-Michel.

Above all, Grimaud, which takes its name from the powerful Genoese Grimaldi family (now rulers of Monaco), is dominated by the hilltop ruins of an 11th-century castle. It provides a wonderful viewpoint.

⟦i⟧ *Boulevard des Aliziers*

▶ *Leave Grimaud on the D558 then turn left on the D14. Turn left on the mostly unsurfaced D214 signed 'La Verne'.*

10 **Chartreuse de la Verne,** Provence-Alpes

The road is lonely, slow and dusty to this remote and impressive monastery established by the Carthusians as long ago as 1170. At the time of the French Revolution it was deprived of its revenues, and the monks left secretly, disguised as peasants. The buildings then passed through several hands, and are now owned by a trust and are being renovated. In 1983 another order of monks – the Order of St Bruno – moved in. There are guided tours (for visitors discreetly dressed) showing the historic buildings and the breathtaking view of high ridges and deep valleys, covered by the forest of the Massif des Maures.

▶ *Rejoin the D14 and follow it through Collobrières to Pierrefeu. Turn right on the D12 through Puget-Ville and Rocbaron to Forcalqueiret. Go*

left on the **D554** *and continue to Méounes-les-Montrieux, then right on the* **D2** *via Signes, and right at Le Camp on the* **N8** *to Aubagne.*

SPECIAL TO...

Collobrières, near Chartreuse de la Verne in the Maures massif, has many varieties of the chestnut candies called *marrons glacés*. Two major producers in the village sell chestnut-based sweets, syrups and creams.

⓫ **Aubagne,** Provence-Alpes At the heart of this town, surrounded by a cat's-cradle of motorway bypasses, there are public gardens and cool tree-shaded squares. In one of them the tourist office pavilion houses a colourful display – using the painted clay-model figures called *santons* which are made in great numbers by craftsmen in the town – of

scenes from the films of the writer and director Marcel Pagnol, a native of Aubagne. After the world-wide screening in the 1980s of new versions of his stories *Jean de Florette* and *Manon des Sources*, interest in Pagnol, who died in 1974, spread widely. Guided tours are organised round the real-life locations he used in the countryside near Aubagne. In the

---

FOR CHILDREN

On the N98 before Aubagne, the OK Corral has far more attractions than simply the Wild West elements its name suggests. As well as a 'western' street and railway, pony rides, cowboys and Indians, there are swooping roller-coasters which produce a total white-knuckle experience.

St-Tropez owes its popularity to its sheltered harbour and marina

western outskirts of the town, the Musée de la Légion Etrangère (Foreign Legion Museum) has displays on its years of service in the baking Sahara sands.

ⓘ *Avenue du 8 Mai*

▶ *Leave Aubagne on the* **D2** *and return to Marseille.*

RECOMMENDED WALKS

There is access at Collobrières to the long-distance footpaths which explore the deep wooded valleys and ridgetops of the Massif des Maures. For instance, GR90, offers a strenuous half-day hike out and back to the hermitage of Notre-Dame-des-Anges. Further on, Signes on the D2 is the starting point of forest and hill walks on the Massif de la Sainte Baume.

SCENIC ROUTES

The D559 leaves Marseille by the winding climb, under wooded cliffs and banks of valerian and broom, to the Col de la Gineste.
The climb to Cap Canaille – as well as the summit view – is one of the most spectacular on the coast.
Look for the views to the island of Bendor from the bay after Bandol.
Where clear of woodland, the RF32 on the way to the Col du Canadel has a glorious outlook to the sea.
The high road from Gassin to Ramatuelle looks over a beautiful settled landscape of woodlands, farms and farmyards.
The D14 to Collobrières gives a fine impression of the wooded ridges and deep lonely valleys of the Massif des Maures. Then from Pierrefeu towards Rocbaron, the D12 climbs sharply as it overlooks the vineyard plain it is leaving behind.

The Riviera & its Hinterland

From Cannes and other coastal resorts, by way of artists' and craft-workers' villages, this tour climbs into the glorious mountain scenery that forms the backdrop to the Côte d'Azur. Limestone cliffs and ridges, spectacular valleys and ranges of faraway mountains reach a landscape climax in the magnificent Gorges du Verdon.

4/5 DAYS • 440KM • 273 MILES

ITINERARY		
CANNES	▶	**Cap d'Antibes (14km-9m)**
CAP D'ANTIBES	▶	**Antibes (5km-3m)**
ANTIBES	▶	**Biot (7km-4m)**
BIOT	▶	**Grasse (20km-12m)**
GRASSE	▶	**Gourdon (12km-8m)**
GOURDON	▶	**Plateau de Caussols (14km-9m)**
PLATEAU DE CAUSSOLS	▶	**Castellane (52km-32m)**
CASTELLANE	▶	**St-André-les-Alpes (22km-14m)**
ST-ANDRÉ-LES-ALPES	▶	**Riez (60km-37m)**
RIEZ	▶	**Moustiers-Ste-Marie (15km-9m)**
MOUSTIERS-STE-MARIE	▶	**Gorges du Verdon (42km-26m)**
GORGES DU VERDON	▶	**Draguignan (72km-45m)**
DRAGUIGNAN	▶	**Fayence (38km-24m)**
FAYENCE	▶	**Mons (15km-9m)**
MONS	▶	**Cannes (52km-32m)**

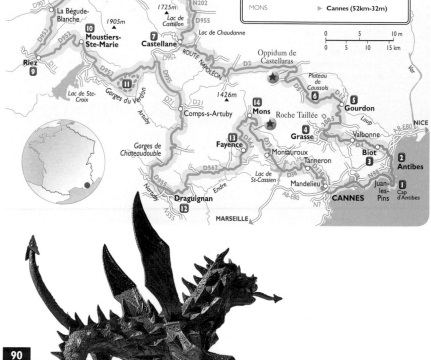

Boulevard de la Croisette, Cannes

▶ *Leave Cannes on the* ***N7*** *towards Golfe-Juan, then bear right on the* ***N98*** *signed 'Antibes par Bord de Mer'. In Juan-les-Pins watch carefully for all the 'Cap d'Antibes' signs and join the Cap d'Antibes coast road,* ***D2559****.*

1 Cap d'Antibes, Côte d'Azur

There are tiny family-style beaches and boat moorings on the east side of the Cape, which also includes security-guarded millionaires' retreats and, at the Hôtel du Cap and the Eden Roc restaurant, two of the most exclusive establishments of their kind on the coast. A fine museum devoted to Napoleonic and naval history – Musée Naval et Napoléonien – occupies an old gun battery, perhaps surprising visitors from the United Kingdom with contemporary cartoons showing the British as the enemy. Around the Villa Thuret there is a botanical garden, and right on the summit of the Cape the Sanctuaire de la Garoupe, a seafarers' chapel beside the lighthouse tower, which is a marvellous viewpoint, houses a collection of simple but affecting thanks-offerings, often for a safe return from a voyage.

American writers and artists were attracted to the Cape from the 1920s onwards. Scott Fitzgerald's novel *Tender is the Night* had its real-life setting here. It is possible to trace the exact course of the disastrous car journey described in James Thurber's *A Ride with Olympy*. And Orson Welles once arrived in a hurry for a cash-raising meeting in the Hôtel du Cap, having come by taxi all the way from Rome!

▶ *Continue on the* ***D2559*** *into Antibes.*

2 Antibes, Côte d'Azur

The old town here, with its narrow streets, cafés and restaurants, is one of the most attractive and least pretentious on the coast. Antibes' connection with the ancient Greeks – it was founded as *Antipolis* by Greek colonists from Marseille in the 4th century BC – attracted the Cretan writer Nikos Kazantzakis, author of *Zorba the Greek*, to settle here, as did the British novelist Graham Greene. While the archaeological museum in the old fortification of the Bastion St André may look gloomy from the outside, it has a wonderful collection of thousands of exhibits going back to Etruscan, Greek and Roman times, many recovered from the sea. The old castle was a stronghold of the powerful Genoese Grimaldi family. With the little 'cathedral', it watches over the bustling market place, and was long since turned into the Musée Picasso. The artist used part of it as a studio for six amazingly fruitful months in 1946, and now it contains many of his – and other artists' – paintings and ceramics, making it one of the most important Picasso collections anywhere. The so-called cathedral is, in fact, a church, with a Romanesque tower and east end and 17th-century façade.

Place de Gaulle

Paintings in Notre Dame de Bon Port, Cap d'Antibes

RECOMMENDED WALKS

On the south side of the Cap d'Antibes, turn off the Boulevard J F Kennedy for the Sentiers des Douaniers the Excisemen's Path. Starting alongside the wall of a private estate, it leads to a beautiful little park set among rocks above the sea, with a lovely bay stretching to the west.

▶ *Leave Antibes on the* ***N98*** *as for 'Nice par Bord de Mer'. Take the left-hand lane, turn left at the traffic lights for Biot, then right and left on the* ***D4*** *to Biot.*

FOR CHILDREN

Marineland, to the right of the D4 on the way to Biot, has penguins, seals, sea lions and a dolphin show. Near by are a butterfly jungle, a little Provençal farm, water chutes and an assault-course style of mini-golf layout. This was Europe's first marine park.

3 Biot, Côte d'Azur

On the approach road to Biot, a road to the right leads to the Musée National Fernand Léger, unmistakable thanks to the huge abstract in multi-coloured

tiling which decorates its frontage. With more than 300 works on display, it celebrates the life of one of France's major 20th-century artists, and was opened in 1960 with fellow-artists Picasso, Braque and Chagall as its honorary presidents. The charming little town of Biot is largely given over to the shops and studios of painters, potters, woodworkers, embroiderers and craftworkers of many other kinds. Even the town maps are on painted ceramic tiles. Glassmaking is important here nowadays and it can be observed at the Verrerie de Biot near the southeast exit from the town. Gates and ramparts of the medieval town survive, and away from the tourist bustle there is a pleasant arcaded square beside a 15th-century parish church. The museum features mementoes of the days when the Romans and, later, the Knights Templar, were established here, and has a dazzling pottery display.

i   *Place de la Chapelle*

▶ *Continue on the **D4** via Valbonne to Grasse, turning right at a T-junction on the outskirts to follow the **D4** towards the town centre.*

4 Grasse, Côte d'Azur
Spread over a south-facing hillside with splendid views over a lovely plain towards the sea, Grasse enjoys a year-long calendar of concerts, drama, dance and exhibitions of every kind. The old town, crammed with 14th- to 18th-century buildings, is Italian in appearance and atmosphere. Around it, Grasse expanded with exuberant 19th-century architecture in typical French Riviera style.

Grasse has the most famous perfume industry in the world, and one museum, Musée International de la Parfumerie, traces its history as well as the processes by which huge amounts of flower petals are distilled down to tiny volumes of the ultimate essence. The Maison Fragonard, named after the rococo painter who was born in the town, is a perfume factory open to the public. The Musée d'Art et d'Histoire de Provence, housed in an 18th-century mansion, celebrates the art and history of Provence.

Another museum, the Musée de la Marine, has gathered an intriguing collection of ship models to illustrate the career of the 18th-century Admiral de Grasse, an ally of George Washington in the American

Biot is set attractively on a small hill rising in the centre of a valley

War of Independence. A statue on one of the town's outlook terraces reealls Washington's gratitude to him.

i   *Place de la Foux*

FOR CHILDREN

In Grasse, the Musée des Trains Miniatures on the Routes de Cannes has a fascinating model railway collection. The layout includes locomotives and rolling stock from many European countries and from many different eras, right up to the TGV – France's high-speed Train de Grande Vitesse.

▶ *Leave Grasse on the **D2085** as for Nice. At Pré-du-Lac turn left at the roundabout and immediately bear left on the **D3** to Gourdon. Turn right for the car park at the entrance to the village.*

5 Gourdon, Côte d'Azur
Some writers sneer at Gourdon for being a tourist trap. You will probably disagree, because this old Saracen stronghold, set on

the edge of a cliff which gives it tremendous views down into the valley of the Loup, goes about its business quietly. In the narrow lanes of restored and impeccably kept buildings, shops sell lavender, honey, herbs, perfumes, pottery, wines, basketwork and glassware, many of these goods being produced in the district.

The historic Château de Gourdon, with terraced gardens on the edge of the cliff, has architectural details from the 12th century onwards. Here you will see valuable furnishings, as well as collections of arms and armour, and 'naive' paintings by European and American artists.

▶ *Leave Gourdon on the **D12** as for Caussols. In about 8km (5 miles) watch for a junction sign and then go sharp left under a sign giving advice to 'Visiteurs'.*

⑥ Plateau de Caussols,
Côte d'Azur
A notice at the turn-off of the D12 warns that gathering stones, mushrooms and snails is forbidden. Do not worry about the mild potholes on the early stretch of the road; the surface never deteriorates too badly. Here on the high limestone plain is a countryside not many casual tourists know: clumps of pines and rock outcrops, occasional sheep farms, isolated holiday homes, groups of beehives and, here and there, a survivor from the days of the *bories*, the stone-built shepherds' huts. There are mountain ridges to

north and south, with the remote white buildings of the CERGA observatory high on the northern rim. The scenery may be faintly familiar to film buffs: this was the setting of the Charles Bronson thriller *Cold Sweat*.

▶ *Turn right at a T-junction beside a postbox, following an old sign 'St-Lambert'. This is the **D12** again. Turn sharp left as for Thorenc on the **D112**, then follow 'Thorenc' signs on the **D5**. Go left on the **D2**, left on the **D2211**, then right on the **N85** to Castellane.*

⑦ Castellane, Côte d'Azur
A modest little town on the Route Napoléon, Castellane lies in a constricted location where the River Verdon elbows its way through the hills. Directly overlooking the square is a massive

cliff, 184m (604 feet) high, on which the original settlement, dating from Gallo-Roman times, was built.

When the population decided, eventually, to settle in the valley, plague, floods and occupation in the time of the religious wars in the 16th century was their reward. Now the classic outing at Castellane is a walk up the steep and occasionally rough pathway to the 18th-century Chapel of Notre Dame du Roc, a magnificent clifftop viewpoint.

ℹ *Boulevard St Michel*

▶ *Continue on the **N85**, go right on the **D955**. Then left on the **N202** to St-André-les-Alpes.*

Perched high above the River Loup, Gourdon has stunning views of the coast

The Riviera & its Hinterland

8 St-André-les-Alpes,
Côte d'Azur

This is a quiet little inland resort a world away from the hustle of the coast. But St-André was once a busy enough place. The village had four cloth mills, but all that remains of the industry is the canal which supplied their water-power. In the latter part of the 19th century it became the railhead of a line from Nice, and the place from which stagecoaches took passengers further on. This railway, now extended to Digne, is the last survivor of the old inland lines. St-André station is a halt on the year-round railcar service, and there are summer excursions on the steam-hauled Train des Pignes (the Pine Cone Train).

St-André lies in an attractive valley that has helped it achieve its present-day renown as a centre for hang-gliding and free-fall parachuting.

[i] *Place Paslorelli*

▶ Continue on the **N202** to Barrême, then turn right on to the **N85** and left on the **D907**, then in La Bégude-Blanche take the **D953** to Riez.

9 Riez, Provence-Alpes

Two structures show how old the settlement of Riez is. A group of columns now standing isolated at the edge of the field was once part of a 1st-century Roman temple; and there is an early Christian baptistery (dating from some time in the 4th to 7th centuries), complete with the original font, inside a 19th-century building set up to preserve it.

The old town may have a faded look, but its streets

Surely one of nature's most delightful harvests – fields of perfumed lavender at Riez contain medieval doorways and Renaissance frontages, some in the course of restoration. In pre-Roman times, the settlement stood on the summit of the St Maxime hill overlooking the present-day town in the valley below. St Maxime, which is the site of an attractive chapel, is a pleasant place for a stroll. A popular Riez industry is the production of *santons*, characteristic Provençal painted clay figurines, originally made for the traditional Christmas crib, but now sold as souvenirs.

[i] Allées Louis Gadiol

BACK TO NATURE

After Riez, the Lapidaire Pierres de Provence on the D952 displays beautiful examples of rose quartz, agates, amethysts and other semi-precious stones. This is a fine area for minerals and gemstones, but much of it is protected as a geological reserve.

▶ Leave on the D952 to Moustiers-Ste-Marie.

⑩ Moustiers-Ste-Marie, Provence-Alpes

Any history of Moustiers pales before its amazing situation, clustered round the banks of a tumbling mountain stream at the foot of a huge gash in towering limestone cliffs. Footpaths climb to a spectacularly located church, Notre Dame de Beauvoir, set on a high rocky terrace. Across the break in the cliffs, and silhouetted against the sky, a chain supporting a gilded star was, according to tradition, first placed there by a crusader knight, who had sworn to do it when released from weary years of imprisonment.

The town is famous for its glazed pottery, or faienceware. The industry established in the 17th century died out for a generation or two, and restarted in the 1920s, but without equalling the delicacy of the early designs, many of which are on show in the local museum, Musée des Faïences.

[i] Rue du Seigneur de la Clue

▶ Continue on the D952 to La Palud. Go straight on through La Palud, then bear right on the D23, the Route des Crêtes. If you enjoy exposed and narrow roads with steep, unguarded drops, follow the D23 all the way back to La Palud and turn right to rejoin the D952. If you do not enjoy this kind of road, go along the D23 to the first two or three belvederes, then retrace your route and turn right again on to the D952. Only the later part of the D23 is difficult.

⑪ Gorges du Verdon, Provence-Alpes

Landscape superlatives are needed here, because this is France's equivalent, on a smaller scale, to the Grand Canyon in Colorado. The River Verdon, on its way to Castellane, runs through a huge ravine in the limestone mountains, with colossal drops, vertigo-inducing views, exciting low-level footpaths and the possibility of organised expeditions on foot and by canoe, raft or rubber dinghy, right through the heart of the gorge. There are magnificent, high-level roadside views from railed-off belvederes (look-out points), some of which, on the Routes

Moustiers has been famous for its pottery since the 17th century

des Crêtes, have warnings not to throw stones off the edge – they might fall on walkers 715m (2,350 feet) below!

▶ Continue eastwards on the D952. After a stretch of overhanging cliffs, turn right on the D955 to Comps-sur-Artuby and Draguignan.

⑫ Draguignan, Provence-Alpes

Down from the mountains, and the vast military training area of Canjuers which occupies the scrubland plateau south of the River Verdon, Draguignan marks a return to the milder landscapes of mid-Provence. There is a dignified old town here, and a fine museum, housed in the one-time palace of the Bishop of Fréjus, with thousands of exhibits connected with local industries, including a reconstructed olive oil mill. Shaded squares and gardens fend off the sun. On the boulevard John Kennedy, the American military cemetery commemorates the mostly Franco-American Provençal landings of August 1944. In front of the memorial there is an imaginative tribute in the form of a massive relief map, in bronze and copper, illustrating the campaign.

[i] Boulevard Clemenceau

> *Leave Draguignan on the D562 as for Grasse. Go left on the D563 to Fayence.*

The Gorges du Verdon offers a range of activities and natural beauty to take your breath away

13 Fayence, Provence-Alpes
Here is a classic back-from-the-coast village, facing southwards into the sun as its red-roofed houses climb a hillside from the plain. Fayence has a very well-cared-for 18th-century church, a good selection of craft studios and galleries, and terraces which act as splendid viewpoints. You may find it pleasant to laze around them, look out over the plain and watch the gliders soaring from one of France's most important launching fields far below.

> [i] *Place Léon Roux*

> *Continue on the D563 to Mons.*

14 Mons, Provence-Alpes
The colonists from Ventimiglia in what is now Italy, who founded this little hilltop village in the 13th century, picked the location well. The spacious square, in fact a semi-circle, looks out over an extensive view from the islands off Cannes to the Italian Alps, with suggestions that, on a really clear day, Corsica appears as a smudge on the horizon. Mons survived two outbreaks of plague and the desertion of all its citizens after a brigands' raid in 1468, to doze in the sun for centuries before it recently decided to emphasise its situation as one of the 'belvederes of the Côte d'Azur'. There is a maze of cool, narrow alleyways. The historic ramparts are still partly in place. Local arts and crafts are displayed in a gallery. And the streets usually bear two names – one in French and one in Provençal.

> [i] *Centre Culturel*

FOR CHILDREN

In Mons, ask them to find the electricity meter for the house at 22 Su Lou Coustihoun.

FOR HISTORY BUFFS

After Mons, Roche Taillée, to the left of the D56, is a fine example of Roman civil engineering, a deep cutting in a limestone outcrop to take part of the 40km (25-mile) aqueduct which supplied the town of Fréjus near the coast. The aqueduct is still in use today.

> *Leave Mons on the D56 as for Callian, then go left on the D37. Follow the D37 to the left for Montauroux at a T-junction where the right turn is signed 'Callian 0.5km'. Follow the 'Grasse' sign in Montauroux, still on the D37, cross the D562, then go left on the D38 through Tanneron. At a five-road junction after Tanneron bear right for Mandelieu-la-Napoule, then watch for an abrupt left turn avoiding a road straight ahead signed 'Poney Club'. Take the D92 to Mandelieu. Turn right on the N7 then take the fourth exit at a roundabout signed 'Les Plages'. Go right at the T-junction as for Napoule, then keep in the right lane and return to Cannes.*

SPECIAL TO...

From the Lac de St-Cassien to Mandelieu, the beautiful Tanneron massif is planted out with mimosa. In summer there is no trace of the brilliant yellow blooms which light up the winter hillsides.

SCENIC ROUTES

Approaching Gourdon, the D3 looks deep into the valley of the Loup, then reveals a stunning view of the village in the eagle's-eyrie location on the summit of a plummeting cliff.

Exploring the
Côte d'Azur

Often using steep and hairpinned roads, the route climbs spectacular valleys and wooded mountain ridges. Far from the hustle and
bustle of holiday crowds, the valley of the Gordolasque is a cleft in
the wildest part of the Maritime Alps, and the pilgrimage church of
Madone d'Utelle crowns a remote and atmospheric hilltop.

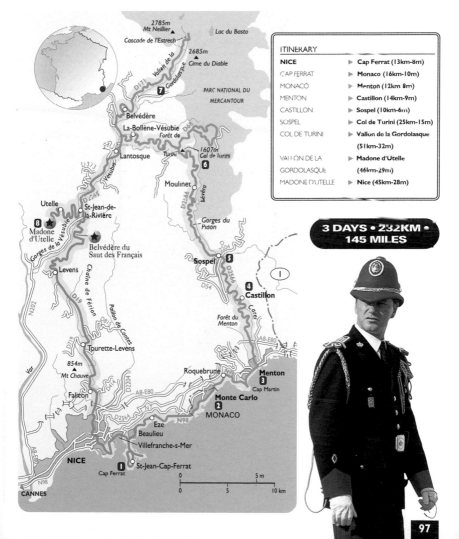

2785m
Mt Neillier
Lac du Basto
Cascade de l'Estrech
Vallon de la Gordolasque
2685m
Cime du Diable
7
PARC NATIONAL DU
MERCANTOUR
Belvédère
La-Bollène-Vésubie
Forêt de
Turini
1607m
Col de Turini
6
Lantosque
Moulinet
Utelle
St-Jean-de-
la-Rivière
8 ★
Madone
d'Utelle
★
Belvédère du
Saut des Français
Gorges du
Piaon
Levens
Gorges de la Vésubie
Sospel **5**
Chaîne de Férion
4
Castillon
Paillon de Contes
Forêt du
Menton
Tourrette-Levens
854m
Mt Chauve
Roquebrune
Menton
3
Cap Martin
Falicon
Monte Carlo
2
MONACO
Eze
Beaulieu
Villefranche-s-Mer
NICE
St-Jean-Cap-Ferrat
Cap Ferrat
1
CANNES
Var
1

ITINERARY		
NICE	▶	**Cap Ferrat (13km-8m)**
CAP FERRAT	▶	Monaco (16km-10m)
MONACO	▶	Menton (12km-8m)
MENTON	▶	Castillon (14km-9m)
CASTILLON	▶	Sospel (10km-6m)
SOSPEL	▶	Col de Turini (25km-15m)
COL DE TURINI	▶	Vallon de la Gordolasque
		(51km-32m)
VALLON DE LA	▶	Madone d'Utelle
GORDOLASQUE		(46km-29m)
MADONE D'UTELLE	▶	Nice (45km-28m)

**3 DAYS • 232KM •
145 MILES**

Exploring the Côte d'Azur

ⓘ *Avenue Thiers, Nice*

▶ *Leave Nice following the **N98**, the Corniche Inférieure, to Villefranche. Bear right for St-Jean-Cap-Ferrat.*

❶ **Cap Ferrat,** Côte d'Azur
Cap Ferrat is a cape extending about 3km (2 miles) south of Beaulieu. All the capes along the Côte d'Azur are favoured residential areas, with imposing villas in discreet well-wooded grounds. At Cap Ferrat one of the most majestic of these, once the home of the Baroness Béatrice Ephrussi-de-Rothschild, was built early this century to house a massive collection of furnishings, tapestries, costumes, paintings and porcelain.

The house and contents were left to the Académie des Beaux Arts and now form the Musée 'Ile de France'. It stands among 7 hectares (17 acres) of gardens, and the collection, although it has a strong bias to the 18th century, includes Impressionist paintings and oriental *objets d'art*. St-Jean-Cap-Ferrat, the resort village facing the towering cliffs that

march to Monaco and the Italian frontier, is on an arm of the cape going off to the east. It has two promenades, the upper one on the roof of a line of shops, cafés and restaurants looking out to the yachts and cruisers bobbing in the harbour.

ⓘ *Avenue Denis Seméria*

FOR CHILDREN

Cap Ferrat Zoo, in a former estate of King Leopold II of the Belgians, raises many young animals, including llamas, kangaroos, gazelles and monkeys. Children enjoy its daily 'chimpanzee school'.

RECOMMENDED WALKS

On Cap Ferrat, the Maurice Rouvier walk is a promenade from the harbour to Beaulieu, while the Pointe St-Hospice walk from the Paloma beach circles a rocky peninsula below the villa gardens.

▶ *Return to Villefranche and bear right on the **D125**, then follow signs through Beaulieu for Monaco.*

FOR HISTORY BUFFS

On a rocky promontory in Beaulieu, which lies between Cap Ferrat and Monaco, the Villa Kérylos is a modern replica of a Greek palace of the 5th century BC, created early in the 20th century by archaeologist Théodore Reinach. Its pillars, mosaics, frescos and furnishings, marble and alabaster benefit from their location by the deep blue Mediterranean, and there are some granite antiquities among the reproductions.

❷ **Monaco**
If you are a first-time visitor to Monaco, forget any idea that it is some kind of comic-opera place where only high-society millionaires feel at home. This is an ancient and sovereign

Spectacular view over Monaco from the Jardin Exotique

Every year Menton hosts an elaborate lemon festival in February

state, ruled by the Grimaldi family for over 700 years. The Grimaldis originated in Genoa in Italy, one of their number seizing the Rock of Monaco in 1297.

Despite being so tiny – no larger than many a farm – the vastly wealthy principality is divided into four main districts: Monte Carlo, where the casino and the sumptuous Hôtel de Paris are located; La Condamine, around the harbour with its tens of millions of pounds' worth of yachts; the lovely old town on Le Rocher, the original Rock of Monaco, and Fontvieille, a new suburb.

Prince Rainier III's palace is reached from La Condamine up a steep ramp. It is mostly of the 16th and 17th centuries, and has several magnificent rooms open to the public, as well as a museum devoted to Napoleon, who was related to the Grimaldis. A fascinating archive collection documents centuries of Monagasque history. Throughout the palace and, indeed, throughout Monaco itself there are reminders of Princess Grace, the former film actress Grace Kelly whose fairytale marriage to Prince Rainier delighted the world.

Also in the old town are the elegant cathedral, built in neo-Romanesque style in the 19th century and containing the tomb of Princess Grace, and the splendid Musée Océanographique (Oceanographic Museum), rising dramatically from the sea-cliffs. The latter, with an aquarium as well as fascinating museum exhibits, is directed by the famous underwater explorer Jacques Cousteau. Around it lie the beautiful St Martin gardens. They look down on the marina and Fontvieille, which is packed with housing and industry but has a large sports stadium and marina to its credit.

ⓘ *Boulevard des Moulins*

▶ *Leave Monaco on the N98 as for Menton. In Roquebrune bear right for Cap Martin.*

▶ *Follow 'Menton' signs to the shore road, then keep right along the seafront to Menton.*

❸ Menton, Côte d'Azur
An old rhyme about the Riviera resorts claimed that 'Menton's dowdy, Monte's brass, Nice is rowdy, Cannes is class'. For years, Menton did have rather a faded air, brought about partly because its most faithful visitors were invalids and elderly people, from all corners of Europe. Famous visitors of the past include the writer Katherine Mansfield and the illustrator Aubrey Beardsley. Now Menton has revitalised itself, but, nevertheless retains a less hectic pace than most other Côte d'Azur resorts. In addition, it has a lovely climate and Italian-style architecture; the Italian border is in its eastern outskirts.

Menton has beautiful gardens including the Biovès Gardens in the town centre, a casino, fine museums, one of which is dedicated to the work

TOUR

15 Exploring the Côte d'Azur

of Jean Cocteau, and churches, promenades and squares. Around it lie the lemon groves – susceptible to very rare winter frosts – which give the town its most famous product. A Lemon Fair is held in February.

ℹ️ *Avenue Boyer*

▶ *Leave Menton on the D2566 as for Sospel. Watch for the sharp right turn into Castillon.*

4 Castillon, Côte d'Azur
The original Castillon was wrecked in a 19th-century earthquake, and the rebuilt town destroyed during World War II. Their replacement is a charming modern village with lanes and stairways, a tiny square and a beautiful southern outlook, as well as shops and studios offering paintings,

sculptures, ceramics, leatherwork, stained glass and jewellery.

▶ *Return to the D2566, bearing right to the Col de Castillon. Go through the tunnel and turn right to Sospel.*

5 Sospel, Côte d'Azur
For a town in such an agreeable situation, at the junction of two river valleys surrounded by exhilarating mountain scenery, Sospel gives a scruffy impression to the visitor. However, there is an intriguing old quarter with houses alongside the River Bévéra which is crossed by an 11th-century toll bridge, and in the Église St Michel the town

Sospel has a bohemian charm that inspires one to reach for paintbrush and canvas or camera

has a former cathedral whose grand baroque interior comes as a perplexing surprise. At the railway station a group of coaches in a siding form a museum about the Orient Express. On the outskirts, Fort St Roch is an astonishing underground artillery installation, part of the Maginot Line of defences built in the 1930s between the Belgian border and Corsica.

ℹ️ *Le Pont Vieux*

▶ *Leave Sospel on the D2566 via Moulinet to the Col de Turini.*

6 Col de Turini, Côte d'Azur
In the high pine and larch forests at 1,607m (5,270 feet) above sea-level, Turini is a winter sports resort and a cool bolt-hole in summer from the heat of the coast. Four roads radiate from the hamlet at the summit, one to the still-higher circuit of l'Authion, just inside the huge Parc National du Mercantour. There are magnificent viewpoints here, as well as ruins of military fortifications battled over during the Revolution and in the last bitter days of fighting in 1944.

> ### SPECIAL TO...
>
> The Col de Turini is the most famous stage, every January, in the Monte Carlo Rally. You may see messages painted on the road – encouragement to top drivers from their fans.

> ### BACK TO NATURE
>
> Reached from the Col de Turini, the mountainous Parc National du Mercantour is home to chamois, ibex, ptarmigan and eagles. Alpine flowers and butterflies are at their best from June to August.

▶ *Leave the Col de Turini on the D70 through La Bollène-*

Vésubie, where you should turn sharp right following 'St-Martin' sign. Go right on the **D2565** as for St-Martin-Vésubie, then sharp right on the **D71**, follow signs to Belvédère and go right at the T-junction for Gordolasque. This is the narrow **D171**. Follow it to a car park before the bridge where the public road ends.

7 Vallon de la Gordolasque, Côte d'Azur

This dead-end valley road follows a rocky mountain stream past steep scree-slopes, crags and boulder-runs where the woodland cover peters out in scattered pines and larches. The public road ends at the 1,700m (5,575-foot) Pont du Countet, beside a relief map of the bare,

RECOMMENDED WALKS

In the valley of the Gordolasque, a long distance footpath on the east bank can be split into individual stretches for shorter walks. Look for the footbridges which cross the river and take you past scree-runs, boulder fields and thinning pinewoods on the other side.

impressive upper valley still to come. An easy stroll gives a grand view of the dashing falls at the Cascade de l'Estrech.

▶ Return through Belvédère to the **D2565** and turn left as for Nice. At St-Jean-de-la-Rivière take the **D32**, the hairpinned climb past Utelle. Go left on the **D132** to Madone d'Utelle.

8 Madone d'Utelle, Côte d'Azur

The silence, air of tranquillity and tremendous views make the journey to this remote hilltop well worthwhile. Madone d'Utelle has been a place of pilgrimage since the 9th century. The present church, with its many thanks-offerings, was built in 1806 and is the goal of four major pilgrimages every year. It shares the hilltop with a mountain 'refuge' and a domed orientation table which identifies the major summits among the all but unaccountable mountain peaks included in the glorious 360-degree skyline view.

▶ Return to St-Jean-de-la-Rivière and turn right on the **D2565**. After a 'Nice par Levens' sign, bear left on the **D19** and follow it back to Nice.

La Bollène-Vesubie is an enchanting village in the Col de Turini region. For all its sophisticated reputation, villages like this are the real south of France

SCENIC ROUTES

From the immaculate villas of the Cap de Nice, the N98 swings round to open up a gorgeous view of Villefranche bay.
Leaving Menton, the D2566 climbs past woodlands and soaring limestone ridges which stretch to the Italian border. After the tunnel at the top of the Col de Castillon, be ready for a striking northwards view past dramatic wooded ridges to lonely skyline peaks.
Beyond Sospel the D2566 cuts through a seemingly impenetrable mountain wall by hairpinning up the Gorges du Piaon. There is a remarkable view back down the ravine from the little Chapel of Notre-Dame de la Menour, reached by an arched staircase bridge across the road.
The Col de Turini descends a forested mountainside towards the red-roofed village of La Bollène-Vésubie.
As it rises, the hairpinned climb to Madone d'Utelle opens up more and more dramatic views.

Through
Historic Provence

The Romans left some of their most imposing monuments in the region they called *Provincia* – at Nîmes, Arles and Pont du Gard. Avignon retains the architectural grandeur given it by popes in voluntary exile from Rome. In the south, one of France's finest regional nature parks includes most of the Camargue.

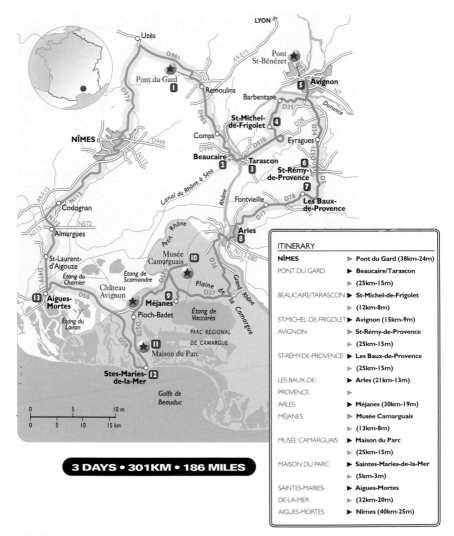

ITINERARY	
NÎMES	▶ **Pont du Gard (38km-24m)**
PONT DU GARD	▶ **Beaucaire/Tarascon**
	▶ **(25km-15m)**
BEAUCAIRE/TARASCON	▶ **St-Michel-de-Frigolet**
	▶ **(12km-8m)**
ST-MICHEL-DE-FRIGOLET	▶ **Avignon (15km-9m)**
AVIGNON	▶ **St-Rémy-de-Provence**
	▶ **(25km-15m)**
ST-RÉMY-DE-PROVENCE	▶ **Les Baux-de-Provence**
	▶ **(25km-15m)**
LES BAUX-DE-PROVENCE	▶ **Arles (21km-13m)**
	▶
ARLES	▶ **Méjanes (30km-19m)**
MÉJANES	▶ **Musée Camarguais**
	▶ **(13km-8m)**
MUSÉE CAMARGUAIS	▶ **Maison du Parc**
	▶ **(25km-15m)**
MAISON DU PARC	▶ **Saintes-Maries-de-la-Mer**
	▶ **(5km-3m)**
SAINTES-MARIES-DE-LA-MER	▶ **Aigues-Mortes**
	▶ **(32km-20m)**
AIGUES-MORTES	▶ **Nîmes (40km-25m)**

3 DAYS • 301KM • 186 MILES

i Rue Auguste, Nîmes

▶ Leave Nîmes on the **D979** as
for Uzès. Turn right on the
D981, then watch for a right
turn following it to Pont du
Gard.

❶ Pont du Gard,
Languedoc-Roussillon
In civil engineering the Romans
thought big. Their settlement at
Nîmes needed water, and the
magnificent three-tiered aqueduct at Pont du Gard, built
around 20BC, was the most spectacular section of the 50km (30
miles) of channels which
brought it from faraway springs.
The first and second levels of
arched bridges are simply
supports for the topmost water
channel which now, out of use,
is open to pedestrians. In the
modern world, few utilitarian
structures have such abiding
elegance.

▶ Continue to Remoulins. Go
straight on along the **N86**,
then follow signs for
Beaucaire.

❷ Beaucaire, Languedoc-
Roussillon
Road traffic here defers to the
Canal du Rhône à Sète (Rhône-
Sète canal). Beaucaire's one-way
street system circles an attractive canal basin where barges
and holiday cruisers are moored.
The two great interests of the
town are bullfighting and music.
Beaucaire was where the
Camargue style of bullfighting
began, free from weapons and
any taint of 'blood on the sand'.
One statue in the town celebrates 'Clairon' – not a famous
bullfighter, but a bull! Classical
and jazz concerts are held at
various venues all over the town
throughout the season.
Beaucaire's part-ruined hilltop castle offers a good view
over the lower Rhône, and the
town museum holds many
souvenirs of the days when traffic on the Roman highway – the
Via Domitia – passed through
between Italy and Spain. The
town hosted a famous fair from

1217 to the mid-19th century
and the museum has exhibits
illustrating this.

i Cours Gambetta

▶ Leave Beaucaire following
signs to Tarascon.

❸ Tarascon, Provence
The twin, and often the rival, of
Beaucaire across the Rhône,
Tarascon is famous for two
fictional characters – the river
monster called the Tarasqe,
which is paraded through the
town during the annual fair on
the last Sunday in June, and
Tartarin of Tarascon, the protag-
onist of *Aventures Prodigieuses de
Tartarin de Tarascon* by
Alphonse Daudet. The hero of
these 'prodigious adventures'
features in a musuem in the

town. Tarascon has cool plane-
tree avenues where the summer
sun is held at bay. Its 15th-
century castle on a dramatic
riverside site displays valuable
17th-century tapestries and
houses regular art exhibitions.
Close by, the church dedicated
to St Martha has a very impressive crypt which is the traditional burial place of Martha
herself, the sister of Mary and
Lazarus in the Bible story.

i Rue des Halles

▶ Leave Tarascon on the **D970**
as for Avignon. Turn right for
St Michel-de-Frigolet, looping
over the **D970** on an elevated
bridge.

Practical and beautiful: the Roman
aqueduct at Pont du Gard

4 St-Michel-de-Frigolet, Provence

Among the trees, the spires and towers of a complex of abbey buildings suddenly comes into view. A religious community has lived here among the sweet scents of herbs and pinewood since as early as 1133, although there were some years in the 20th century when the monks were dispersed elsewhere. In the public areas of the abbey the buildings include a beautifully decorated basilica completed only in 1866. The old abbey farm is now a café; and the shop sells the modern version of Père Gaucher's Elixir, which featured in one of Daudet's best-known stories.

i Le Magasin

▶ Continue to Barbentane, where you should ignore the 'Toutes Directions' sign and go straight on, following the 'Château' sign, then turn right and follow signs into Avignon.

5 Avignon, Provence

Avignon's heyday was in the 14th century, when the papacy moved the court here from Rome. The heart of the city is dominated by the grand 14th-century palace complex built by Popes Benedict XII and Clement VI and the towers, chapels, churches, cloisters and elegant courtyards which grew up to support it. What matters here is the architecture, since the restored buildings are mostly unfurnished, although Gobelin tapestries hang in the banqueting hall. Near by, the famous bridge of St-Bénézet stretches its remaining arches across the Rhône. Visitors from all over the world come to stroll 'sur le pont d'Avignon', as in the old song.

The modern town has museums of all kinds, and a hectic summer programme of concerts, plays, dance, painting and sculpture exhibitions.

i Cours Jean-Jaurès

▶ Return from Avignon on the **N570** as for Arles. Turn left on the **D571**, then right for St-Rémy-de-Provence on the **D34**, entering the town on the **D571**.

6 St-Rémy-de-Provence, Provence

St-Rémy is a place that knows how to cope with the relentless summer sun of Provence. There

The well preserved Château de Tarascon, sitting on the bank of the River Rhône

are virtual tunnels of shady plane trees, and cooling water runs down channels in the alleyways of the old town. The Musée des Alpilles, named after the limestone sierra that rises to the south, contains permanent exhibitions on St-Rémy's history and domestic life. Among townspeople commemorated is the 16th-century seer Nostradamus, whose birthplace can still be seen.

On the outskirts of St-Rémy one road leads to a woodland lake at the foot of the Alpilles, another to the former Monastery of St Paul de Mausole, converted into the mental home where Vincent van Gogh spun out his last demented days. In the countryside you are likely to see amateur artists, serious under floppy hats, painting their own versions of the scenes van Gogh put on canvas.

South of the town lie the extensive ruins of the Greek and Roman settlement of *Glanum*. Many of the artefacts are displayed in Le Musée Archéologique in town.

i Place Jean-Jaurès

RECOMMENDED WALKS

From the tourist office in St-Rémy there is a walk through the outskirts of the town (finishing back on the main Boulevard Mirabeau), which visits the scenes of many of Vincent van Gogh's paintings – farms, poppy fields, plane and olive trees, and the quarry which appealed to him because of the Japanese-style arrangement of the rocks.

BACK TO NATURE

All over the Camargue you will see the characteristic white horses, often ridden by *gardians* – the Camargue equivalent of cowboys. But look out for the foals. They are born black or grey, and may take as long as five years to grow a fully white coat.

FOR CHILDREN

The easiest thing to arrange in the Camargue is an escorted ride on one of the mysterious Camargue white horses, with a *gardian* to act as guide. Sessions as short as half an hour are offered, and many visit farms where bulls are reared for the ring.

▶ Leave St-Rémy on the **D5**, then go right on the **D27a** to Les Baux-de-Provence.

7 Les Baux-de-Provence, Provence

On a ridge that towers above the southern plain, this hill settlement is split into two distinct parts, each of limestone masonry hard to distinguish at a distance from the living rock. The inhabited quarter, dating mostly from the 16th and 17th centuries, crams shops, museums, galleries, cafés, hotels and restaurants into its narrow lanes. The eerie 'Ville Morte' ('dead city') on the crown of the ridge was the medieval stronghold, which became famous for its 'Courts of Love', courtly rituals in which troubadours vied in composing ardent, flowery verses for aristocratic ladies. It is a now a ruin. In the 15th century Louis XIII crushed the power and influence of Les Baux, but the 'dead city' remains a haunting place with magnificent views over the surrounding countryside.

Just outside the town, on the D27, the Cathédrale des Images offers a majestic audio-visual presentation. In chilly halls cut into the old bauxite quarries (Les Baux was where that aluminium ore was first discovered), 40 projectors continuously show historical and nature-based films.

i Hôtel de Manville

▶ From Les Baux-de-Provence, follow the signs to Arles, entering the town on the **N570**.

8 Arles, Provence

Phoenicians, Greeks and Romans all established themselves here, but it is the Romans who made Arles the capital of *Provincia*, who have left the most abiding monuments. The elliptical amphitheatre (Arènes) built by the Emperor Hadrian in the 1st century AD still survives, used, alas, for bull-fights in the Spanish style as well as the bloodless style of the Camargue; and you can attend concerts and festivals in the semi-circular Augustan theatre (Théâtre Antique). The town's summer calendar is crammed with events having an international flavour as well as those firmly rooted in the traditions of Provence. One of these is the parade of *gardians* – the

Carving on the main doorway of the Romanesque cathedral of St-Trophime, in Arles

Camargue 'cowboys' – on their white horses.

Arles is very well supplied with museums strong on paintings, sculptures and Provençal life. The former cathedral and cloisters of St-Trophime, one of the finest cloisters in the south of France, are decorated with beautiful stone carvings. A favourite walk is along the tree-lined avenue of Les Alyscamps, flanked by ancient tombstones, the remains of Arles' once wide-spread necropolis.

There are more memories of van Gogh here; it was in Arles that, after a fight with his friend Gauguin, he slashed off his own ear. A memorial to his tormented spirit stands in the quiet and shaded public gardens.

i Boulevard des Lices

▶ *Leave Arles on the **D570** as for Saintes-Maries-de-la-Mer. Go left on the **D36**, right on the **D36b**, then right on the **D37**. Turn left on the **C5** to Méjanes.*

9 Méjanes, Provence

In the very heart of the Camargue, and including some of the shoreline of the lagoon called Étang de Vaccarès, this estate doubles as a leisure centre and a farm. It has its own bull-ring, in which events are held every weekend during the summer, a restaurant and stables where horses may be hired for short or full-day rides.

▶ *Rejoin the **D37**. Turn right on the **D570** to the Musée Camarguais.*

10 Musée Camarguais, Provence

Based on an old sheepfold, the Camargue Museum is the best place to find out about the geology and history of this curious area and about the lives of the farmers and how intensive draining turned great areas of previously useless marsh into productive grazing and arable land. A walk from the museum follows the banks of a drainage canal dug as long ago as 1543, and shows the difference between reclaimed land and the original marsh. The museum is

one of the main centres of the Réserve zoologique et botanique de la Camargue (Camargue Regional Nature Park) which covers more than 83,000 hectares (205,000 acres) of the Rhône delta.

▶ *Return along the **D570** and watch for the Maison du Parc on the left of the road at Pont du Gau.*

11 Maison du Parc, Provence

Complementary to the Musée Camarguais, this centre explains and illustrates the fascinating wildlife of the park, with an audio-visual theatre and a display on all the brands used on the Camargue horses. Throughout, the emphasis is on the fragility of this marvellous habitat. The good advice is offered that anti-mosquito creams are a wise precaution for anybody exploring the Camargue, particularly in September and October; but to avoid the insects, there is indoor wildlife watching here too. The

picture windows at the rear of the centre overlook a pool where flamingos are often seen.

Close by, there is a privately owned Parc Ornithologique where many species of resident and migrant birds are on show.

▶ *Continue to Saintes-Maries-de-la-Mer.*

12 Saintes-Marie-de-la-Mer, Provence

Often packed with summer visitors, the former fishing village of Saintes-Maries takes its name from the tradition that the three Marys from the Bible story, together with Martha (the sister of Mary and Lazarus), sailed here from Palestine and began evangelising the Camargue.

But for the gypsy people of Europe the significant figure in the story is Sarah. In one version an Egyptian or Ethiopian servant who accompanied the Marys; in another, a local woman who helped them ashore. Sarah is venerated as the patron saint of gypsies. Her statue, dressed in rich robes, is

paraded through the town during two festivals in May and October. For the rest of the year it rests in the claustrophobic undercroft of the 9th-century church, illuminated by candles which also throw an eerie glow on a head of Sarah sculpted from Silesian coal.

Just south of the church, the Musée Baroncelli concentrates on local and natural history and folklore.

On the outskirts of the town, the Musée de Cire has a glorious mixture of exhibits, from waxwork tableaux of local tales, comprehensive displays of old farming equipment and farmhouse furnishings, to a chamber of horrors with torture scenes, a victim on a rack ... and more that you can see yourself.

The Musée Camarguais shows the beauty of the Camargue through displays and films.

i Avenue van Gogh

Les Baux-de-Provence, one of France's most famous hill villages

▶ Follow 'Aigues-Mortes' signs from Saintes-Maries, keeping on the **D38, D38c** and **D58**.

SPECIAL TO...

At Pioch-Badet, off the D570 before Saintes-Maries-la-Mer, is the Musée Tsigane, housed in a group of caravans. The museum tells the story of a thousand years of gypsy travel, history, music and crafts.

FOR CHILDREN

Just beyond Saintes-Maries-de-la-Mer, look for the sign to the pier where *Tiki III*, a little Mississippi-style sternwheeler, starts its cruises around the mouth of the Petit Rhône. This is an ideal way to wander past the grazings of Camargue horses and bulls.

13 **Aigues-Mortes,**
Languedoc-Roussillon
This town is an amazing survival, extended hardly at all beyond the original rampart walls constructed in the 13th century by Louis IX of France who called here on the seventh and eighth crusades. The walls, towers and fortified gateways remain in place. Inside them, a pleasant town retains the old medieval grid pattern of streets. A statue of St Louis looks down on the activity round the central square, just as his gilded statue graces the arcaded interior of the church. The best view of Aigues-Mortes is from the gallery of the Tour de Constance, once a political and religious prison, which overlooks the town and also puts it in a geographical context among the low-lying lagoons and lakes of the Camargue. But where is the sea? Over the years the Mediterranean has receded, stranding the town. In terms of the sea, Aigues-Mortes became what its name implies – the 'Dead Waters'. The history of

the place is explained in the Musée Jadis Aigues-Mortes.

i Porte de la Gardette

▶ Return from Aigues-Mortes following 'Nîmes' signs on the **D979, N313** and **N113**, avoiding the 'peage' signs, to Nîmes itself.

SPECIAL TO...

Not only in the Camargue itself, but also in the inland towns, are regular and well-attended bullfights. However, these are not usually of the bloodstained Spanish variety you may find distasteful. Here the aim of the bullfighter (the *rasetteur*) is not to kill the bull but to get away unscathed with a rosette or some other favour that is tied to its horns. Bulls thus live to fight many times and become skilled operators.

SCENIC ROUTES

North of Nîmes the D979 crosses the limestone scrubland of the Garrigues, then descends to the gorges of the Gardon and continues through totally different country of fields and vineyards. On the way to Frigolet and Barbentane, to the south of Avignon, the road runs through pleasant pinewoods with long stretches of picnic sites.

BACK TO NATURE

Of the many species of birds which live in the southern part of the Camargue, the most often illustrated are the flamingos. Watch out also for herons and egrets standing motionless in the water before darting down to spear their prey. Bee-eaters are perhaps the most colourful – look for them perched beside roadsides.

THE ALPS TO ALSACE

Alsace, Savoie, Burgundy, Lorraine — these towns include four provinces, each with its own independent heritage, separate for centuries from that of France. On the French-German border, Alsace and Lorraine were long contended territories, and even after they merged with France, they were lost again during the years of German occupation following the disastrous war of 1870 until the Allied victory in 1918. The battlefields around Verdun and St-Mihiel were the scene of indescribable carnage during World War I.

For 2,000 years and more, the Rhône/Saône valleys have been major highways, and it is still easy to drive quickly and unseeingly through them. However, off the main route, there is a jigsaw of medieval fishponds, and small towns of great interest.

East of Grenoble lie the majestic passes of the Alps and one of the highest roads in Europe. An exploration of the country of the lost duchy of Savoie, shows how France's massive hydro-electric schemes are landscaped so as not to spoil the glorious mountain scenery in which they are set.

Alsace is a different country once again, France with German names, sweeping vineyards and a strong preoccupation with storks. The Vosges mountains here may pale beside the Alps, but their forests and often cloudy upland ridges have an individual appeal.

Driving conditions are very varied. There are roads across the plains, among great acreages of arable land. Others wind through the vine-clad foothills. But on the Col de l'Iseran and the upper reaches of the Col de la Croix de Fer, you are in genuine Alpine country. The first of these passes can be swept by icy winds, the second can create a curious vertigo. All the roads, though, cope with summer tourist traffic.

There is splendid vineyard country here, producing wines as different as Burgundy and the Rieslings of Alsace. Many sophisticated gourmets consider that the country's finest 'table' is in Lyon.

Nancy

If you are expecting some modest provincial town, Nancy will come as a surprise. At the heart of this historic capital of Lorraine, richly-gilded Place Stanislas is one of the most elegant squares in France. Look for the lovely late Gothic Palais Ducal containing the Musée Historique Lorrain, for the Église des Cordeliers with the tomb of the dukes of Lorraine, for the superb medieval gateway and former prison of the Porte de la Craffe, and for the beautiful buildings of the old town. The Musée de Fer illustrates the history of iron, for generations a major industry in Lorraine. You can watch the glass-blowers in the crystal works of Daum.

Lyon

Lyon is a handsome city. It has sweeping quays on two rivers, the Rhône and the Saône, whose waters converge in the southern suburbs. Many notable buildings stand on the Presqu'île, the peninsula between the rivers. Here is the Musée des Beaux Arts with others devoted to textiles and decorative arts, printing and the history of banknotes. The 19th-century Basilica of Notre-Dame-des-Fourvière stands on the skyline above the streets of the old quarter in the loop of the Saône. A funicular links it with the lower town. Another climbs to twin Roman theatres still in use today.

The Lumière brothers, pioneers of moving film, worked in Lyon. There is a decorative mosaic, featuring famous figures such as Buster Keaton, near the Institut Lumière which regularly shows vintage films.

Grenoble

Grenoble, at the confluence of the Rivers Isère and Drac, is dominated by the soaring cliffs of the Massif de la Chartreuse. Cable cars whisk you to the viewpoint Fort de la Bastille, looking to the mountain ranges of Chamrousse and Vercors.

Beautifully sited, and with extensive parks and gardens, Grenoble offers music and drama, the Musée de Grenoble which contains paintings and sculpture, and has well-presented museums of science and technology, natural history, the Resistance and the region of Dauphiné.

Explore the gracious old quarter, admire Grenoble's modern architecture, and note its revived enthusiasm for the urban tram.

Strasbourg

Seat of the Council of Europe and the European Parliament, Strasbourg is also where Gutenberg, in the 15th century, invented modern printing. His memory is still revered.

The heart of the city is a river island. Look for the intriguing quarter called La Petite-France, where lovely old houses stand by the restored navigation canal.

Strasbourg has beautiful Renaissance and half-timbered buildings, a glorious cathedral and a cluster of museums in the 18th-century Château des Rohan. You can take a river cruise, stroll through botanic gardens and enjoy the Parc de l'Orangerie created in 1804 for Napoleon's Josephine.

Opposite: the cathedral of St-Etienne, in Toul, has a splendid Flamboyant frontage
Below: Nancy prides itself on its classical townscape

Visions of
War & Peace

Except for part of the valley of the Moselle, this tour avoids the industrial districts of Lorraine in favour of the agricultural south around Nancy. There are peaceful rural landscapes here, but they have bitter memories. The Franco-Prussian War of 1870 ravaged Lorraine, as did the battles of the 20th century.

3 DAYS • 300KM • 187 MILES

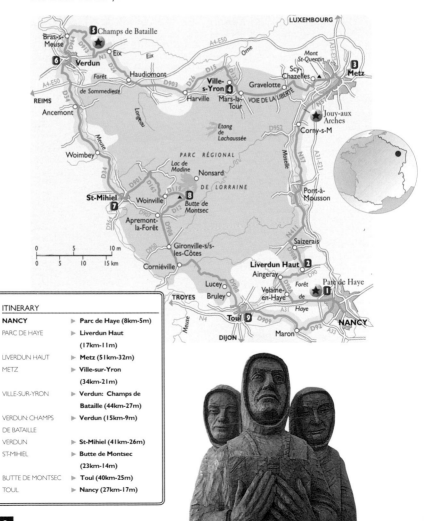

ITINERARY		
NANCY	▶	**Parc de Haye (8km-5m)**
PARC DE HAYE	▶	**Liverdun Haut** **(17km-11m)**
LIVERDUN HAUT	▶	**Metz (51km-32m)**
METZ	▶	**Ville-sur-Yron** **(34km-21m)**
VILLE-SUR-YRON	▶	**Verdun: Champs de Bataille (44km-27m)**
VERDUN: CHAMPS DE BATAILLE	▶	**Verdun (15km-9m)**
VERDUN	▶	**St-Mihiel (41km-26m)**
ST-MIHIEL	▶	**Butte de Montsec (23km-14m)**
BUTTE DE MONTSEC	▶	**Toul (40km-25m)**
TOUL	▶	**Nancy (27km-17m)**

ℹ️ *Place Stanislas, Nancy*

▶ *Leave Nancy as for Paris on the **A31**. Take the 'Parc de Haye' exit.*

❶ Parc de Haye, Lorraine
This extensive leisure park is laid out on the site of a World War II American army camp; so it is appropriate that its motor museum should have both civil and military themes. You will see examples of Bugatti, Delahaye and Jaguar among the cars. The Zoo de Haye, with its deer and wild boar, rare domestic breeds and well-stocked aviary, is an unusual one. Almost all its wild animals and birds are being cared for after accidents with cars, poisons or high-voltage lines and it is hoped they might be returned to their natural habitat.

FOR CHILDREN

Parc de Haye has a children's play area and farm, mini golf and a miniature railway.

▶ *Turn right from the park exit following the **D400** sign, then right through Velaine-en-Haye and Aingeray. Go left over the bridge on the **D90b**, through traffic lights, then left for Liverdun Haut.*

❷ Liverdun Haut, Lorraine
Crowning a bluff above a wooded curve of the Moselle, and providing lovely views over the river, this little medieval town was once the favoured summer residence of the bishops of Toul. Many old buildings survive. The tourist office is in the 16th-century fortified gateway, and there is an arcaded square of the same period. Dedicated to St Euchaire, the church is basically 12th-century. Look for the saint's tomb with his beheaded effigy. Euchaire was martyred at nearby Pompey in AD362.

ℹ️ *Porte Haute*

BACK TO NATURE

See how the currents of air sweeping up the wooded ridge from the Moselle suit the birds of Liverdun Haut. Kestrels nest in the old buildings and hunt above the woodlands. Kites are here too, as well as swifts, swallows and martins darting around the streets.

Medieval Liverdun, once favoured by the bishops of Toul

▶ *Return to the **D90b** and continue through Saizerais. Go right on the **D907** then, immediately after the 'Saizerais' board, turn left along Route de Villers. Go right at a give way sign, then left on the **N57** to Metz.*

FOR HISTORY BUFFS

Jouy-aux-Arches on the N57 takes it name from the high masonry arches, built almost 1,900 years ago in the reign of the emperor Trajan as part of the Roman aqueduct to Metz. Metz was already an old town when Julius Caesar conquered Gaul. The Romans fortified it, their walls forming the battlefield fortifications.

---

❸ Metz, Lorraine
Old fortifications are a reminder that Metz has been besieged, captured and relieved many times over the centuries, most recently in our own century. A memorial in the Place d'Armes recalls how, in 1918, Marshal Foch, Commander-in-Chief of the Allied armies on the

a landlord's and a labourer's farm, the 12th-century church and the simple château built in 1762 by the bishop of Metz.

SPECIAL TO...

Along the D903 near Verdun are certain kilometre stones which nominate the road the 'Voie de la Liberté' (Freedom Way). Allied troops swept the German forces along it in 1944.

FOR HISTORY BUFFS

Turn left along the Rue Robert Schuman in Scy-Chazelles, on the way from Metz to Ville-sur-Yron, to visit the modest home, now a museum, where the great French statesman (1886–1963) worked out his plans for a united Europe. Schuman played an important role in the creation of NATO, the Council of Europe and the European Coal and Steel Community, the first step towards the EU.
The Musée Militaire in Gravelotte recalls the disastrous Franco-Prussian War of 1870, which led to the downfall of Napoleon III.

Western front at the end of World War I, said that to see French troops on parade again at Metz was his greatest reward (the city had been in German hands for 47 years). Another memorial commemorates the liberation of Metz in 1944.

Despite being an industrial centre, Metz has a colourful selection of parks and gardens, a sizeable lake and attractive riverside promenades. The cathedral (St-Étienne), of soft yellow stone, features a soaring interior with intricate stained glass including an impressive rose window. Archaeology, art and history are all to be found under one roof at the Musée de Metz. The Renaissance section is particularly enchanting, as is Roman Metz, displayed through sarcophagi, pottery and architecture.

[i] Place d'Armes

▶ Leave Metz by the **N3** through Longeville. At traffic lights in Le Ban-St-Martin,

Metz has been the prize of armies since Roman times

*turn right on the **D103w** for Mont St-Quentin, following the hairpinned Rue Fort. Down from Mont St-Quentin, turn right at the Stop sign in the village (this is Scy-Chazelles), go left down Rue Leduchat and continue downhill at the next Stop sign. Pass Rue Robert Schuman on your left. At traffic lights turn right and follow 'Verdun' signs to Gravelotte, then go straight on along the **D903** through Mars-la-Tour. Turn right on the **D952**, then left on the **D132** to Ville-sur-Yron.*

4 **Ville-sur-Yron,** Lorraine
In 1990, in this village tucked away among the fields, a fascinating trail was laid out which allows you to 'read' the architecture, building materials, history and way of life of a typical Lorraine agricultural settlement. It leads over the 19th-century bridge to the watermill,

▶ *Continue on the **D132**, then go left on the **D15**, which becomes the **D26** to Harville. Rejoin the **D903** as for Verdun. Go right on the **D24**, then left on the **D24a** and left on the **N3** into Verdun. Turn right at the traffic lights as for Paris, then watch for a sharp right turn following 'Champs de Bataille' boards. This is the **D112**. Go left at the crossroads on to the **D913**, follow 'Ossuaire' signs, then go left as for Verdun.*

5 **Verdun: Champs de Bataille,** Lorraine
In 1916 the Germans launched a ferocious attack against the French lines northeast of Verdun: colossal artillery bombardments, mines, flame-

throwers and poison gas were all employed. In the next few months, literally hundreds of thousands of troops died in the trenches, but the French essentially held the line. After the war, the ground of the battlefields was so ravaged that it was forested over.

Along the D112 and the D913 you will find forts, trenches, memorials and utterly devastated villages. The hilltop Ossuaire (Ossuary) de Douaumont is the last resting place for the bones of 130,000 soldiers on both sides, and offers a regular audio-visual programme on life in the trenches. As you walk to the Fort de Douaumont, you might wonder why the French high command in 1915 decided to leave this greatest underground stronghold in Europe virtually unguarded.

▶ *Continue to Bras-sur-Meuse and turn left to Verdun.*

6 Verdun, Lorraine
Linked with other 'martyred towns' such as Hiroshima, Nagasaki, Coventry and Warsaw, Verdun is the Capital of Peace. Its vast underground citadel has tableaux of wartime scenes, and of the sombre moment in 1920 when France's Unknown Soldier was chosen. He now lies under the Arc de Triomphe in Paris.

Attractively sited on a curve of the Meuse, Verdun enjoys riverside quays, a fine Romanesque cathedral and the former bishop's palace, gardens and sports grounds, as well as prehistoric displays, paintings, furnishings and ceramics in the 16th-century Hôtel de la Princerie. Try the *dragées* – the sugared almonds which have been made in Verdun to a secret recipe since the 13th century.

[i] *Place de la Nation*

▶ *Leave Verdun on the **D34** through Dugny, then go left on the **D901** to St-Mihiel.*

7 St-Mihiel, Lorraine
Best known in history for its strategic position in the St-Mihiel salient – the defensive ring created by the Germans in 1918 – this little town also has the notable Benedictine abbey church of St Michel, with a 12th-century Romanesque portal and, in its light and airy interior, 80 beautifully carved choir stalls from the time of Louis XV. Here and in the Church of St Étienne, look for works by the local 16th-century sculptor Ligier Richier, a pupil of Michelangelo.

The Benedictines' library, itself a masterpiece of Lorraine design, survives with 8,000 valuable books and illuminated manuscripts.

[i] *Place Jacques-Bailleux*

▶ *Leave St-Mihiel as for Chaillon. Go right on the **D162** and left on the **D119** through Woinville to Montsec. Turn right on the **D12** then follow 'American monument' signs.*

FOR CHILDREN

Turn left off the route at Woinville for Nonsard on the northeast shore of the reservoir called Étang de Madine. Here youngsters can enjoy mini golf, cyclocross and pedaloes, as relief from the grim memories of war all around.

The impressive Benedictine library in St-Mihiel

8 **Butte de Montsec,** Lorraine

It was the Americans who smashed through the St-Mihiel salient in September 1918. The US 1st Army's memorial is a massive rotunda on this beautiful viewpoint summit overlooking the Étang de Madine, with a relief map illustrating the course of the battle. Ironically, American troops had to fire on the memorial to subdue a German machine-gun post here in 1944. It was later completely restored.

▶ Return to the **D12** and turn right. Go left on the **D908** to Toul.

9 **Toul,** Lorraine

Almost ringed by the Moselle, the Canal de l'Est and the canal linking the Marne with the Rhine, the fortress city of Toul once had the status of an independent enclave within the dukedom of Lorraine and as the heart of a diocese and a free imperial city was very important in medieval times. Old town gateways survive, as do the 17th-century walls, and the cathedral (St-Étienne) shows a splendid 15th-century Flamboyant frontage to the Place de Gaulle.

You should look at the decorated cloisters of the town's other principal church, St Gengoult. With all the water near by, Toul welcomes anglers, and the yacht basin is enlivened by the spray of a fountain in the centre.

i *Parvis de la Cathédrale*

▶ Leave Toul on the **N4** as for Nancy. Go under the bridge, then right on the **D909** to Maron. Turn left on the **D92** and return to Nancy.

The town centre of Toul

Secrets of the
Rhône Valley

The landscape changes from level plains scattered with ponds, to beautiful vineyards in the foothills and gentle forest passes. Wildlife parks display waterfowl and birds of prey. There is a spa, and one of the loveliest towns in the Lyonnais commemorates a saintly man whose life's work relieved the sufferings of the poor.

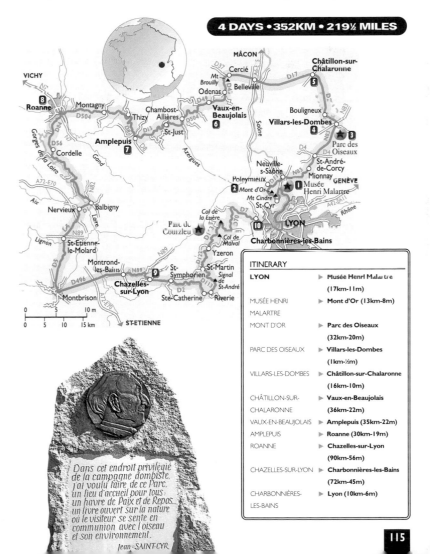

4 DAYS • 352KM • 219½ MILES

ITINERARY	
LYON	▶ Musée Henri Malartre (17km-11m)
MUSÉE HENRI MALARTRE	▶ Mont d'Or (13km-8m)
MONT D'OR	▶ Parc des Oiseaux (32km-20m)
PARC DES OISEAUX	▶ Villars-les-Dombes (1km-½m)
VILLARS-LES-DOMBES	▶ Châtillon-sur-Chalaronne (16km-10m)
CHÂTILLON-SUR-CHALARONNE	▶ Vaux-en-Beaujolais (36km-22m)
VAUX-EN-BEAUJOLAIS	▶ Amplepuis (35km-22m)
AMPLEPUIS	▶ Roanne (30km-19m)
ROANNE	▶ Chazelles-sur-Lyon (90km-56m)
CHAZELLES-SUR-LYON	▶ Charbonnières-les-Bains (72km-45m)
CHARBONNIÈRES-LES-BAINS	▶ Lyon (10km-6m)

Dans cet endroit privilégié
de la campagne dombiste.
J'ai voulu faire de ce Parc.
un lieu d'accueil pour tous :
un havre de Paix et de Repos.
un livre ouvert sur la nature
où le visiteur se sente en
communion avec l'oiseau
et son environnement.

Jean SAINT-CYR

*Turn right on the **D89**. In St-Cyr, go right on the **D65**. Continue straight on uphill at the Stop sign, then keep right on the **D92** for Mont Cindre. After Mont Cindre, go straight on at a crossroads on the **D90** signed 'Fortin du Mont Thou'. Return to the cross-roads and turn right, then go right on the **D73** to Poleymieux-au-Mont-d'Or.*

2 Mont d'Or, Rhône Valley
Follow the main route to Poleymieux over Mont d'Or ('Golden Hill') above Lyon, but be sure to stop off for occasional strolls, and to admire the views. There are several pleasant villages on the hillsides, as well as farms and woodlands. Mont Cindre, beside a telecommunications tower, is a favourite place for people from Lyon who take to the hills at weekends. Many of them enjoy the walk which starts at the hermitage. The best 360-degree panoramic view is from Mont Thou, as you walk over the grasslands beside a hilltop military camp.

| i | *Place Bellecourt, Lyon*

Lyon is a handsome city in the valley of the Rhône

FOR CHILDREN

The Parc de la Tête d'Or, on the banks of the Rhône in Lyon, has a lake, a small zoo, go-cart track, botanical gardens and pony rides.

▶ *Leave Lyon on the **D433** as for Neuville. Go through Caluire-en-Cuire, then turn right at 'Musée de l'Automobile' sign and follow 'Musée' signs along a complicated route to the Musée Henri Malartre.*

1 Musée Henri Malartre, Rhône Valley
In the attractive, high-set Château Rochetaillée and the exhibition halls in its grounds, is an impeccably maintained collection of really rare cars. The Hugot, Thieulin, Noël Beret and the very early steam-powered Secretand, displayed in the Musée Henri Malarte, are the only survivors of these makes in the world. The separate hall displays several Gordini racing cars, built by the dogged but perpetually broke French constructor after whom it is named.

Hitler's Mercedes is here, as well as examples of Packard, Lincoln and the 1912 Alco built by the American Locomotive Corporation. Look for the bizarre gyroscope-equipped 1926 Monotrace tandem car, and the huge battery-powered Stela which ran as a taxi in Lyon till 1953. There is also a strong collection of cycles and motorcycles (1898–1954).

▶ *Return by the same route to the **D433** and turn left. Go right over the suspension bridge into Couzon, then left on the **D51** into St-Romain.*

FOR CHILDREN

At the Maison d'Ampère in Poleymieux children are encouraged to try 18 of Ampère's original electrical experiments, including some with magnets. This is fun as well as a fine learning experience, and perfectly safe at the power levels employed.

FOR HISTORY BUFFS

In Poleymieux the Maison d'Ampère is devoted both to the brilliant and engagingly eccentric Lyon-born physicist André-Marie Ampère (1775–1836) – who gave his name to the standard unit of electric current – and to an amazing display of historic electrical equipment.

▶ In Poleymieux-au-Mont-d'Or bend right after gantry traffic lights, still on the **D73**, and continue via Curis-au-Mont-d'Or to Neuville-centre on the **D16**. Go straight on along the **D16e** through Montanay, then left at the T-junction (this is the **N83**) through Mionnay. Turn right into the Parc des Oiseaux.

3 Parc des Oiseaux, Rhône Valley

Far more than simply the ornithological park its name suggests, this public estate near Villars-les-Dombes takes full advantage of its situation in woodland circling an attractive lake. Eagles, vultures, parrots and parakeets have enclosures in the woods, and there is a tropical bird house, while pelicans, swans, geese and flamingos favour the water. The guided tour, by 'tourist train', takes 30 minutes. A walk round to see the park in all its details might occupy two hours. There is an adventure playground and a picnic area. At the entrance to the park, the Maison de l'Arrisanat stocks high-quality ceramics, glassware and even boomerangs made by local craftworkers

▶ Continue to Villars-les-Dombes, eventually leaving the village on the **D2** as for Châtillon.

4 Villars-les-Dombes, Rhône Valley

With a fine Gothic church, a road system which craftily keeps through traffic away from the narrow streets of the pleasant and colourful centre, and an excellent natural history bookshop, Villars is where to start any exploration of the curious plateau district known as Les Dombes.

Here there are a thousand pools, lakes or meres dug as fishponds from the 12th century onwards. They are now split between angling waters and commercial fisheries for carp, tench, roach and pike. Around 2,000 tonnes are taken every year, to make this one of the great inland fishery districts of France. Ask locally about dishes such as fillet of royal carp.

☐ *Parc des Oiseaux*

▶ Continue on the **D2** to Châtillon-sur-Chalaronne.

Baby ostriches at the Parc des Oiseaux – Villars les Dombes

5 Châtillon-sur-Chalaronne, Rhône Valley

Few small towns in France have been awarded four stars in the national *villages fleuris* ('villages in bloom') competition, but Châtillon deserves every one. You should spend time admiring the blaze of blossoms in parks and gardens, beside the banks of the River Chalaronne and its tributary streams, in window boxes and hanging baskets, and decorating all the bridges.

Châtillon cherishes some beautifully maintained buildings to match the flowers. The covered market hall of 1670 is a gem, some of the old town ramparts survive, and the brickwork Church of St André dates from the 16th century. The famous Châtillon triptych of 1527 is displayed in the dignified town hall. Its three Biblical

scenes – the sleeping apostles, Christ taken from the cross and the Resurrection – are beautifully painted and restored.

Gathered in the intriguing old Apothecairerie is a fine collection of earthenware pots from which 18th-century pharmacists concocted their mixtures of gentian, sassafras, asafoetida and other plants. You can see where some of the prescribed salts ate away the painted surface of the pots!

prises here continue the *Clochemerle* name. This is one of the most beautifully located of the Beaujolais wine-growing villages. There is a lively fraternity of enthusiasts for wine, and much of it may be tasted locally at the Caveau de Clochemerle.

However, *Clochemerle* is perhaps best remembered for the ceremonial inauguration of the public toilet. La Pisotière de Clochemerle stands on a terrace above the beautiful wine-planted valley, and is still popular with visitors today.

▶ Take the Lamure road, leaving Vaux on the 'Le Sottier poids lourds' road. This is the **D49**. Follow 'Lamure' signs – ignoring a left turn for Les Buissières – then go left on the **D44** to St-Cyr. Turn right on the **D504** to Allières, left on the **D485**, then right on the **D98** and over the level crossing. Go straight on through St-Just, then follow signs to Amplepuis.

The delightfully fragrant town of Châtillon-sur-Chalaronne

ℹ *Place du Champ de Foire*

▶ Leave Châtillon on the **D17**, which becomes the **D37** through Belleville and Cercié, then go left on the **D43** and left on the **D43e** to Mont Brouilly. Return to the **D43** and turn left. Turn right on the **D19**, then right on the **D49** to Vaux-en-Beaujolais.

❻ Vaux-en-Beaujolais,
Rhône Valley
Gabriel Chevallier immortalised this village among the hillside vineyards as the fictional setting for his famous satirical novel *Clochemerle*, and several enter-

❼ Amplepuis, Rhône Valley
In this little industrial town, the Musée de la Machine à Coudre celebrates a most heroic failure. Barthélèmy Thimonnier was an apprentice tailor here. In 1825, having seen the laborious work of the seamstresses, he invented the sewing machine.

He was spurned in Paris. London businessmen paid him an insulting sum for his design. Soon after his dejected return to France, the sewing machine revolutionised the production of clothes. But by then

Thimonnier had died – still poor, still unappreciated and still unknown.

▶ *Leave Amplepuis on the D8, then take the D504 to Roanne.*

8 Roanne, Rhône Valley
Backing on to the Loire, Roanne is also on a well-maintained canal along which visitor cruises are run. It is an historic textile town, and old techniques of spinning and weaving are demonstrated at the Écomusée. If you enjoy ceramics, visit the elegant château of the Musée Déchelette, which has beautiful displays of French and Italian ware. Modern craftworkers congregate in the Maison des Métiers d'Art.

Roanne keeps a foothold in the wine business, although the great days when it shipped barge-loads of barrels to Paris are long since gone. You can taste some of the *Côte Roannaise* wine in the town-centre *caveau*, housed in a lovely little half-timbered building with a steeply pitched red-tiled roof.

i Cours de la République

The countryside round Roanne reflects its heyday as a major producer of wine

SPECIAL TO.....

Many gourmet centres were originally on the main road from Paris to the Riviera. Roanne on the N7 is now avoided by the traffic on the Autoroute de Soleil, but it remains a famous gastronomic town. The restaurant of the Troisgros brothers' hotel is classed as one of the finest tables in France.

▶ *Leave Roanne on the N7 as for Lyon. Go right on the D43 as for Varennes then right on the D84 as for Vernay. As soon as you enter Commelle-Vernay turn left as for Cordelle. Follow the D56 and N82 into Balbigny. Go right at the traffic lights to Nervieux, then left on the D5 through St-Étienne-le-Molard. Go left on the D8 into Montbrison, left on the D496, then straight ahead on the N89. Go right to Chazelles-sur-Lyon.*

FOR CHILDREN

The Musée d'Allard on the Boulevard de la Préfecture in Montbrison, on the way to Chazelles-sur-Lyon, has several individual themes, but is best known for its collection of dolls and puppets from countries all over the world.

9 Chazelles-sur-Lyon,
Rhône Valley
Off the main roads in the wooded hills north of St-Étienne, Chazelles owes a great deal to the crusaders who brought back from the east the secret of making felt. Chazelles used this new-found expertise to turn itself into a great hat-making centre. The extensive Musée du Chapeau explains, with guided tours, audio-visual presentations and working machinery, all the techniques of preparation, manufacture and fashion, and has a gallery of more than 500 specimen felt hats of all styles, including a collection of chefs' *toques*. The museum also devotes space to the history of the town, from its days as a junction of Roman roads.

i Place J B Galland

▶ *Leave Chazelles on the* **D103**, *which becomes the* **D2**, *to Ste-Catherine. Go straight on as for Mornant, then turn left on the* **D63** *into Riverie and left on the* **D113** *via St-André-la-Côte to St-Martin. Follow signs to Yzeron, go left as for Plan d'Eau, left on the* **D489** *as for Duerne, then right on the* **D113**. *Continue straight on at Col de Malval, then at Col de la Luère go straight on along the* **D24** *as for Lyon. Watch for a sudden left turn on to the* **D70**. *Go through Poillonnay then turn right on the* **D7** *as for Lyon into Charbonnières-les-Bains, then left for Charbonnières-centre.*

BACK TO NATURE

Turn left at Col de Malval for the Parc de Courzieu. Here, not only are wolves, lynx and wildcats on show, but free-flying displays by eagles, vultures and falcons also take place in a thousand-seat auditorium.

---

⑩ Charbonnières-les-Bains, Rhône Valley

Lyon is one of several French cities to have a totally different-looking spa town just beyond its outskirts, well away from the familiar busy streets. The first mineral spring here was traditionally discovered by a donkey on its last legs, which regained its vigour by drinking from it.

Whatever its origins, Charbonnières developed into a full-scale spa and health resort with thermal baths, a pump house, a casino and elegant villas in discreetly wooded

---

RECOMMENDED WALKS

Stop off on the way from Chazelles to Charbonnières and in St-André-la-Côte, or from a left-hand bend on the route beyond it, take the waymarked path to the Signal de St-André. In clear weather the dramatic view extends from a series of hill villages to the mountain wall of the Alps.

---

grounds. It has good sports facilities, shaded footpaths and a fine array of shops.

ⅈ *Parc Thermal*

▶ *Follow 'Lyon-centre' signs and return to Lyon.*

SCENIC ROUTES

From Mont Cindre wonderful views open up of Lyon, the Rhône valley and the Alps. After Châtillon there is a splendid outlook to the hillside vineyards of Beaujolais.

On the D504 to Roanne, look for the gorgeous hilltop setting of Thizy.

The Lac de Villarest reservoir is very attractive from the D56 between Roanne and Chazelles; a view of wooded gorges with an abandoned castle standing on a flooded rock.

There is a magnificent valley view to the right of the D113 after Riverie, on the way from Chazelles to Charbonnières.

Vineyard in the Beaujolais region

The French Alps

This is essentially a mountain tour among the wild and magnificent landscapes of the French Alps. Check the *ouvert-fermé* (open/closed) signs – in most years the route is not fully open till mid-June – and be ready for some steep gradients and exposed hairpinned climbs.

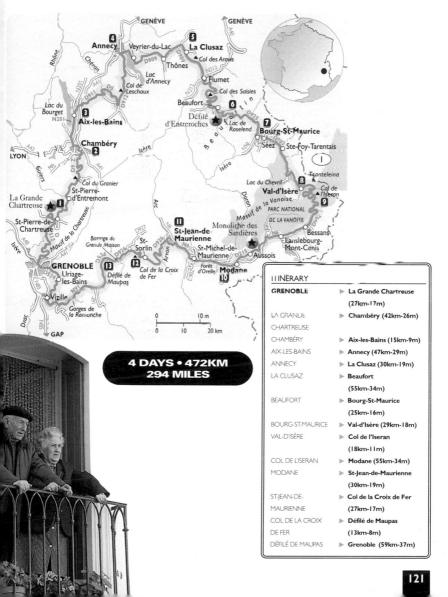

4 DAYS • 472KM 294 MILES

i *Rue de la République, Grenoble*

▶ *Leave Grenoble for Le Sappey on the D512, then continue to St-Pierre-de-Chartreuse. Turn left and follow signs to the Musée de la Grande Chartreuse, using the one-way system.*

☐ La Grande Chartreuse, Rhône-Alpes

High on the west side of the Massif de la Chartreuse stands La Grande Chartreuse, the grand mother house of the Carthusian monks. It has been established in this remote location, on ground under snow for more than half the year, since its founder St Bruno built the first monastery here in 1084.

The monks lead an austere life of study, meditation, solitude and prayer. No visitors are allowed in La Grande Chartreuse itself, and cars may not use the road to it. However, a fine museum has been created at La Correrie, by the end of the public road. It explains and illustrates the monastic life, as well as the history of the Order and the difficulties experienced by the monks here (they were expelled from the monastery during the Revolution, and again between 1903 and 1940).

The famous Chartreuse liqueurs, the profits from whose sales fund the Order's charitable works, are distilled elsewhere.

▶ *Return to St-Pierre-de-Chartreuse and turn left to rejoin the D512. Follow this road and the D912 to Chambéry.*

② Chambéry, Rhône-Alpes

Why the elephants, you may wonder, on the great fountain in the pleasant centre here? They commemorate the Duc de Boigne, who made his military reputation and his fortune in the East, before retiring to Chambéry to indulge his passion for town planning.

Wander through the arcaded streets, intriguing alleyways and courtyards of the old quarter. Above them stands the castle of the dukes of Savoie. The guided tour explains how Savoie was once an independent state whose territory stretched from Lake Geneva to the Mediterranean and included regions of modern Italy.

The Italian connection persists in the Musée des Beaux-Arts, which has a splendid display of Italian paintings. Local history collections are housed in the Musée Savoisien.

Fontaine des Éléphants, one of the sights of Chambéry

In the cathedral (look for more elephant motifs), some interior details such as the apparently vaulted ceiling are actually 19th-century attempts at *trompe l'oeil* paintwork. If nothing more, they have achieved some historical curiosity value of their own.

i *Boulevard de la Colonne*

▶ *Leave Chambéry for Aix-les-Bains on the N201.*

BACK TO NATURE

Approaching Aix-les-Bains, the N201 runs beside the shore of Lac du Bourget. Just before Tresserve, stroll over to look on the reed beds and watch the comings and goings of the great crested grebes. Coots, pochards and little grebes can also be seen on the water, and there are grey herons around the margins.

☐ Aix-les-Bains, Rhône-Alpes

Starting at the banks of the Lac du Bourget, the most extensive mountain lake in France, the town rises from a cruise-boat harbour and a lakeside promenade to a very stylish town centre. Aix-les-Bains is an elegant and well equipped spa resort. Its springs were known to the Romans, and later patrons were Napoleon's family and Queen Victoria.

Colourful gardens, old and new-style fountains and pleasant woodland walks are scattered around. Top-class sports facilities are provided, especially winter sports on the lake, and the mountains are always in view. Relics of Roman times include a Temple of Diana and a restored archway facing the Thermes Nationaux. Guided tours – on which you are encouraged to wear a toga – explore the Roman remains, the original baths and the statues preserved in the Musée Lapidaire.

On a hillside boulevard, the Musée Faure houses a valuable art collection. Look for fine paintings and sculpture by Degas, Pissarro, Rodin and Corot.

[i] *Place Mullard*

▶ *Continue on the N201, then go right on the D911. Turn left on the D31, right on the D5 and go straight on as for Le Châtelard on the D911. Turn sharp left on the D912 over Col de Leschaux. Go left on the N508 to Annecy.*

4 Annecy, Rhône-Alpes
You can see how dearly the Annéciens love their pure and beautiful mountain-rimmed lake (Lac d'Annecy). They have spurned any encroachment on the lakeside parks and gardens which are areas of general relaxation as well as wonderful mountain viewpoints; and they make an attractive feature of the rivers and canals which thread through the lovely old quarter of the town.

Lake cruises are a favourite excursion here, but in a place ideally laid out for aimless strolling around, or for clip-clopping along in the calèches (open carriages) which ply for hire, there are also specific attractions on land. Visit the castle museum, for instance. Go to prison – or, at least, to the Palais de l'Ile, the old jail, mint and courthouse (which now houses a small history museum). The restored château houses a local museum.

In the evenings, the old town (pedestrianised) is lively and chattering as its pavement restaurants and cafés fill up. Then the lights reflect in the waters lapping quietly by.

[i] *Centre Bonlieu, rue Jean-Jaurès*

▶ *Leave Annecy for Veyrier-du-Lac on the D909. Continue through Thônes to La Clusaz.*

5 La Clusaz, Rhône-Alpes
Here is the first of many Alpine ski resorts on this tour, occupying a valley site crammed between jagged peaks. In summer when, as throughout the region, the weather can be very changeable, La Clusaz seems to be waiting impatiently until the snows return, bringing with them thousands of winter sports enthusiasts.

However, summer visitors are by no means neglected. The Bureau des Guides will introduce you to rock-climbing in half-day courses, and grass skis are available for hire. You can also, briefly or at length, try your hand at canoeing, fishing, skating, tennis, horse- or pony-

Aix-les-Bains is a great centre for boat trips on the Lac du Bourget

riding, fencing, archery, pistol-shooting and pottery. Folklore groups enliven the evenings.

In among the typical shops, chalets, bars, cafés, hotels and restaurants of a ski resort, La Clusaz has a most attractive modern church. Look for the beautiful stained-glass windows, illustrating work in the mountains, fields and forests.

i Parc de l'Église

La Clusaz is one of Haute Savoie's oldest and biggest ski resorts

▶ *Continue on the **D909** over the Col des Aravis to Flumet, then go straight ahead on the **D218B** over the Col des Saisies and follow signs to Beaufort. Go through Beaufort as for Bourg-St-Maurice.*

6 Beaufort, Rhône-Alpes
At Beaufort, a village in a spruce-clad mountain valley, you may wonder where the road can possibly go next. In fact, it slices through the amazing rock cleft of the Défile d'Entreroches, then up a steep hairpinned pass with magnificent views of the valley left behind.

A good excursion centre, Beaufort is the heart of the Beaufortain district. In its cooperative you can watch the making of 'the prince of Gruyères' – Beaufort cheese, produced with milk from the upland farms – and even help in the process.

Eastwards, the Lac de Roselend reservoir lies in a deep depression among the mountains. Then the road battles up through 10 hairpin bends towards a notch in the skyline. This is an exciting landscape of mountain torrents, scree slopes and high snow-filled gullies. Wildflowers put on their brave summer display.

i On the D925 in Beaufort

► *Continue to Bourg-St-Maurice.*

⁷ Bourg-St-Maurice,
Rhône-Alpes

Bourg-St-Maurice lies in a spectacular setting overlooked by cliffs and tiers of chalets. Green in summer, the hill slopes to the southeast are in the easily-reached skiing area of Les Arcs, upgraded for the 1992 Winter Olympics.

Down in the town itself there is a woodland park beside the compensation reservoir of a hydro-electric scheme. Bourg-St-Maurice is keen on sports such as white-water canoeing and rafting. Horse and pony trips can also be arranged. There is a minerals and crystals display, and another co-operative where Beaufort cheese is made.

The satellite village of Vulmis, along a steep road to the southwest, has a chapel with beautiful 15th-century frescos.

And at Hauteville-Gondon, to the south, you will find a costume museum and an unexpectedly baroque 17th-century church.

ⓘ *Place de la Gare*

FOR CHILDREN

Bourg-St-Maurice has installed a modern funicular railway. Children will enjoy the ride as the train climbs above the river then plunges into a mountain tunnel on its way up to the ski areas of Les Arcs.

► *Leave Bourg-St-Maurice on the N90 to Séez. Go right on the D902 to Val-d'Isère.*

⁸ Val-d'Isère, Rhône-Alpes
The resort of Val-d'Isère lies 1,850m (6,068 feet) above sea level and is one of the most famous locations on the European ski-racing calendar. Cable cars climb from its narrow valley setting to reach spectacular viewpoint summits such as Bellevarde at 2,827m (9,270 feet). The eastern mountain ridge, marking the frontier with Italy, soars to over 3,350m (11,000 feet).

Val-d'Isère is simply a series of long lines of apartment blocks, chalets, shops, hotels and restaurants. Many of the latest buildings, though, are quite sensitively designed in traditional mountain-country idiom.

Summer sports facilities are more for weekly residents than for transients, although horse and pony hire, archery and tennis lessons and mountain biking may be tackled in shorter bursts.

ⓘ *Maison de Val-d'Isère*

► *Continue on the D902 to Col de l'Iseran.*

⁹ Col de l'Iseran, Rhône-Alpes
When the road over the Col de l'Iseran was opened in 1937, it had taken 20 years to build. At 2,770m (9,085 feet) in the wildest country, it was the highest road in Europe. Today, only a handful surpass it. The Iseran is usually under impenetrable snow till mid-June, but even a month later chill winds may sweep down from the still higher glaciers and snowfields.

In clear weather the Iseran is exhilarating, although the climb is on a broken surface. There is a summit shop. An austere, four-square chapel stands a little way apart. This is the only through road which penetrates the huge nature reserve of the Parc National de la Vanoise. The mountain scenery is magnificent, and the descent is fortunately on a much better-surfaced road.

► *Continue on the D902. In Bessans follow the 'Chambéry' sign. Go through Lanslevillard,*

which you will see directly across the valley. Another excursion worth making is to the complex of forts at l'Esseillon, built in the 1820s to defend the forgotten kingdom of Piedmont-Sardinia against possible invasion from France.

ⓘ *Place du Replaton*

▶ *Leave Modane on the N6, then turn left into St-Jean-de-Maurienne.*

⑪ St-Jean-de-Maurienne, Rhône-Alpes

Although the world's most modern aluminium factory is sited here, it is well away from the charming heart of St-Jean-de-Maurienne. As you approach, you will see, rising above the town, a great sweep of pasture land dotted with higher and higher hamlets and farms.

The town square dips down to a fine modern war memorial outlined against the northern mountains. During the holidays, schoolchildren act as earnest and well-informed guides to the cathedral and the one-time bishop's palace whose elegant salon and connecting rooms house a comprehensive local museum. Displays include traditional women's dresses from villages round about, showing how each place had its individual style. The Opinel company based here exports its wooden-handled clasp knives all over the world. The factory museum shows how its extensive range is produced.

ⓘ *Place de la Cathédrale*

▶ *Leave St-Jean for Col de la Croix de Fer on the D926.*

then, in Lanslebourg-Mont-Cenis, join the **N6** as for Chambéry. In Sollières, turn right on the **D83**. In Sardières, go right as for Hôtel du Parc, then left past La Monolithe. Turn right at the T-junction, rejoining the **D83** to Aussois, then go straight ahead on the **D215** to Modane.

BACK TO NATURE

Pause after Sardières, on your way to Modane, to look at the *monolithe*, a huge isolated limestone pillar soaring to 83m (272 feet) in the heart of a pinewood. This strange weathered feature is not uncommon here. You will see more of them among the pines further on.

⑩ Modane, Rhône-Alpes

This is where the busy road and rail tunnels to Bardonecchia in Italy begin. The 12.8km (8-mile) road tunnel opened in 1980. Go to the old ornamental rail tunnel entrance above the town, and you will see the coats of arms of the main cities on the Calais-Paris-Rome line.

Modane had a hard time in World War II. It was heavily bombed by the Allies in 1943, in an attempt to disrupt the German-Italian rail supply system, and the Germans fired colossal demolition charges at the rail tunnel entrance in 1944. You can still see a concrete blockhouse, intact but flung askew by the tremendous force of the explosion.

There is a glorious view from here, over Modane in its deep winding valley to the skyline of the Vanoise peaks. The town is an access point to the mountain footpaths of the Vanoise. Local walks include a hairpinned climb to the Fort du Replaton

Val-d'Isère has developed into a popular summer and winter resort

SPECIAL TO...

Transhumance – the bringing down of sheep from the lush summer mountain pastures – is still practised in the Maurienne. However, nowadays, the flocks arrive by train.

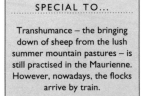

12 Col de la Croix de Fer,
Rhône-Alpes

Take care in the five rock tunnels above the stunning Arvan gorge, with the needle peaks of the Aiguilles d'Arves on the skyline. Alpine meadows towards Entraigues, and the little ski resort of St-Sorlin, come and go. Then comes the narrow and dizzying zigzag road up the boulder fields to the summit of the pass. Here you can relax by the restaurant, note the cross of iron which gave the col its name, and marvel at the outlook over a sea of Alpine summits. To the south-south-east, the 3,983m (13,065-foot) peak of La Meije is just in view.

▶ *Beyond the col, turn left as for Grenoble.*

13 Défilé de Maupas,
Rhône-Alpes

The final exposed climb to the Croix de Fer may have left you wondering what lies on the other side. In fact, the descent is on a road of a much higher stan-

dard, although the grandeur of the mountain scenery and of the majestic gorge which takes the route back down to a lower level is even more impressive.

Pause at the Barrage de Grand'Maison. Displays here explain how this is the top reservoir of the most powerful hydroelectric scheme in France, fed by cascades from the permanent snowfields.

FOR HISTORY BUFFS

On the return route to Grenoble, the 17th-century château at Vizille houses a comprehensive museum of the French Revolution. In 1788, a year before the Revolution, the three Estates – nobles, clergy and commoners – met In this castle to denounce Louis XIV's suppression of parliament and proclaim individual liberty. With tableaux, sculptures, paintings and posters as well as weaponry, the museum stresses the artistic environment of revolutionary France no less than the events and personalities.

Grenoble is a modern city dedicated to superlative winter sports

▶ *Continue downhill. Avoid the road for Le Verney and take the road signed 'Hydrolec'. Turn left as for Grenoble, then join the N91. Go through Le Péage de Vizille, then turn right to Vizille-centre on the D101. Continue to Uriage on the D524 and return to Grenoble.*

SCENIC ROUTES

From Grenoble to Chambéry the route, runs over a massif of hills, forests, deep-cut valleys and towering limestone cliffs.
On the D34, after Aix-les-Bains, look for the dramatic valley of the Chéran, overlooked by the rock pillars called the Fairies' Chimneys.
The superlative mountain landscapes beyond La Clusaz include glimpses on the eastern horizon of Mont Blanc.
Even the spectacular climb to the Col de la Croix de Fer is surpassed by the descent through precipitous gorges to the N91.

The German
Connection

From the Rhineland plain south of Strasbourg to the viewpoint roads high in the Vosges mountains, this tour explores some of the most beautiful areas of Alsace. There have been vineyards in the eastern foothills of the Vosges since Roman times. At higher altitudes lie forests and upland pastures covered by winter snows.

3/4 DAYS • 420KM • 260 MILES

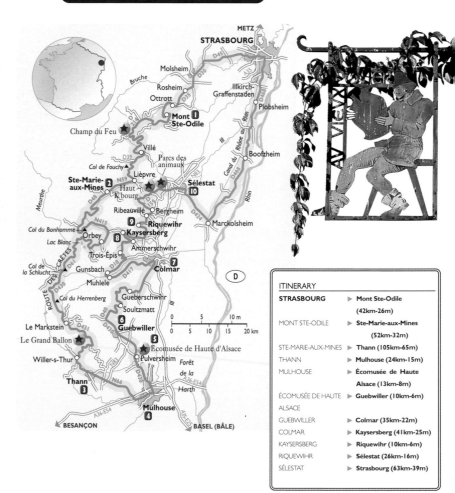

ITINERARY		
STRASBOURG	▶	**Mont Ste-Odile (42km-26m)**
MONT STE-ODILE	▶	**Ste-Marie-aux-Mines (52km-32m)**
STE-MARIE-AUX-MINES	▶	**Thann (105km-65m)**
THANN	▶	**Mulhouse (24km-15m)**
MULHOUSE	▶	**Écomusée de Haute Alsace (13km-8m)**
ÉCOMUSÉE DE HAUTE ALSACE	▶	**Guebwiller (10km-6m)**
GUEBWILLER	▶	**Colmar (35km-22m)**
COLMAR	▶	**Kaysersberg (41km-25m)**
KAYSERSBERG	▶	**Riquewihr (10km-6m)**
RIQUEWIHR	▶	**Sélestat (26km-16m)**
SÉLESTAT	▶	**Strasbourg (63km-39m)**

i Place de la Cathédrale, Strasbourg

▶ Leave Strasbourg for Eckbolsheim on the D45. Continue to Ergersheim, then take the D30 to Molsheim. Follow the 'Strasbourg' sign, then take the D422 and D35 through Rosheim to Ottrott. Turn right in Ottrott on the D426, then follow the D426a to Ste-Odile.

SPECIAL TO...

Molsheim, to the southwest of Strasbourg, was the home of Bugatti, the marque which epitomises *pur sang* (the thoroughbred ideal) in car design. Cars are no longer built in what is now the Messier-Bugatti factory, but Bugatti owners regularly make the pilgrimage to Molsheim.

❶ Mont Ste-Odile, Alsace

You may be surprised by the press of traffic on this out-of-the-way woodland hilltop. The cluster of buildings here is one of France's great pilgrimage centres: the historic convent which guards the tomb of Odile, the patron saint of Odile.

Odile, abbess of the original religious house of this splendid site, died around the year 720. The present buildings, in fine order, are from much later centuries, including our own. With cloister and courtyard gardens, an excellent paved walk around viewpoint terraces, a pilgrims' hall and several individual chapels, this is a place of beauty, dignity and repose. The site appealed to earlier civilisations, too. As you approach the summit, look for carefully worked masonry of the imposing Mur Païen (Pagan Wall) constructed in prehistoric times.

▶ Return downhill, bear slightly left and follow signs to Champ du Feu. Go straight ahead and there follow signs to Villé. Turn right on the D39

Strasbourg, capital of Alsace and sophisticated seat of government

RECOMMENDED WALKS

At Mont Ste-Odile you can step into the network of way-marked trails which explore this beautifully wooded hill. Some were originally pilgrims' paths, others follow the Pagan Wall, and all offer splendid views to the valleys.

as for St-Dié. In Fouchy, go left on the D155 to Col de Fouchy, then follow signs to Lièpvre and go right to Ste-Marie-aux-Mines on the N59. Approaching Ste-Marie, avoid the tunnel.

❷ Ste-Marie-aux-Mines, Alsace

From the 16th century onwards, this little town was famous for the richest seams of silver in France. You can join a guided tour of the old St Bartélemy mine. Safety helmets and waterproof capes are provided, and you start by walking in through a hillside tunnel to the levels and galleries beyond.

There is also a fine Musée Minéralogique in the town, and the Maison du Pays (not quite the 'country house' which the local English translation suggests) mounts displays on

the mining era and on the spinning, dyeing, weaving and hosiery which, combined, formed Ste-Marie's other 'boom' industry.

Look for the restrained baroque style of the Church of La Madeleine, for intriguing old buildings such as the towered Pharmacie by the main square, and for the little public gardens which include one, beside the town hall, with a floral peacock on display.

ⓘ *Rue Wilson*

▶ *Leave Ste-Marie-aux-Mines as for Le Bonhomme. Turn right at Col des Bagenelles to Col du Bonhomme. Turn left on the N415. At the roundabout go right on the D48 to Orbey, then follow signs 'Les Lacs' and 'Lac Blanc'. Go left on the D418 to Col de la Schlucht. Turn right on the D417 as for Épinal and almost immediately left on the D430 to Le Markstein. Continue straight ahead on the D431 to le Grand Ballon, then follow signs to Thann.*

❸ Thann, Alsace
On the banks of the fast-flowing River Thur, overlooked by a hillside Cross of Lorraine, Thann was wrested back from German control by Marshal Joffre's troops in 1914. The text of his emotional proclamation is

Superb carvings on the choir stalls in Thann's Gothic cathedral

carved on a war memorial. Thann's history is even more complex than that of other places in Alsace, as it was Austrian territory from 1324 to 1648.

The splendid collegiate Church of St Thiébaut features immensely detailed sculptured façades and portals, polychrome roof tiling and superb carved-oak choir stalls. Look there for the figures of the gossip, the fiddler and the spectacled man. Thann's local history museum is in the arcaded corn market (Halle aux blés) of 1519. Two towers survive of its medieval ramparts, and several fine buildings from the 16th century onwards remain.

ⓘ *Place Joffre*

▶ *Leave Thann on the N66. Go over the autoroute and continue to Mulhouse.*

❹ Mulhouse, Alsace
Despite its parks and gardens, zoo and yacht basin and attractive old quarter, 'Moo-loose' is an industrial town which may take some time to grow on you. Look round its museums, and you will realise that this is one of the most amazingly well-endowed towns in Europe as regards museums of technology.

History, fine arts, painted wall-coverings and printed fabrics all have extensive museums of their own, but the Musée des Beaux-Arts is an excellent starting-point. Railway enthusiasts should head for the excellent Musée Français du Chemin de Fer. Close by, the Musée du Sapeur-Pompier has a fine display of fire engines.

However, the pride of Mulhouse is the Musée National de l'Automobile, the most stupendous motor museum in the world. On display are over a hundred Bugattis, whole collections of Rolls-Royces, Alfa Romeos, Maseratis, Mercedes-Benz, Gordinis and the rest – more than 500 splendid vehicles of almost 100 different makes. The fine tradition continues, as new Peugeots are also made in Mulhouse.

☐ *Avenue Maréchal-Foch*

▶ *Leave Mulhouse as for Guebwiller on the **D430**. Turn on to the **D430bis** and follow 'Éco-musée' signs.*

⑤ Écomusée de Haute Alsace, Alsace

Occupying a roomy site on the Alsace plain, here is a fascinating replica village of more than 60 traditionally styled buildings – houses, farms, barns and workshops – created to show the domestic life of past generations, as well as the work of the blacksmith and cart builder, baker, clog-maker and weaver, and all the half-forgotten farming trades.

Favourite local dishes are cooked for the restaurants, and Alsace wines are served. There is a keen interest in wildlife conservation: storks, for instance, are encouraged to nest.

During the 1990s a major project is the restoration of the potassium mine whose derelict buildings you will see on the approach road.

▶ *Return to the **D430** and continue to Guebwiller.*

⑥ Guebwiller, Alsace

A place full of squares, and bright with window-boxes, Guebwiller is partly built of a soft local stone which gives the Église St-Léger, for instance, a warmer 'feel' than most French churches. St-Léger also has stately arcaded aisles and some worthwhile stained-glass windows.

Overlooked by hillside vineyards, the town enjoys some beautiful parkland. The Parc de la Marseillaise features fine examples of cypress, lime, cedar and sequoia trees.

Guebwiller was the birthplace of the 19th-century ceramic artist Théodore Deck. Examples of his work, and historical mementoes of the district, are on display in the Musée du Florival.

☐ *Place St-Leger*

▶ *Continue on the **D430** as for Le Markstein. Turn right on the **D40** to Soultzmatt, left on*

the **D18bis** to Osenbach, then right on the **D40** again. Bear right to Gueberschwihr, turn left as for Hattstatt, then join the **N83** for Colmar, and enter it on the **D30**.

⑦ Colmar, Alsace

In colour, design, construction, layout and state of preservation, Colmar is one of the world's most beguiling towns. The narrow streets, some darting off at eccentric angles, are lined with colour-washed half-timbered houses of the 16th and 17th centuries, most of them banked with flowers.

Look in particular for the balconied Maison Pfister of 1537, the riverside houses of the Quai de la Poissonnerie and 'La Petite Venise' (Little Venice) to which they lead, and for the lovely cluster of buildings by the pastry shop at the corner of Rue Kléber. The 15th-century Koïfhus – the old customs house, used as the town hall – is topped by glorious polychrome roof tiling.

Colmar's fine town hall

Colmar has a museum and art gallery in the old Dominican convent of Unterlinden (Musée d'Unterlinden), noted for its 16th-century altarpiece by Matthias Grünewald – the Isenheim Altarpiece. The sculptor Auguste Bartholdi was born here, in a courtyard house which is now a museum recalling that his most famous work was the Statue of Liberty.

i *Rue des Unterlinden*

Take the first left under the archway, follow the 'Toutes Directions' sign, then turn left and continue to Kaysersberg.

8 Kaysersberg, Alsace
As you stroll through this attractive little flower-decked medieval 'city', past the *caves* of wine growers and liqueur distillers, you will encounter many houses, gateways, bridges, towers and chapels of the 13th to 15th centuries.

9 Riquewihr, Alsace
Enclosed in 16th-century ramparts, this charming old town is the 'pearl of the Alsace vineyards'. Wine cellars stock the produce of its Riesling, Muscat, Tokay and Gewürztraminer grapes.

Local history is the concern of the Musée Dolder. The Tour des Voleurs (Thieves' Tower) houses an 'authentic' torture chamber. Installed in a princely palace, the Musée d'Histoire

RECOMMENDED WALKS

The hilltop resort of Les Trois-Épis, between Colmar and Kaysersberg, concentrates on sports and open-air activities. Ask at the tourist office about the 50km (31 miles) of footpaths on its invigorating woodland ridges.

▶ *Leave Colmar as for Épinal on the **D417**. Turn right to Gunsbach, then right at the crossroads on the **D10**. Go left on the **D11** to Trois-Épis, then right to Ammerschwihr.*

The Église Ste-Croix has a magnificent altarpiece of 1518. Other works of religious art are displayed in the local museum.

Kaysersberg is twinned with Lambaréné in Gabon because of the town's links with Dr Albert Schweitzer. He was born in Kaysersberg in 1875 and spent most of his working life at his hospital in West Africa. A room in his birthplace is preserved in his memory.

i *Place de la Mairie*

▶ *Leave Kaysersberg as for Ribeauvillé on the **D28**. Go left at the roundabout and left on the **D3** to Riquewihr.*

Kaysersberg, once the home of kings, is now a small wine-growing centre

des PTT d'Alsace includes lavish displays of stage coaches, maps, models, uniforms, electric and wireless telegraphy systems, telephones, teleprinters and a miniature of the Ariane space rocket, telling the story of 2,000 years of message deliveries since Gallo-Roman times.

i *Place de la 1ère Armée*

▶ *Leave Riquewihr for Ribeauvillé and Bergheim. In Bergheim, go left on the **D42** as for Haut Koenigsbourg.*

SPECIAL TO...

The population of storks, which have nested for centuries on the rooftops and chimneys of Alsace, dwindled alarmingly in the 1970s. However, the birds are strongly established once again.

After Riquewihr, turn left as for Hunawihr to visit the Centre de Réintroduction des Cigognes.

Turn right on the D159 and continue to Sélestat, entering it on the N83.

FOR CHILDREN

Off the D159 on the way to Sélestat, the Montagne des Singes allows 300 Barbary apes to roam in 20 hectares (50 acres) of forest. At the nearby Volerie des Aigles, in the grounds of a castle, eagles, vultures, kites and falcons give flying displays.

10 **Sélestat,** Alsace
Unremarkable in its suburbs, Sélestat becomes much more interesting as you explore its historic centre. Here there are beautiful medieval, Renaissance and 18th-century houses and public buildings, the Romanesque Church of Ste-Foy and the later Gothic Church of St-Georges. The town's water towers are unexpectedly ornate.

Sélestat is the main centre where modern Alsace artists show their paintings, and its 15th-century Bibliothèque Humaniste, housed in the old corn market (Halle aux blés), Sélestat's greatest glory is its Humanist library

is one of the most valuable libraries of books and manuscripts in France.

i *Boulevard Leclerc*

▶ *Leave Sélestat on the D424 as for Marckolsheim. At the roundabout, turn left on the D468 and return to Strasbourg.*

FOR HISTORY BUFFS

On the way to Sélestat, turn left off the D159 for the spectacular hilltop castle of Haut-Koenigsbourg. The 12th-century fortress was destroyed in the 17th century, and was completely restored early this century on the orders of Kaiser Wilhelm II. It looks like a film set, and was in fact used by the great director Jean Renoir for *La Grande Illusion.*

On the return route to Strasbourg, turn right into Marckolsheim then left on the D10 to the Musée de la Ligne Maginot, the French defensive line bypassed by the Germans in 1940, but the scene of fierce fighting in 1944.

SCENIC ROUTES

Early on, the D45 opens up long views over villages and vineyards to the forested range of the Vosges.

On the way to Thann, the D48 rises through beautiful miniature landscapes in the valley of the Petite Lièpvre. After the Col de la Schlucht, admire the 'top of the world' views over the deep western valleys from the 'Route des Crêtes', then on to the descent of Le Grand Ballon.

From the approach to Guebwiller, you are in the delicious foothills country of the 'Route du Vin'. The flat return to Strasbourg is enhanced by unexpectedly bright and flower-filled villages.

THE NORTH, BURGUNDY & CHAMPAGNE

This area of northern France, just back from, or along the coast, has long been fought over, and frequently devastated by war. Here you will find historic battlefields, Crécy, Valmy and Sédan, and more from the World War I Somme campaign, whose British and Commonwealth victims are remembered in dignified parkland memorials such as Vimy Ridge.

Huge areas of land are occupied by arable farms. This is the country's bread-basket, and the source of many of its fine vegetables. Here and there, modest woodlands break up the view, and the high points are more likely to be the water towers known grandly as *châteaux d'eau*.

Elsewhere, there are full-scale state forests, including some of the most beautiful in France. The forest around Fontainebleau attracted the royal and imperial courts. Then it was the turn of the 19th-century artists to enjoy the forest and the atmospheric towns and villages close by. Some of France's most lavish state residences are here: Fontainebleau, Rambouillet, Pierrefonds.

Near the border, France shares with Belgium the lovely winding, wooded river valleys of the Ardennes. Other hill country includes quiet areas off the Paris-Riviera autoroute and the mazy lanes of the Morvan.

You can hardly miss the vineyards in the foothills of the Côte d'Or and the great champagne estates round Reims. On the coast you will find resorts as different as stylish Le Touquet and simple Le Crotoy by the Somme. Inland towns, such as Pierrefonds, Compiègne and Moret-sur-Loing, have their following too.

You will encounter the long-lost melding of French and English history – Richard the Lionheart conferred with the French king at Vézelay before they set off to lead their joint army in the Third Crusade. And you can learn how Revolutionaries pursued and captured the fleeing Louis XVI, how artists such as Millet shrugged off the studios of Paris and came to paint from real life in the countryside.

Calais

Under English occupation for more than 200 years, Calais has always looked across the Channel. The Dover-Calais route was the first Continental service to be operated by a steamship, the *Rob Roy*, in 1821. One of the most famous sights is Rodin's great statue of the Burghers of Calais, who pleaded with Edward III of England to spare the town after its surrender in 1347. There is a confidently ornate town hall, a fine arts museum displaying the lacework for which Calais is famous, and a little parkland museum of the town's travails in World War II.

Amiens

Amiens is centred on the majestic Cathédrale Notre-Dame, largest of all the Gothic churches in France. Even its grubby exterior cannot hide the wonderful fretted upper reaches. Inside, there are beautifully carved oakwood choir stalls.

Museums and galleries concentrate on local art and history: Amiens is the capital of Picardy. Quaysides and inlets of the Somme thread through the northern suburbs, and there is an eastern quarter of market gardens first cultivated in medieval times.

Reims

Reims is not just outwardly the city of champagne. Millions of francs' worth lies in cellars underground. Visitors are welcome at the champagne houses which even commissioned stained-glass panels of the different vineyard areas for the cathedral. Two of the old city abbeys have been turned into museums. You can see where the German capitulation order was signed in 1945. And Reims has a major motor museum devoted entirely to French marques.

Chalon-sur-Saône

Baseball in France? Yes, in a beautiful park at Chalon-sur-Saône, which also features a magnificent riverside garden with 25,000 roses from Europe, America, Japan and the Himalayas.

By the Saône, visit the museum commemorating the pioneer of photography, Nicéphore Niepce. Exhibits range from his first camera of 1822 to the Apollo equipment taken to the moon.

There is an exhibition centre for the 44 vineyard villages known collectively as the Côte Chalonnaise. On the little St Laurent island, the topmost gallery of the Tour du Doyenné is an unusual viewpoint over the town.

Chartres

Chartres is, first and foremost, its cathedral, Notre Dame, whose twin towers are seen for miles across the plain. Connoisseurs consider that the stained-glass windows at Chartres are the finest in the world. An art gallery concentrates on stained glass of classical and modern designs, and there are studios where present-day artists work.

Look for the Maison Picassiette with its décor picked out in fragments of glass and china. Admire the paintings, sculptures and tapestries in the fine arts museum, and stroll by the quays, mills and wash-houses on the River Eure.

Opposite: Flavigny sits on a rocky outcrop above wooded valleys
Below: Caves of Moet & Chandon

The English
Connection

This tour from Calais, busiest of all the French car ferry ports, visits resorts both sophisticated and family-style. The chalk headlands match the white cliffs of Dover, which can be seen on a clear day, glistening in the sun. Behind the coast there are inland river valleys where quiet villages doze in the shelter of gently wooded hills.

3 DAYS • 272KM • 170 MILES

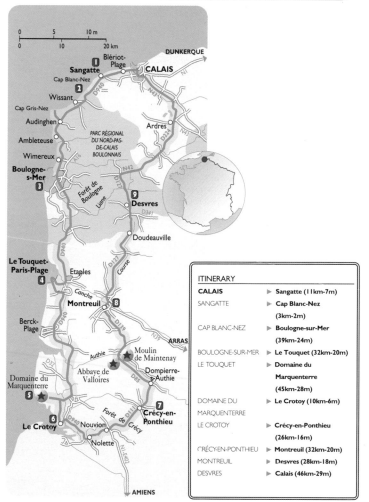

ITINERARY

CALAIS	▶	**Sangatte** (11km-7m)
SANGATTE	▶	**Cap Blanc-Nez** (3km-2m)
CAP BLANC-NEZ	▶	**Boulogne-sur-Mer** (39km-24m)
BOULOGNE-SUR-MER	▶	**Le Touquet** (32km-20m)
LE TOUQUET	▶	**Domaine du Marquenterre** (45km-28m)
DOMAINE DU MARQUENTERRE	▶	**Le Crotoy** (10km-6m)
LE CROTOY	▶	**Crécy-en-Ponthieu** (26km-16m)
CRÉCY-EN-PONTHIEU	▶	**Montreuil** (32km-20m)
MONTREUIL	▶	**Desvres** (28km-18m)
DESVRES	▶	**Calais** (46km-29m)

ⓘ *Boulevard Clemenceau, Calais*

▶ *Leave Calais on the* **D940** *through Sangatte.*

SPECIAL TO...

West of Calais there are several smaller fishing ports. One local speciality is *moules* (mussels), often sold from stalls outside the fishermen's homes.

---

❶ Sangatte, Pas de Calais
Here is the huge landward base of the French Channel Tunnel. At the information centre a comprehensive display explains what massive investment and civil engineering expertise were needed for the opening.

ⓘ *Rue du Vigier*

▶ *Continue on the* **D940** *to Cap Blanc-Nez.*

❷ Cap Blanc-Nez, Pas de Calais
This sweeping chalk headland is introduced by a fine windswept statue of the pioneer French aviator, Hubert Latham, who was famous, like Blériot, for his 'audacious flights' above the Channel. Turn right for the splendid viewpoint memorial to the French sailors of the World War I Dover Patrol. Turn left for the Musée du Transmanche devoted to the history of the Channel Tunnel plans from the earliest hare-brained schemes involving horse-drawn carriages.

BACK TO NATURE

The chalk cliffs around Cap Blanc-Nez and Cap Gris-Nez are a nesting ground for gulls and fulmars which skim the waves and soar on the up-currents of air. Kestrels also nest here, and you may be lucky enough to see one hovering over the grassy cliff-tops before plunging on its prey. The clifftop flora is outstanding during the summer months.

▶ *Continue on the* **D940** *through Audinghen, where the* **D191** *on the right leads to Cap Gris-Nez. Beyond Wimereux the left turn signed 'vers A16' leads towards the Colonne de la Grande Armée. The* **D940** *continues to Boulogne-sur-Mer.*

SPECIAL TO...

The Pas de Calais district played a great part in World War II, and there are several museums about the conflict. Two on the route are at Ambleteuse and in a former German blockhouse at Audinghen.

---

❸ Boulogne, Pas de Calais
France's most important fishing port has a bustling and complex harbour front. Every morning fishermen's stalls offer the freshest possible produce of the sea.

Turn uphill through the busy shopping streets, and you will come to one of the best-preserved historic citadels in the north of France. The castle

Calais' ornate *Hôtel de Ville* (town hall)

museum covers a bewildering variety of subjects including archaeology, ethnology, painting and sculpture and local souvenirs from the time of Napoleon. A pleasant stroll round the towers and fortified gateways of the preserved 13th-century ramparts, which enclose the medieval Haute Ville, gives views of the catamarans below discharging and loading.

ⓘ *Quai de la Poste*

FOR HISTORY BUFFS

On the outskirts of Boulogne, the Colonne de la Grande Armée is a towering monument topped by a statue of Napoleon in characteristic pose. He assembled his army here in 1803 for an invasion of Britain which never took place.

▶ *Leave Boulogne on the* **N1**, *then take the* **D940** *and* **N39** *to Le Touquet-Paris-Plage.*

4 **Le Touquet,** Pas de Calais
Le Touquet grew up in the 19th
century, largely as a haven for
British gamblers taking advantage of the more lenient French
gambling laws. Developed
jointly by French and British
interests Le Touquet has unpar-
alleled facilities for all kinds of
sport, including a huge annual
motor-sport 'enduro' race on its
extensive sands. Three well-
kept golf courses occupy the
southern outskirts. The beaches
are glorious.

You may think that some of
the seafront apartment blocks
contrast hideously with the few
remaining 19th-century buildings there. The heart of the
town, however, retains its
elegant shops, cafés and restaurants. Discreet wooded footpaths are threaded through the
pine- and birch-woods of the
handsome residential suburbs.

FOR CHILDREN

Aqualud on the seafront at Le
Touquet is a modern swimming
pool complex. Its water
fountains and a 90m (98-yard)
curving chute are great fun for
the children; adults might enjoy
the sauna.

FOR CHILDREN

On the D940 south of Le
Touquet, the extensive fun park
at Bagatelle features a roller-
coaster ride which finishes with
a belly-flop into a lake, a mono-
rail, a mirror maze,
roundabouts, an aviary and a
zoo.

Le Touquet is a fine example of a
turn-of-the-century seaside resort

ⅰ *Palais de l'Europe*

▶ *Leave Le Touquet following
Berck and Hesdin signs, and
rejoin the **D940** as for Rue.
Turn right, following signs to
Domaine du Marquenterre.*

5 **Domaine du
Marquenterre,** Picardy
Reached by a rather rough
approach road, this private
estate is one of the finest bird
reserves in Europe. La parc
ornithologique de Marquenterre
was created behind a screen of
pine trees on land reclaimed as
recently as the 1970s from the
estuary of the Somme.
Residents and migrants include
ducks, geese, swans, gulls and
waders, hoopoes, avocets,
spoonbills, storks and dozens of
other species of shore, lake and
salt-marsh. Entry is free and you
may rent binoculars.

▶ *Return from the Domaine
and follow signs to Le Crotoy.*

6 **Le Crotoy,** Picardy
Very much a French family
resort, Le Crotoy has a good
beach, fishing and yacht
harbours by the River Somme.
Fresh fish and shellfish are
available from roadside stalls
and in the restaurants. You
should take care before imitat-
ing the locals' casual-seeming
gumbooted strolls across the
tidal inlets. Make sure not to be
caught by the incoming tide.
The old station is a terminus for
the summer railway whose
steam-hauled trains explore the
pleasant countryside inland.

**RECOMMENDED
WALKS**

Local tourist offices have maps
of the network of walks inland
from Le Crotoy, in the lovely
pastureland behind the Somme
estuary. They wander past
fields, woodlands and water
channels in what was
unproductive marshland just a
few generations ago.

▶ Leave Le Crotoy by 'Sortie Ville' signs. Turn right on the **D940**, then left on the **D140** to Noyelles. Turn left over a level crossing, then left on the **D111** through Nolette to Crécy-en-Ponthieu.

7 Crécy, Picardy

On the exit from the village a view-point tower (Le Moulin Édouard III) stands at Edward III's traditional vantage point over the battlefield of Crécy in

1346, when his English archers routed the French cross-bowmen in one of the most decisive battles of the Hundred Years' War. Edward's son, the Black Prince, who was then little more than a boy, won his spurs here.

▶ Continue on the **D111** to Dompierre, then go left on the **D85** to Valloires. After the Abbaye de Valloires turn sharp right to Moulin de Maintenuy, right at a roundabout and left on the **D139** to Montreuil.

8 Montreuil, Pas de Calais

Formerly Montreuil-sur-Mer, the town is now 14km (9 miles) from the sea. It retains many picturesque houses on cobbled and steeply cambered streets; some of the action of Victor Hugo's *Les Misérables* is set here. A statue of Sir Douglas Haig is a reminder that the British commander-in-chief in World War I made his headquarters near by. Montreuil's historic ramparts provide a beautiful hour-long walk, partly edged with trees and giving splendid sunset views. The abbey church dates back to the 11th century.

ℹ Place Darnétal

▶ Leave Montreuil on the **N39**, then take the **N1** as for

Le Crotoy is a bustling fishing and yacht harbour on the River Somme

Boulogne. Bear right off the **N1** for Ixent, then follow the **D127** to Desvres.

9 Desvres, Pas de Calais

The square here is the site of regular morning markets, but since the 18th century the main business of the town has been in faïence or glazed pottery. Several workshops welcome visitors, and there is a purpose-built pottery museum.

ℹ Rue Jean Macé

▶ Leave Desvres on the **D127**. Turn right on the **N42** and then take the **D224** to Ardres. In Ardres turn left on the **N43** and return to Calais.

Towns of Picardy

Centred on the cathedral city of Amiens, this tour is through districts often missed by visitors to France. It features wide rural landscapes in areas such as the Picardy plateau, goes through the fringes of the northern industrial belt and takes in elegant towns.

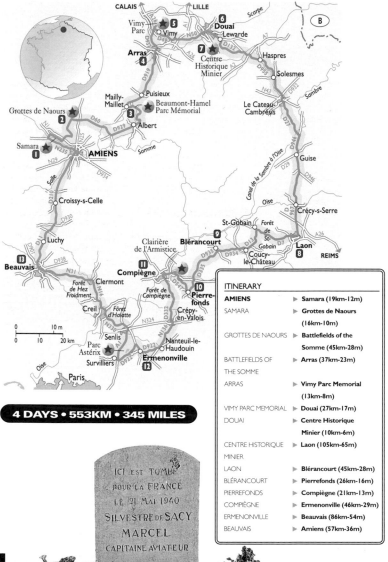

4 DAYS • 553KM • 345 MILES

ITINERARY	
AMIENS	▶ **Samara (19km-12m)**
SAMARA	▶ **Grottes de Naours (16km-10m)**
GROTTES DE NAOURS	▶ **Battlefields of the Somme (45km-28m)**
BATTLEFIELDS OF THE SOMME	▶ **Arras (37km-23m)**
ARRAS	▶ **Vimy Parc Memorial (13km-8m)**
VIMY PARC MEMORIAL	▶ **Douai (27km-17m)**
DOUAI	▶ **Centre Historique Minier (10km-6m)**
CENTRE HISTORIQUE MINIER	▶ **Laon (105km-65m)**
LAON	▶ **Blérancourt (45km-28m)**
BLÉRANCOURT	▶ **Pierrefonds (26km-16m)**
PIERREFONDS	▶ **Compiègne (21km-13m)**
COMPIÈGNE	▶ **Ermenonville (46km-29m)**
ERMENONVILLE	▶ **Beauvais (86km-54m)**
BEAUVAIS	▶ **Amiens (57km-36m)**

ICI EST TOMBÉ
POUR LA FRANCE
LE 21 MAI 1940
SILVESTRE DE SACY
MARCEL
CAPITAINE AVIATEUR

i Rue Catelas, Amiens

▶ Leave Amiens on the **N235** through Picquigny, then go right on the **D191** to Samara.

❶ Samara, Picardy
Laid out among scrubland, marsh and ponds, Samara is a fascinating historical park which looks at thousands of years of human life and activity in the valley of the River Somme. There are accurate representations of ancient dwellings and demonstrations of prehistoric trades such as flint cutting. There is a botanical garden and arboretum. Along the pathways is an excavated Celtic town and a modern pavilion whose exhibits look not only into the distant past but also at what life may be like in the future.

i la Chaussée Tirancourt, Picquigny

▶ Continue on the **D191** to St-Sauveur, go left on the **D97** at 'Grottes de Naours' sign, left on to the **D933** to Flesselles, straight on along the **D117** to Naours, right on the **D60**,

Amiens, a pleasing mixture of ancient riverside streets and modern development

then sharp left to the Grottes de Naours.

❷ Grottes de Naours, Picardy
Burrowed into a wooded hillside above the village, the Underground City of Naours (Grottes de Naours) is one of the most amazing places in France. About 30 tunnels and 300 separate rooms – including chapels and stables – have been used as refuges in times of danger and invasion from the Gallo-Roman era to the 18th century. They were the haunt of salt smugglers and used as stores for the British Army in World War II.

▶ Return from the car park, go left at the Stop sign and follow the **D60** to Contay. Turn right on the **D919**, immediately left on the **D23** to Franvillers and left on the **D929** through Albert. Go left on the **D20**, right on the **D151** to Thiepval, left on the **D73** and follow signs to Beaumont-Hamel memorial park.

❸ Battlefields of the Somme, Picardy
The countryside hereabouts is scattered with war graves and monuments recalling the first

day of July 1916, the opening of the Battle of the Somme. Among the most impressive are Sir Edward Lutyens's massive brick-and-stone memorial at Thiepval; the Ulster Tower also near Thiepval; and the Newfoundland Memorial Park at Beaumont-Hamel, where almost the whole of the 1st Newfoundland Regiment were mown down by enemy machine-gun fire and shrapnel.

▶ Continue on the **D53** to Mailly-Maillet. Turn right on the **D129**, then right on the **D919** to Arras.

❹ Arras, Picardy
Arras, the capital of Artois, would be a finer place if its two most spectacular squares – la Grand Place and la Place de Héros – had gleaming stonework to match the elegance of their arcaded buildings. The Hôtel de Ville (town hall) is a handsome affair, and there is a good view from its belfry. Part of the former Benedictine Abbaye de St-Vaast is now a cathedral (18th- to 19th-century); in the south wing of the abbey is a well-stocked fine arts museum with extensive collections of French and Flemish paintings, medieval

wood carvings and a superb display of local porcelain and tapestry.

[i] Place des Héros

▶ Leave Arras on the **N425**, then take the **D937** as for Béthune. Turn right on the **D55** following the 'Memorial Canadien' sign to Vimy Parc.

5 Vimy Parc Memorial, Picardy

One of the largest war memorial areas in France, Vimy Parc commemorates, in particular, the tremendous assault of 9 April 1917 when all four divisions of the Canadian Corps stormed the German defences on Vimy Ridge. Keep to the paths, as there is still a chance of encountering unexploded shells and ammunition. Guided tours explore the underground galleries. On the crown of the ridge, the Mémorial et Parc Canadien, whose soaring pillars bear the maple leaf of Canada and the fleur-de-lys of France, is the most majestic of all the monuments raised after the Great War.

▶ From the memorial, return down the **D55** as for Arras, then go left at the first junction following the 'Gendarmerie' sign. Turn right on the **N17** to Thélus, left on the **D49**, right on the **D33**, go under a bridge, then turn left and join the **N50** dual carriageway to Douai.

The Vimy Parc Memorial honours the 75,000 Canadians who died in 1917

6 Douai, Picardy

An industrial town brightened by judiciously placed gardens, flowery roundabouts and avenues of trees, Douai is, at its heart, an island bounded by the River Scarpe and its associated canals, lined with old quaysides. The most impressive building is the ornate Gothic belltower, completed in 1410. Escorted tours show visitors the view from the top, over the town, and also the fine interior of the historic Hôtel de Ville (town hall). In the old Carthusian convent (Chartreuse) – a mixture of three centuries of architectural ideas – more than a dozen exhibition halls show off French, Flemish and Italian Renaissance paintings as well as sculptures, earthenware and ivories. There is a splendid antique map of Douai, drawn in 1709 to Louis XIV's command.

[i] Place des Armes

SPECIAL TO...

The belfry at Douai houses the largest carillon in France, using no fewer than 62 individual bells. Douai's official carillonist is the 34th in a line which started in 1391. Douai also owns the first mobile carillon in France, with 50 bells.

▶ Leave Douai on the **N45**. In Lewarde turn right on the **D135** and follow 'Centre Historique Minier' signs on to the **D132**.

7 Centre Historique Minier, Picardy

On the site of the old Delloye pit (Fosse Delloye) near Lewarde, you will find an extensive indoor, outdoor and underground museum dedicated to coal-mining in the north of France. Former miners guide visitors round displays about the geology and exploitation of the coal-seams, the machinery and processing plant used in the mines, and the working conditions of miners through the centuries.

Finally, you can descend into one of the original pits where 450m (490 yards) of galleries have been reconstructed as they would have been in their heyday.

▶ Continue on the **D132** to Bouchain. Go right on the **D943**, left on the **N30**, then right to Haspres. Go left for Saulzoir and right before the FINA station, leaving Haspres on the **D955** to Solesmes. Then follow signs to Le Cateau-Cambrésis. Leave Le Cateau on the **D12**, which becomes the **D27**, then follow the **D946** and the **D967** to Laon.

8 Laon, Picardy

The attractions of Laon are partly in its situation, partly in the architecture of the old city (Ville Haute) surrounded by medieval ramparts and imposing entrance gates. Laon lies on a long narrow ridge which dominates the surrounding plain and is an excellent natural viewpoint. The many-towered 12th- to 14th-century cathedral, one of the great Gothic edifices of France, has a nave of immense grandeur and some beautiful medieval stained-glass windows. Beside an old garden chapel of the Knights Templar (Chapelle des Templiers), the museum holds extensive archaeological and arts collections.

ℹ️ *Place de la Cathédrale*

▶ *Leave Laon on the **D7** for St-Gobain. Go left on the **D13**, then right on the **D5** to Coucy. Join the **D937** as for Folembray, then turn left on the **D934** to Blérancourt.*

9 Blérancourt, Picardy
Headquarters during World War I of the American volunteer ambulance corps, the pavilions, restored ground floor and gardens of the largely dismantled Château de Blérancourt are now the national Museum of Franco-American Co-operation. Notable Americans such as George Washington, Benjamin Franklin, John Paul Jones and Thomas Jefferson are honoured. There is a substantial library, as well as many documents and souvenirs of battles in which the two nations fought side by side, notably in the two World Wars.

▶ *Leave Blérancourt on the **D935**, which becomes the **D335**, to Pierrefonds.*

10 Pierrefonds, Picardy
Drive slowly down the hill into Pierrefonds, so as not to miss the first stunning glimpse of the massive castle which towers over this engaging island resort. Handsome villas in discreet wooded grounds overlook a lake, which rowing boats and pedaloes share with the coots and mallards. The Parc Rainette is home to a herd of stately fallow deer. However, it is the château which dominates the town. Napoleon I bought it in ruins, but it was Napoleon II who commissioned the great architect Viollet-le-Duc to oversee its transformation into a grand imperial residence. Guided tours show off the whole lavish project; one room is dedicated to the architect himself, but the château itself is his memorial.

ℹ️ *Place de l'Hôtel-de-Ville*

▶ *Leave Pierrefonds on the **D973** as for Compiègne. Go right on the **D547** to Vieux Moulin, then left on the **N31** and right on the **V4** to Clairière de l'Armistice. Then follow signs to Compiègne.*

11 Compiègne, Picardy
Here is a dignified and spacious town with a fine riverside frontage on the River Oise, spreading parkland and suburbs to south and west where villa gardens drift into the glorious Forêt de Compiègne. Louis XV and Louis XVI commissioned the building of a palace here, facing a wide cobbled square. It was completed in the fateful year of 1789. After the Revolution, Napoleon I had it rebuilt, and later still it was the favourite residence of Napoleon III and Empress Eugénie.

Open to the public, the royal and imperial apartments recall all these personages, and there is a separate Musée du Second Empire. Elsewhere in the complex of buildings a first-class motor and carriage museum (Musée National de la Voiture et du Tourisme) includes splendid exhibits of vehicles from the horse-drawn age, and cars which are a reminder that, although Germany was the birthplace of the automobile, the French were livelier designers and experimenters.

Another memorable museum in Compiègne is the Musée Vivenel, which includes exceptional collections of archaeological items and classical ceramics.

For 200 years until AD987, Laon was actually capital of France

i Place de l'Hôtel de Ville

▶ Leave Compiègne on the
D332 as for Meaux. In Crépy-
en-Valois follow 'Paris' signs
and take the D136 into
Nanteuil, ignoring the bypass.
Watch the navigation here.
About 55m (60 yards) after a
Fiat garage, turn right follow-
ing the sign 'Ermenonville
Tourisme'. Go left on the
D922, then right on the
N330 through Ermenonville.

RECOMMENDED WALKS

Ask at the tourist office
in Pierrefonds for the
Itinéraires circuits pédestres
booklet describing four
waymarked walks in the
eastern part of the Forêt de
Compiègne. One follows an
ancient Roman road, another
goes past the Empress
Eugénie's hunting pavilion.

The elegant town of Compiègne

12 Ermenonville, Picardy
Ermenonville has been done no
favours by the planners, who
have signposted the road here
as being a convenient way to
bypass other towns. Traffic is
usually heavy. However, the
town itself has one haven of
tranquillity. To the left of the
main road is a park, introduced
by a carved stone which says
'here begins the course of a
sweet and rustic leisure' with
woodland paths, ponds and
streams.

Beyond Ermenonville is a
small zoo (Zoo Jean-Richard).
The Abbey of Chaalis, just
north of the town, in a gracious
parkland which contains one of
France's finest rose gardens, is a
classical 18th-century château
on the site of an old Cistercian
monastery.

▶ Turn sharp left for
Mortefontaine. Join the D922
and in Plailly follow the blue

and white 'A1' signs. Join the
A1 autoroute as for Lille. Parc
Astérix is reached by the first
exit. After Parc Astérix take
the next autoroute exit as for
Senlis. After the toll booths
follow the 'Creil' sign on the
N330, then the Beauvais
signs via Clermont into
Beauvais itself.

FOR CHILDREN

Parc Astérix, off the A1, on the
way from Ermenonville to
Beauvais, is an expensive but
massive theme park based on
the adventures of the ancient
Gauls – Astérix, Obélix and
Toutatix – made famous by
Goscinny and Underzo.

13 Beauvais, Picardy
One victim of World War II was
the tapestry industry at
Beauvais, removed elsewhere
and never brought back here.
The Galérie Nationale de la
Tapisserie, a gallery of French
tapestries from the 15th century
onwards, is one of the sights of
the town. Stained glass was
another Beauvais interest, and
much of it survives, both in the
Church of St-Etienne and as a
feature of the superb interior of
the cathedral (St Pierre), which
has a tremendous height for the
area of its base. The cathedral's
astronomical clock, gilded and
astonishingly complicated, was
completely restored in 1989.

Beside the cathedral, the old
bishop's palace houses the
Musée Départementale de
l'Oise, the principal museum in
the *département* of the Oise
region. There are wide-ranging
displays of classical and
contemporary art, art nouveau
and art deco, as well as a glorious exhibition of ceramics.

i Rue Beauregard

▶ Leave Beauvais on the D901
as for Abbeville, then take the
D149 as for Crèvecoeur-le-
Grand and the D11/D210
back to Amiens.

A Taste of
Champagne

Although Reims itself is the heart of champagne country, in the early part of the tour you will find many vineyards occupying sloping fields on the edge of the Montagne de Reims, south of the city. Arable plains stretch north to the hill and river country which France shares with Belgium in the Ardennes.

3/4 DAYS • 386KM • 240 MILES

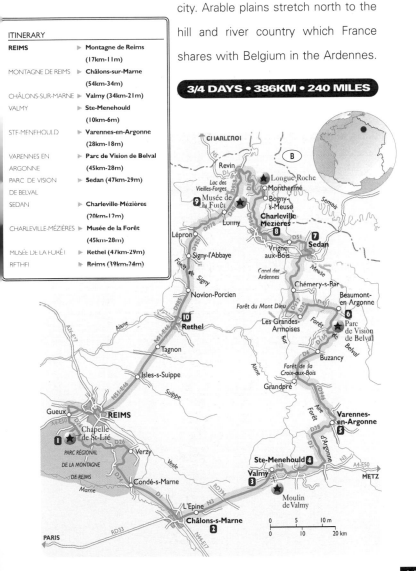

ⓘ *Place Guillaume de Machault, Reims*

▶ *Leave Reims on the N31 as for Soissons. Turn left on the D27 to Gueux, then left on the D26 through Vrigny. Turn right into Ville-Dommange, follow 'Courmas' sign, then go right to the Chapelle de St-Lié.*

❶ Montagne de Reims, Champagne-Ardenne

From the viewpoint below the Chapelle St-Lié there is a glorious outlook down over the vineyards on the lowest slope of the wooded hills south of Reims, and of the city itself, separate on the plain. Many of the villages are the home of champagnes little known abroad – Rilly for *Vilmart*, Ludes for *Blondel*, Villedommange immediately below for *Champagne de la Chapelle*. St-Lié, a church on the summit of a wooded hill sacred from pagan days, is being sympathetically restored.

The hilly woodlands and the villages are all included in the Parc Naturel Régional de Montagne de Reims. Many waymarked walks have been laid out in it. St-Lié is on the *sentier petite montagne* which meanders along the north-facing slopes.

▶ *Return to the D26 and turn right. Follow this road, not always numbered on signs, through Villers-Allerand, Ludes, Rilly-la-Montagne and Verzenay to Verzy. In Verzy, watch for a right turn on the D34 to Louvois and Condé. Go left on the D1 to Châlons-sur-Marne.*

BACK TO NATURE

On the way to Châlons, turn left off the D34 for Les Faux de Verzy. These are bizarrely mutated beeches, first mentioned in monastic writings of the 6th century, with thin corkscrewed trunks and umbrella-like foliage.

❷ Châlons-sur-Marne, Champagne-Ardenne

An old-established town – the main street is on the line of the Romans' Via Agrippa from Milan to Boulogne – Châlons sometimes calls itself Châlons-en-Champagne. It does have extensive champagne cellars to be visited. The largely 13th-century cathedral (St Étienne) with lovely stained glass which you can easily admire, because it is at less than the usual neck-craning angle, has a march of flying buttresses and a later north front uncomfortably out of tune with the rest. You may find Notre-Dame-en-Vaux just as interesting. In a cloister museum reached by a lane beside this multi-towered church, more than 50 carved columns featuring saints, prophets and medieval personalities are on display. Châlons has many waterfronts along the River Marne and the canals connected with it. Look for the series of parks and formal gardens called the Jards.

ⓘ *Quai des Arts*

▶ *Leave Châlons on the N3 as for Metz. After Auve, watch for a left turn signed for Valmy. This is the D284. Turn right for Moulin de Valmy.*

FOR HISTORY BUFFS

In the village of L'Épine, on the N3 after Châlons, the pilgrimage church is an astonishing miniature cathedral in Flamboyant Gothic style. It houses a statue of the Virgin found miraculously unharmed in a burning thorn bush (*épine*).

❸ Valmy, Champagne-Ardenne

The reconstructed windmill (*moulin*) on the hilltop at Valmy, marks the site of the most significant engagement in the war which Revolutionary France fought against the Prussians and Austrians. Plaques show the line-up of troops on 20

September 1792, when General Kellermann's inexperienced French army faced the battle-hardened Prussians under the Duke of Brunswick. Expecting an easy victory, the Prussians were in fact repulsed, and the young Revolutionary forces proved they could defend the homeland. Within a few hours, the Republic was proclaimed. The French troops, and Kellermann himself (by a spirited statue) are commemorated near by. There is a museum of the battle on the D31 in the little village of Valmy.

☐ *Maison du Meunier*

▶ *Continue on the D284, follow signs to Braux-Ste-Cohiere, then follow sign 'Vers N3'. Go left on the N3 to Ste-Menehould.*

❹ Ste-Menehould,
Champagne-Ardenne
A statue of Dom Pérignon recalls the fact that this Benedictine monk, to whom we owe the modern method of blending different wines into champagne, was born here in the 17th century. Incongruously, perhaps, you will find many shops selling a quite different speciality – pigs' trotters. It was at the now-restored Maison de Poste that the ill-fated Louis XVI and Marie Antoinette were recognised, to be arrested later.

At Ste-Menehould you will see a river flowing in different directions. Thanks to canal works, the Aisne splits into two channels which encircle the town and join up again after it. Since the Auve joins the Aisne here, Ste-Menehould has many pleasant waterways.

Its plateau location and a woodland fringe keep the old upper town almost out of sight, but a good self-guided walk links it with the lower town, whose elegant public buildings were raised after a disastrous fire in 1719.

A picturesque windmill (*moulin*) still operates in Verzenay

☐ *Place Leclerc*

▶ *Continue on the N3. In Les Islettes turn left for Varennes, following the D2 and then the D38.*

❺ Varennes-en-Argonne,
Champagne-Ardenne
In June 1791, when Louis XVI and his family fled secretly from Paris to try to join loyal troops at Metz, it was in Varennes that their coaches were stopped. Arrest, trial and the guillotine followed. The Musée d'Argonne is an excellent local museum, which describes the drama, and gives a balanced account of a king who forcefully supported the Americans in the War of Independence but made many political blunders at home. It also has intriguing displays on the old crafts and industries of the Forest of Argonne, and on the devastating effect on the district of World War I.

French and American flags fly at the entrance to the little grassy park leading to the pillared Pennsylvania Monument. It was troops from that US state who liberated Varennes in 1918.

☐ *Musée d'Argonne*

▶ *Leave Varennes on the D946. Turn right on the D6 to Buzancy, left on the D947, then right and left on the D155 to Fossé, taking care on the bumpy roads. Go left on the D55, left on the D4 and follow it right as for Beaumont, to the Parc de Vision de Belval.*

❻ Parc de Vision de Belval, Champagne-Ardenne
In 350 hectares (865 acres) of woodland and clearings, with a lake to accommodate its ducks and geese, this extensive wildlife park houses around 400 wild animals belonging to species which either still live in the northern forests or are known to have lived in them within the last 2,000 years.

Because the red, roe and fallow deer, the wild boars, the moufflons, the bison and the other animals all live in semi-freedom inside the boundary fence, visitors drive slowly along the viewing roads, follow a fenced-in walking route or travel on the little 'train', whose locomotive is a thinly-disguised tractor. The only animal kept in a separate secure enclosure is a brown bear, which might otherwise become testy if annoyed!

▶ *Continue on the **D4** through Beaumont, then go straight on to the **D30** as for Le Chesne. Beyond Les Grandes-Armoises, after the bend sign, take the first right to pass an '8t' sign. Turn right at the Give Way sign. This is the **D977**. Follow the signs to Sedan.*

RECOMMENDED WALKS

After joining the D977 for Sedan, turn right on the D230 into the Forêt de Mont-Dieu. The Circuit de la Chartreuse walk wanders through the forest and overlooks the historic monastery of Mont-Dieu.

Sedan, dominated by its fortress, has had a turbulent history

7 Sedan, Champagne-Ardenne

Some quarters of the town are fairly depressing, but Sedan can barely dispel the memories of its past. This is where Napoleon III capitulated to end the Franco-Prussian War of 1870. In World War I the huge Château-Fort, in area the biggest castle in the whole of Europe, was a brutal forced-labour camp. And in the next war, this was where the Germans burst through the French lines in the invasion of 1940. Now the castle houses a museum on Sedan's military history, and there is a guided tour.

Away from these melancholy recollections, Sedan is famous for its high-quality woollen rugs; the workshop where rugs are still made as they were a century ago is open to visitors. There are pleasant promenades by the River Meuse.

ⓘ *Rue Rousseau*

▶ *Leave Sedan for Floing on the **D5** and continue on this road to Charleville-Mézières. Avoid the autoroute.*

---

8 Charleville-Mézières, Champagne-Ardenne

Two once-separate towns, around loops of the River Meuse, have merged here. Mézières to the south is virtually on two islands. Within its 16th-century ramparts, the Flamboyant Gothic Church of Notre-Dame d'Espérance will surprise you with its abstract and geometrical stained-glass windows by René Dürrbach, a collaborator of Picasso's.

At Charleville the elegant, arcaded Place Ducale remains virtually as it was completed in 1628 (pity about the faded and obsolete shop signs).

The grand watermill (Vieux Moulin) on the Meuse is a local museum (Musée Ardenne), partly dedicated to the poet Arthur Rimbaud, who was born at Charleville.

ⓘ *Place Ducale*

FOR CHILDREN

Charleville-Mézières is the world capital of puppetry. Its Institut International de la Marionette has details of the summer puppet festival.

▶ *Leave Charleville on the D988 and follow signs to Monthermé along the D989. In Monthermé watch for a sharp left turn on the D1 to Revin. Go left on the D988 as for Les Mazures, then join the D40 as for Renwez and turn left at the junction with the D140 into the Musée de la Forêt.*

9 Musée de la Forêt, Champagne-Ardenne

As much a museum 'in' the forest as 'of' the forest, this 5-hectare (12-acre) area of woodland is devoted to showing – partly with the aid of cheery wooden sculptures – the traditional crafts and harvesting methods of a few unmechanised generations ago. Strolling round, you will see how birchwood brushes were made, how oak bark was peeled, how charcoal burners went about their trade, the kind of huts woodcutters lived in, and a selection of axes and single- and two-man saws.

The museum holds occasional wood-chopping contests, where competitors test their speed and accuracy as they axe their way through felled logs.

▶ *Continue on the D40. Go straight through Lonny. Turn right into Sormonne and left on the D978 as for Laon. Go left on the D985 and continue to Rethel.*

10 Rethel, Champagne-Ardenne

An inscription at the bridge over the River Aisne here is a simple list of seven years between 1411 and 1940 – the years when war came to Rethel. In the 1930s the town hall was proudly re-created in Renaissance style; then in May 1940 more than three-quarters of the buildings in Rethel were flattened. But the town bobbed up again, as it always has.

The fine old Church of St-Nicholas was restored. The local museum was restocked, although it has very restricted opening times. Walks along the river and the nearby canal were opened up, including the tree-lined Promenade des Isles.

There are sports facilities here for everything from tennis and rugby to show-jumping and archery, and the modern swimming pool is partly under cover, partly in the open air.

Rethel is famous for its *boudin blanc*, a white sausage made from pork, eggs, shallots and seasoning.

ℹ *Avenue Gambetta*

▶ *Leave Rethel on the N51 to Reims.*

Monthermé is a popular resort in the Meuse valley

The Heart
of Burgundy

North of Chalon-sur-Saône, this tour runs through the famous Burgundy vineyards. Then it crosses upland areas off the usual tourist track, and wanders through the farm and forest country of the extensive Parc Naturel Régional du Morvan.

3 DAYS • 408KM • 255 MILES

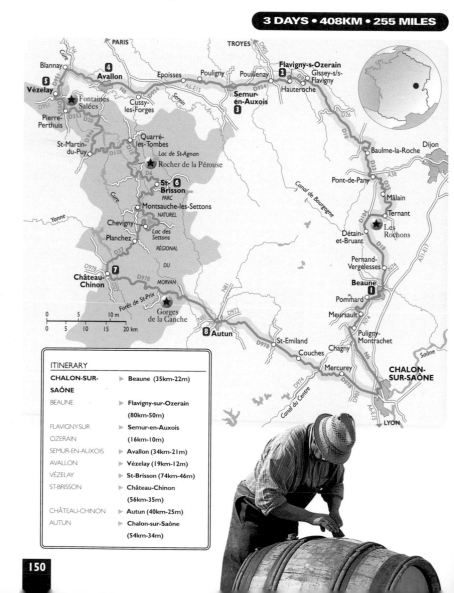

ITINERARY

CHALON-SUR-SAÔNE	▶ Beaune (35km-22m)
BEAUNE	▶ Flavigny-sur-Ozerain (80km-50m)
FLAVIGNY-SUR-OZERAIN	▶ Semur-en-Auxois (16km-10m)
SEMUR-EN-AUXOIS	▶ Avallon (34km-21m)
AVALLON	▶ Vézelay (19km-12m)
VÉZELAY	▶ St-Brisson (74km-46m)
ST-BRISSON	▶ Château-Chinon (56km-35m)
CHÂTEAU-CHINON	▶ Autun (40km-25m)
AUTUN	▶ Chalon-sur-Saône (54km-34m)

ⓘ *Square Chabas, Chalon-sur Saône*

▶ *Leave Chalon on the N6 as for Beaune. Turn right on the N74, left on the C2 to Puligny-Montrachet, then take the D113b to Meursault. Go straight ahead on the D23, turn right on the D17, continue through Pommard and go left into Beaune.*

❶ **Beaune,** Burgundy
Hundreds of thousands of visitors come every year to Beaune. Many go to the Hôtel-Dieu, opened in 1443 as a charitable hospital. Containing displays which show how the nuns looked after their aged patients in years gone by, as well as Rogier van der Weyden's stunning 15th-century altarpiece of the *Last Judgement*, the building is a ravishing mixture of polychrome tiling, intricate window details and appealing galleries. Beaune is honeycombed with wine cellars, some of them in the town walls. The Musée du Vin occupies an old town mansion of the dukes of Burgundy, while the Athenaeum is a cultural centre linking wine, literature and local history.

Magnificent tapestries hang in the Church of Notre-Dame. Beaune also has a fine arts museum and the Musée Marey is a tribute to Beaune-born pioneer of moving pictures, Étienne Jules Marey.

ⓘ *Place de la Halle*

SPECIAL TO...

Puligny-Montrachet, Meursault and Pommard are vineyard villages of the Côte d'Or, whose white burgundies are held in high regard. More than a dozen *grand crus* and *premiers crus* come from Puligny-Montrachet, while the Meursault growers are keenest on welcoming visitors. Details of wine tours are available from the tourist information in Beaune.

▶ *Leave Beaune on the D18 going north, passing Pernand-Vergelesses. Continue on the D18 through Changey, turn right on to the D8, then take the D25F and the D25 to Bruant. Go left on the D8 again, fork right on the D104, right on the D104b to*

Ternant, then take the D35 to Pont-de-Pany. Go left on the D905, and immediately after leaving Pont-de-Pany turn right over the autoroute to Mâluin. Continue through Baulme-la-Roche. Turn left on the D10 to Gissey-sous-Flavigny. Bear left at the roundabout, past Café de l'Oze, on to the D10e to Hauteroche. Turn sharp right and follow signs to Flavigny, entering it on the D9.

FOR HISTORY BUFFS

Look for the dolmens in the woodland left of the D104b before Ternant. These great balanced-stone chambers remain impressive and mysterious after 6,000 years.

❷ **Flavigny-sur-Ozerain,** Burgundy
History has moved on, isolating this little medieval hilltop town. Park outside, study the labyrinthine medieval street plan and feel the centuries drift

away as you stroll through an ancient gateway, along narrow streets and alleyways, to the 13th-century church in the square. Local farm produce is sold here. Guided tours are arranged of an eerie 8th-century crypt. There are farm-track walks on the plateau, one to a site said to be a Roman camp from Julius Caesar's time.

i *Place de l'Église*

SPECIAL TO...

Lliquorice is Flavigny's most famous product. The old abbey makes aniseed in many forms – sweets, candies and flavourings. The genuine article – *véritable marque des anis* – is on sale in local groceries.

▶ Continue on the **D9** and **D954** to Semur-en-Auxois.

🔒 Semur-en-Auxois, Burgundy

Semur occupies a pinched-in red granite promontory at a hairpin bend on the River Armançon. Its 18th-century Pont Joly looks to banked up houses and massive rampart towers of a former castle. You can visit the Tour de l'Orle d'Ore.

The 13th-century Church of Notre-Dame features an eccentrically narrow nave and good stained-glass windows including a rather frank account of the work of the butchers' guild. There are medieval houses and a rampart walk. From the Pont

The Church of St-Lazare, Avallon, has fine carvings on its doorway

Joly, Semur probably looks its best floodlit or at sunset.

i *Place Gaveau*

FOR HISTORY BUFFS

At Époisses, on the D954 on the way to Avallon, pause to visit the dry-moated château, with its dovecote exhibition and 13th-century parish church. Madame de Sévigny was a frequent visitor to the château. Even when the château itself is closed, you can visit its grounds, which form a Burgundy village in miniature.

▶ Continue on the **D954** and **N6** to Avallon.

🔒 Avallon, Burgundy

Those Burgundians who fortified Avallon would be surprised that so many of their rampart walls, towers, bastions and gateways survive in the very agreeable old town today. Perimeter walks and stairways look down on the attractive valley of the River Cousin, with its woods and terraced gardens.

Avallon is packed with fascinating old buildings, such as the clock tower of 1456, formerly a town gate, through which a street leads to the well-endowed Musée de l'Avallonnais and the 12th-century Church of St-Lazare. Part of St-Lazare houses the etchings for 20th-century artist Georges Rouault's harrowing but highly regarded series of prints entitled *Miserere*.

i *Grande Rue Aristide-Briand*

▶ Continue on the **N6** as for Auxerre, then turn left on the **D951** to Vézelay.

🔒 Vézelay, Burgundy

Climbing sinuously to a hilltop, the main street of this little town passes artists' studios, galleries and displays of semi-precious stones before it reaches the Basilica of Ste-Madeleine, one of the all-time glories of Romanesque design. The church, a great pilgrimage goal when it was believed to contain the remains of Mary Magdalen, survived fire, plunder and virtual destruction during the Revolution, to be completely restored in the 19th century. Look for its splendid doorways, intricately carved capitals, impressive crypt and the view from the tower, but most of all for the mellow light that pours into the interior.

Stylised carving over a doorway at the Basilica of St Madeleine

[i] *Rue St Pierre*

▶ *Leave Vézelay on the D957 to St-Père, then go right on the D958 to Pierre-Perthuis. Turn left on the D353 and immediately right following 'Les Ponts' sign. Go through Précy-le-Moult, then turn right on the D36 which becomes the D20. At a crossroads, turn right on the D944. In St-Martin-du-Puy, watch for a sharp left turn to Quarré-les-Tombes. In Quarré, turn right through Les Levaults on the D10, then right on the D211. Go straight ahead on the D6 to the Maison du Parc.*

6 St-Brisson, Burgundy
On the edge of St-Brisson, a fine old red-roofed farm complex is the headquarters of the Parc Naturel Régional du Morvan, the Morvan being the wooded mountain region between the rivers Loire and Saône. The Maison du Parc illustrates wildlife, crafts, conservation and the rural way of life. The grounds include a herb garden, animal enclosures,

a waterfowl pond with pochard, mallard and shelduck, and pathways down to the lake. Near by, the Musée de la Résistance tells the story of the Morvan's secret war in World War II.

[i] *Maison du Parc*

▶ *Return from Maison du Parc, take the first left, go left at the T-junction through St-Brisson, then bear right on the C1 and continue to Montsauche-les-Settons. Go left on the D37, then left on the D193. Keep Lac des Settons on your right, then watch for a sharp right turn following the 'Rive Gauche' sign. At the give way sign turn left on the D520 and continue to Château-Chinon.*

7 Château-Chinon, Burgundy
Capital of the Morvan, Château-Chinon rises to a parkland with walks and drives and gorgeous views over the surrounding countryside.

The Musée du Costume also has displays on local arts and traditions. In the Musée du Septennat you will find an exhibition of the ceremonial gifts lavished at home and abroad on François Mitterand during his first term as President of France. Previously a local politician here, he donated them all to the *département*.

[i] *Place Gudin*

▶ *Leave Château-Chinon on the D978 to Autun.*

8 Autun, Burgundy
Founded by the Emperor Augustus as *Augustodunum*, Autun retains Roman archways such as the Porte St-André and the Porte d'Arroux, still used by traffic and pedestrians. The Musée Rolin, housed in a 15th-century mansion, specialises in Roman exhibits, and the original riverside theatre is still in use. Look for the majestic portal of the 12th-century Cathédrale St-Lazare, the medieval rampart walk, the immaculate military academy, and the 18th-century Lycée Bonaparte where Napoleon was a pupil.

[i] *Avenue Charles de Gaulle*

▶ *Leave Autun following signs to Chalon-sur-Saône.*

The Historic
Centre of France

Many strands of French life and history combine in this tour from Chartres – the palace of Fontainebleau, the castle at Rambouillet, Barbizon and Moret-sur-Loing. You will find pleasant roads which run through cool shady woodlands, and others which cross skyline-to-skyline arable plains, wide open to the summer sun.

2/3 DAYS • 312KM • 194 MILES

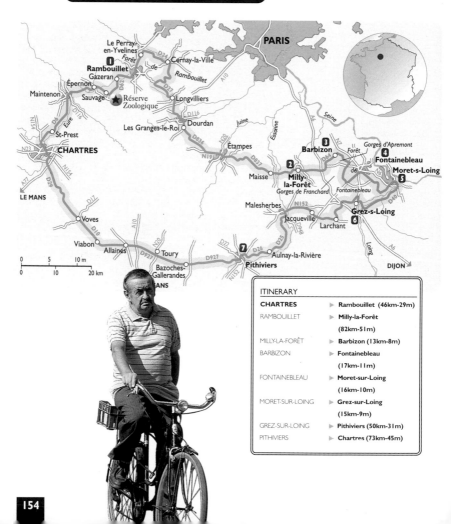

ITINERARY

CHARTRES	▶ **Rambouillet** (46km-29m)
RAMBOUILLET	▶ **Milly-la-Forêt**
	(82km-51m)
MILLY-LA-FORÊT	▶ **Barbizon** (13km-8m)
BARBIZON	▶ **Fontainebleau**
	(17km-11m)
FONTAINEBLEAU	▶ **Moret-sur-Loing**
	(16km-10m)
MORET-SUR-LOING	▶ **Grez-sur-Loing**
	(15km-9m)
GREZ-SUR-LOING	▶ **Pithiviers** (50km-31m)
PITHIVIERS	▶ **Chartres** (73km-45m)

i Place de la Cathédrale,
Chartres

▶ *Leave Chartres on the N154.
At the traffic lights, turn right
for St-Prest and continue on
the D6 to Maintenon. Turn
right to Épernon. Turn right on
the D176, then continue
through Droue to Émancé. Go
as for Orphin, turn left on the
D62 to Gazeran, then follow
the signs to Rambouillet.*

1 Rambouillet, Île de France
This is France's 'presidential
town'. Its elegant château,
standing among extensive
woodlands, lawns and water
gardens, is an official residence
of the president, but is open to
visitors most of the year. Louis
XVI commissioned two buildings in the grounds – the ornamental dairy called the Laiterie
de la Reine, and the Chaumière
des Coquillages ('Cottage of
Shells') with its wall covering of
seashells, mother-of-pearl and
tiny pieces of marble. Also in
the grounds you will see the
Bergerie Nationale, famous for
its pedigree Merino rams.
There is a museum here on the
husbandry and breeding of
sheep. Rambouillet's racecourse
is southeast of the town.
Beyond it (take the D27), a
wildlife reserve shelters red, roe
and fallow deer.

i Place de la Libération

RECOMMENDED WALKS

**After you have left
Rambouillet, where the D24
crosses the D91, turn left, fol
lowing the 'Cascades' sign to
the woodland walks, to the left
of the road, leading by a jumble
of rocks down to a river ravine
and its falls.**

▶ *Leave Rambouillet as for
Paris, join the N10 dual-
carriageway and turn off
through Le Perray-en-Yvelines
on the D910. Go right on the
D24 and continue on to Cernay-
la-Ville. Turn left on to the
D306, then sharp right on
the D72, left on the D61,
then right D72 again to
Clairefontaine-en-Yvelines. Go
left on the D27 and follow
'Dourdan' signs, turning right
on the D149. Go left on the
D836 to Dourdan, then take
the D116 before rejoining the
D836 and taking the N191
through Étampes. Go right on
the D837 and into Milly-la-
Forêt.*

2 Milly-la-Forêt, Île de
France
Expertly trimmed, shade-
providing trees; a 15th-century
market hall; red-tiled houses;
and a wondering stream with
wash-house quays: all these

Rodin called Chartres Cathedral
the 'Acropolis of France'

combine to give this village a
peaceful, attractive and timeless
appearance.
The artist, poet and drama-
tist Jean Cocteau is buried in
the little 12th-century chapel of
St-Blaise-des-Simples, which he
had previously decorated. The
simples are medicinal herbs,
which remain a preoccupation
of Milly today. On the Nemours
road you can visit the
Conservatoire National of medicinal and aromatic plants and
plants used by industry.

SPECIAL TO...

In Le Perray, after Rambouillet,
the Musée des Vieux Métiers is
a working forge with a collection of traditional blacksmith's
tools and equipment. You can
hardly miss the 9m (30-foot)
model of the Eiffel Tower.

▶ *Follow 'Fontainebleau' signs on
the D837. In Arbonne, bear
left as for Melun. Turn right on
the D64 to Barbizon.*

3 Barbizon, Île de France
In the mid-19th century, a group
of landscape artists centred on
the painter Théodore Rousseau,
made this village their base.
They were to become known as

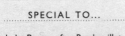

the Barbizon School. Greater figures, such as the Realist painter Jean François Millet, whose *Angelus* was painted near by, were also Barbizon men.

In Rousseau's house, fascinating maps and illustrations shows the village as it was then. Upstairs in his north-light studio is a collection of little gems of landscape art.

The artists' often frugal meals were taken at the village inn run by old Monsieur Ganne. Now the Auberge du Père Ganne houses an atmospheric museum in which it is easy to imagine that the next person at the door is a hungry painter, ready for dinner after a day's sketching in the forests or fields.

i *Grande Rue*

▶ *Leave Barbizon by the Grande Rue and enter the Forêt de Fontainebleau. Turn right at a T-junction following the 'Fontainebleau par route forestière' sign. Go right at the Stop signs for Franchard (this is the D301), then left on the N152 and at the busy roundabout take the N6 for the town of Fontainebleau.*

4 **Fontainebleau,** Île de France

Everything else in this elegant town defers to the spectacular palace in its parkland of lakes, wooded and formal and landscape gardens. A discreet plaque acknowledges John D Rockefeller Jr's generous funding of the palace restoration. The Musée Napoléon houses a massive exhibition on the Bonaparte family. Do not confuse this with the Musée Napoléonien d'Art et d'Histoire, in the town itself, which features grand displays on the French military through the ages.

i *Rue Denecourt*

BACK TO NATURE

Planted with pines, oaks, birches, chestnut trees, hornbeams and – especially – glorious beechwoods, the Forêt de Fontainebleau is one of the most beautiful and most carefully protected woodlands in Europe. It covers about 25,000 hectares (61,775 acres), most of them open to the public.

▶ *Return to the busy roundabout and take the D58 as for Bourron-Marlotte. Go straight ahead on the D148, then turn left on to the D104 to Moret-sur-Loing.*

5 **Moret-sur-Loing,** Île de France

This very appealing little place is an 'ancient and royal city' which once stood on the French frontier, fortified against Burgundy on the far side of a beautiful stretch of the River Loing. Fine medieval gateways, Renaissance and later buildings survive.

By the river, La Grande Batelière is the home of the Clemenceau family, open at weekends to tell the story of France's famous World War I president. Moret also celebrates its connection with the Impressionist painter Alfred Sisley.

i *Avenue Jean-Jaurès*

▶ *Leave Moret on the D302, then immediately turn right at traffic lights for Nemours.*

Napoléon was responsible for Fontainebleau's sumptuous interior

Watch for another right turn as for Nemours along the D40. Go right on to the D40d, then left into Grez-sur-Loing.

FOR CHILDREN

As you approach Grez-sur-Loing, look on the right for Tacot des Lacs, a full-scale railway, whose trains like the 1900 steam locomotive *Clémentine* run weekend trips through scrubland and across the River Loing.

---

6 Grez-sur-Loing, Île de France

Here is a lovely stretch of the Loing with gardens, boathouses, weeping willows and flotillas of geese and mallards. Swallows and damselflies dart above the water, swifts in the higher air. Beyond the old arched bridge rises a pale 12th-century tower.

In the 1870s, Robert Louis Stevenson joined the Bohemian summer colony at Grez. Later, Frederick Delius composed much of his music here.

Stroll to the austere and lofty medieval church, and along the hollyhock lane from the little Place Jolivet. The artists have gone, but the appeal of this charming village never fades.

▶ *Leave Grez as for La Chapelle-la-Reine, taking the D104. After the junction sign watch for a left turn to Larchant. Go right as for La Chapelle on the D16. Turn left on to the D36 and follow signs to Jacqueville. Bear right then left following the 'Malesherbes' sign on the C7. Take care at the level crossing. At the give way sign, go left on to the N152 to Malesherbes. Take the D948 as for Puiseaux, then go right on the D25 through Pinçon and Briarres. Continue through Aulnay-la-Rivière to Pithiviers.*

FOR HISTORY BUFFS

Malesherbes, on the way to Pithiviers, has two castles worthy of a visit on its outskirts. The Château de Malesherbes, off the Puiseaux road, is furnished as it was immediately before the Revolution. Off the D132, the many-turreted Château de Rouville overlooks the valley of the Essone.

Moret-sur-Loing is a favourite destination for Parisians at 'le Weekend'

7 Pithiviers, Île de France

Famous for its fine almond cakes, Pithiviers has an interesting local museum (in the former 18th-century Hôtel-Dieu) which explains the local cuisine and its cooks' pioneering use of saffron – the region was once of European importance for saffron-growing.

Historic steam locomotives from as early as 1870 run on the last 4km (2½-mile) stretch of a light railway opened in 1892. An exhibition displays some elegant old coaches and tells the story of France's branch lines.

i   *Mail Ouest*

▶ *Leave Pithiviers on the D927 to Allaines. Go right at the Stop sign, then left on to the D12 and join the D10 to Voves. Turn right on to the D17 as for Auneau and enter the one-way traffic system in Voves. At the two-way sign turn into a side road on the left. Go right at the Stop sign and return to Chartres.*

FACTS AND FIGURES

Bordered by: Belgium, Germany, Italy, Luxembourg, Spain and Switzerland.

IDD code: 33. To call the UK dial 00*44 (*wait for second dialling tone).

Currency: Franc (*Fr*1 = 100 centimes).

Local time: GMT + 1 (summer GMT + 2).

Emergency services: Police 17; Fire 18; Ambulance – dial number given in callbox, or, if no number given, the police.

Business hours -
Banks: Monday to Friday 9am–noon, 2–4pm.
Shops: Monday to Saturday 9am–6pm (times may vary for food shops).
Post Offices: main Post Offices are open 8am–7pm weekdays, and 8am–noon Saturdays. Some small offices may close for lunch.

Credit and charge cards: these are widely accepted.

Traveller's cheques: either in sterling or local currency are probably the most sensible way to take your money abroad. Note the numbers and keep the note separate from the cheques.

Tourist information:
UK French Government Tourist Office, 178 Piccadilly, London, W1V 0AL. Tel: 0891 244123 (premium information line; 8.30am–9.30pm weekdays, 9am–5pm Saturdays). Monaco Government Tourist and Convention Office, 3-18 Chelsea Harbour, London SW10 0XE. Tel: 0171 352 9962.
USA French Government Tourist Office, 610 First Avenue, New York, NY 10020. Tel: (212) 757 1125.

Camping card: not compulsory, but advisable when using *Castels et Camping* caravanning sites and also the *forts domaniales*. France has an enormous number of campsites, over 10,000 of them, under the auspices of the *French Federation of Camping and Caravanning*.

MOTORING IN FRANCE

ACCIDENTS
If you are involved in an accident you must complete a *constat l'amiable* before moving the vehicle. It must be signed by the other party, and in the event of a dispute or a refusal to complete the form, you should immediately obtain a *constat d'huissier*, a written report from a bailiff (*huissier*).

The police are only called out when someone is injured, a driver is under the influence of alcohol or the accident impedes traffic flow. (See also warning triangles/hazard warning lights.)

BREAKDOWNS
If your car breaks down, try to move it to the side of the road so it obstructs the traffic flow as little as possible. Place a warning triangle to the rear of the vehicle at a suitable distance. You are advised to seek local assistance as, at present, there is no nationwide road assistance service in France.

On autoroutes, ring from emergency phones located every 2km (mile) to contact breakdown service. (See also warning triangles/hazard warning lights.)

CARAVANS
Brakes
Check that the caravan braking mechanism is correctly adjusted. If it has a breakaway safety mechanism, the cable between the car and caravan must be firmly anchored so that the trailer brakes act immediately if the two part company.

Caravan and luggage trailers
Take a list of contents, especially if any valuable or unusual equipment is being carried, as

this may be required on arrival. A towed vehicle should be readily identifiable by a plate in an accessible position showing the name of the make of the vehicle and the production and serial number.

Lights
Make sure that all the lights are working – rear lights, stop lights, numberplate lights, rear fog guard lamps and flashers (check that the flasher rate is correct: 60–120 times a minute).

Speed limits (see general notes on **speed limits**).

Tyres
Both tyres on the caravan should be of the same size and type. Inspect them carefully: if you think they are likely to be more than three-quarters worn before you get back, replace them before you leave. If you notice uneven wear, scuffed treads, or damaged tyres, get expert advice on whether the tyres are suitable for further use. Find out the recommended tyre pressures from the caravan manufacturer.

CAR HIRE AND FLY/DRIVE
If you are not taking your own car, you can make arrangements to hire before departure. Many package holidays include car hire as an option. The main car hire companies are represented in France.

CHILDREN
Children under 10 are not permitted to travel as front seat passengers, with the exception of babies or very young children in an approved rear-facing child seat. Children under the age of 10 in the rear must use a child seat or restraint if fitted. Note: under no circumstances should a rear-facing restraint be used in a seat with an airbag.

CRASH (SAFETY) HELMETS
Visiting motorcyclists and their passengers must wear crash or safety helmets.

DIMENSIONS AND WEIGHT RESTRICTIONS
Private cars and towed trailers or caravans are restricted to the following dimensions: height – no restrictions, but 4m is a recommended maximum; width – 2.5m; length – 12m (excluding towing device). The maximum permitted overall length of a vehicle/trailer or caravan combination is 18m. If the weight of the trailer exceeds that of the towing vehicle, see also **speed limits**.

DOCUMENTS
A valid driver's licence, not provisional, is required. The minimum driving age is 18. An international licence is not required for visitors from the US, UK or Western Europe. You also require the vehicle's registration document, plus a letter of authorisation from the owner, if not accompanying the vehicle, and the current insurance certificate (a green card is not mandatory but remains internationally recognised and can be helpful). Also, a nationality plate or sticker is required. The minimum age at which visitors from the UK or Republic of Ireland may use a temporarily imported motorcycle (over 80cc) or car is 18. Visitors may use temporarily imported motorcycles of up to 80cc at 16. See also **speed limits**.

DRINKING AND DRIVING
The laws in Europe regarding drinking and driving are strict and the penalties severe. They include stiff fines and police escort back to a ferry terminal. The best advice is, as at home, if you drink don't drive.

DRIVING CONDITIONS
Keep to the right (*serrez à droite*).

Though main roads have priority (*passage protégé*), right of way is otherwise given to vehicles coming in from the right (*priorité à droite*).

The *priorité* rule no longer applies at roundabouts with

signs bearing the words '*Vous n'avez pas la priorité*' or '*Cédez le passage*', which means you give way to cars already on the roundabout.

Mountain tours, including the ones in the South of France, call for a properly serviced and not overladen car. Especially in these areas, petrol stations may be far apart. Unleaded fuel is now widely available all over France.

On the Clermont-Ferrand, Pau and Grenoble tours, roadside notices displaying either *Ouvert* (open) or *Fermé* (closed) will show the road conditions ahead. Do not make for a road notified as being closed.

FUEL
You will find comparable grades of petrol in France, with familiar brand names along the main routes. You will normally have to buy a minimum of 5 litres (just over a gallon) but it is wise to keep the tank topped up, particularly in remote areas. Remember when calculating mileage per gallon that the extra weight of a caravan or roof rack increases the petrol consumption. It is best to use a locking filler cap.

Some garages may close between noon and 3pm, but petrol is generally available, with 24-hour service on motorways. Prices for petrol on motorways will normally be higher than elsewhere; self-service pumps will be slightly cheaper.

Leaded gas (*essence super*) is now only sold in one grade (98 octane), while unleaded is sold in two: 95 octane (*essence sans plomb*) and 98 octane (*super sans plomb*). Diesel is much cheaper and readily available. Credit cards are generally accepted, but in rural areas some garages may not accept them.

INSURANCE
Fully comprehensive insurance, which covers you for some of the expenses incurred after a breakdown or an accident, is advisable.

LIGHTS

It is obligatory to use headlights, as driving on sidelights only is not permitted. In fog, mist or poor visibility during the day, either fog lamps or dipped headlights must be switched on in addition to sidelights. It is compulsory for motorcyclists riding machines exceeding 125cc to use dipped headlights during the day. Failure to comply with these regulations will lead to an on-the-spot deposit (see **police fines**).

It is recommended that visiting motorists equip their vehicles with a set of replacement bulbs. Drivers able to replace a faulty bulb when requested to do so by the police will not avoid a fine, but may avoid the cost and inconvenience of a garage call-out. Yellow tinted headlights are no longer necessary.

MOTORING CLUB

The AA is affiliated to the Automobile Club National (ACN) whose office is at 75009 Paris, 5 rue Auber (tel: 44515399).

POLICE FINES

Police in France impose an on-the-spot deposit for minor traffic offences and subsequently levy a fine which may be the same as, or greater or lesser than, the deposit. If the fine is not paid, legal proceedings will usually follow. Once paid, a fine cannot be recovered, but a receipt should be obtained as proof of payment.

ROADS

France has a very comprehensive network of roads, and surfaces are generally good; exceptions are usually signposted *Chausée deformée*.

ROUTE DIRECTIONS

Throughout the book the following abbreviations are used for French roads:
A – Autoroute
N – Route Nationale
D – Route Départementale
C and **V** – smaller roads

SEAT BELTS

It is compulsory to wear seat belts if your car is fitted with them.

SPEED LIMITS

Built-up areas 50kph (31mph). Outside built-up areas on normal roads 90kph (56mph); on dual carriageways separated by a central reservation 110kph (69mph); also motorways without tolls.
Toll motorways 130kph (80mph).

The beginning of a built-up area is indicated by a sign with the place-name in blue letters on a light background; the end is signified by a thin red line diagonally across the place-name sign. Unless otherwise signposted, follow the above speed limits.

Note: the minimum speed in the fast lane on a level stretch of motorway during good daytime visibility is 80kph (49mph), and drivers travelling below this speed are liable to be fined. In fog, when visibility is reduced to 50m (55 yards), the speed limit on all roads is 50kph (31mph).

In wet weather speed limits outside built-up areas are reduced to 80kph (49mph), 100kph (62mph) and 110kph (69mph) on motorways.

These limits also apply to private cars towing a trailer or caravan, if the latter's weight does not exceed that of the car and the total weight is less than 3.5 tonnes. However, if the weight of the trailer exceeds that of the car by less than 30 per cent, the speed limit is 65kph (40mph), if more than 30 per cent the speed limit is 45kph (28mph). Additionally these combinations must:
1 display a disc at the rear of the caravan/trailer showing the maximum speed or
2 not be driven in the fast lane of a 3-lane motorway.
Both French residents and visitors to France who have held a driving licence for less than two years, must not exceed 80kph (49mph) outside built-up areas,
100kph (62mph) on dual carriageways separated by a central reservation and 110kph (69mph) on motorways.

TOLLS

Tolls are payable on many motorways in France. Toll booths will not accept travellers' cheques, but some credit cards are accepted.

WARNING TRIANGLE/ HAZARD WARNING LIGHTS

The use of a warning triangle or hazard warning lights* is compulsory in the event of an accident or breakdown. As hazard warning lights may be damaged or inoperative, it is recommended that a warning triangle be carried. The triangle must be placed on the road 30m (33 yards) behind the vehicle and clearly visible for 100m (110 yards).
*If your vehicle is equipped with hazard warning lights, it is compulsory to use them if you are forced to drive temporarily at a greatly reduced speed. However, when slow moving traffic is established in an uninterrupted lane or lanes, this only applies to the last vehicle in the lane(s).

CAMPING AND CARA-VANNING SITES
Sites

France has an enormous number of campsites, over 10,000 of them under the auspices of the *French Federation of Camping and Caravanning*.

There are *castels et camping* caravanning sites in the grounds of châteaux (castles). On sites in state forests, *forêts domaniales*, it is necessary to apply to the *garde forestier* for permission to camp, and evidence of insurance must be produced (such as the camping card). Opening periods vary widely and some sites are open all year. Local information offices (see individual tours) can supply detailed information about sites in their locality.

Camping information can also be obtained from *Total* petrol service stations which have been equipped with information offices. During July and August there is over-demand around the coast, particularly on the Mediterranean.

All graded sites must display their official classification, site regulations, capacity and current charges at the entrance. Some sites have inclusive prices per pitch, others show basic prices per person, vehicle and space, with extra facilities like showers, swimming pools and ironing incurring additional charges. Most campsites charge from midday to midday, with each part day being counted as a full day.

Reductions for children are usually allowed up to 7 years of age; there is generally no charge for children under 3.

Off-site camping

Off-site camping in the South of France is restricted because of the danger of fire; in other parts, camping is possible, provided that permission has been obtained, although camping is seldom allowed near the water's edge, or at large seaside resorts.

Casual camping is prohibited in state forests, national parks in the Landes and Gironde *départements* and in the Camargue. Camping in an unauthorised place renders offenders liable to prosecution or confiscation of equipment, or both, especially in the South. However, an overnight stop on parking areas of some motorways is tolerated, but make sure you do not contravene local regulations; overnight stops in lay-bys are not permitted.

Camping is not permitted in Monaco. Caravans in transit are allowed but it is forbidden to park them.

SITES

The following sites are located in towns along the routes.

TOUR 1
BAYEUX Calvados
CM Calvados boulevard d'Einhoven (tel: 31920843)
North side of town on Boulevard Circulaire.
Open 15 March to 15 November.

CARENTAN Finistère
CM le Haut Dyck chemin du Grand-Bas Pays (tel: 33421689)
Take village road off N13 towards Le Port.
Open all year.

MONTMARTIN-SUR-MER Manche
Gravelets Les Gravelets (tel: 33477020)
Situated on a reclaimed quarry.
Open April to October.

TOUR 2
DIEPPE Seine-Maritime
At Hautot-sur-Mer (6km SW)
Source Petit-Appeville (tel: 35842704)
Open 15 March to 15 October.

TOUR 3
FOUGÈRES Ille-et-Vilaine
CM Paron (tel: 99994081)
1.5km east via D17.
Open March to November.

LE MONT-ST-MICHEL Manche
Gué de Beauvoir (tel: 33600923)
4km south of Abbey on D776 Pontorson road.
Open Easter to September.

DOL-DE-BRETAGNE Ille-et-Vilaine
Château des Ormes (tel: 99734959)
Site in grounds of château, 7km south on N795 Rennes road.
Open 15 May to 15 September.

CANCALE Ille-et-Vilaine
Notre Dame du Verger (tel: 99897284)
2km from Pointe-du-Grouin on D201.
Open April to September.

ST-MALO Ille-et-Vilaine
CM le Nicet avenue de la Varde (tel: 99402632)
100m from the beach; direct access via staircase.
Open Easter to mid-September.

DINARD Ille-et-Vilaine
Mauny (tel: 99469473)
Off St-Briac road (CD603).
Open Easter to October.

ERQUY Côtes-D'Armor
Pins route du Guen (tel: 96723112)
Situated in a pine forest; 1km northeast of village.
Open Easter to September.

RENNES Ille-et-Vilaine
CM Gayeulles rue du Prof-M-Audin (tel: 99369122)
Northeast via N12.
Open April to September.

TOUR 4
DOUARNENEZ Finistère
Kerleyou (tel: 98741303)
1km west on rue de Préfet-Collignon towards the sea.
Open April to September.

PLONÉVEZ-PORZAY Finistère
International de Kervel (tel: 98925154)
Southwest of village on D107 Douarnenez road for 3km, then towards coast at crossroads.
Open 10 May to 15 September.

PLOMODIERN Finistère
Iroise Plage de Pors-ar-Vag, Port du Bateau (tel: 98815272)
5km southwest, 150m from beach.
Open April to September.

CROZON Finistère
Plage de Goulien Kernavèno (tel: 98271710)
5km west on D308.
Open 10 June to 25 September.

MORGAT Finistère
Bouis (tel: 98261253)
Easter to September.

CAMARET-SUR-MER Finistère
Lambézen (tel: 98279141)
3km northeast on route de Roscanvel (D355).
Open April to September.

SPECIMEN BOOKING LETTER FOR RESERVATIONS

French

Monsieur
Je me propose de séjourner à votre terraine de camping pour .... jours, depuis le .... jusqu'au
....
Nous sommes .... personnes en tout, y compris .... adultes et ...... enfants (âgés de ....) et
nous aurons besoin d'un emplacement pour .... tente(s), et/ou un parking pur notre voiture/cara-
vane/remorque.
Nous voudrions louer une tente/caravane/bungalow.
Veuillez me donner dans votre réponse une idée de vos prix, m'indiquant en même temps le
montant qu'il faut payer en avance, ce qui vous sera envoyé sans délai.

English translation

Dear Sir
I intend to stay at your site for ..... days, arriving on .... (date and month) and departing on ....
(date and month). We are a party of .... people, including .... adults and .... children (aged
..........) and shall require a pitch for .... tent(s), and/or parking space for our car/caravan/caravan
trailer. We should like to hire a tent/caravan/bungalow.
Please quote full charges when replying and advise on the deposit required, which will be
forwarded without delay.

QUIMPER Finistère
Orangerie de Lanniron
Château de Lanniron (tel:
98906202)
2.5km from town centre via
D34.
Open May to 15 September.

TOUR 5
ROYAT Puy-de-Dôme
CM de l'Oclède route de
Gravenoire (tel: 73359705)
Open April to October.

ORCIVAL Puy-de-Dôme
Étang de Fléchat (tel:
73658296)
1.5km south via D27, then
2.5km via D74 towards
Rochefort-Montagne.
Open June to 15 September.

MUROL Puy-de-Dôme
Plage (tel: 73886027)
1.2km from centre of village,
turn off into allée de Plage
before entering village and
follow signposts.
Open May to September.

TOUR 6
MONTAIGUT-LE-BLANC
Puy-de-Dôme (off route)
CM Le Bourg (tel: 73967507)
Open June to 15 September.

TOUR 7
ST-DENIS-D'OLÉRON
Charente-Maritime
Soleil Levant (tel: 46478303)
1km from village adjacent to
D734.
Open all year.

RONCE-LES-BAINES
Charente-Maritime
Pignade avenue des Monards
(tel: 46362525)
1.5km south.
Open 18 May to 14
September.

COGNAC Charente
Cognac route de Ste-Sévère
(tel: 45321632)
2km north on D24.
Open May to 15 October.

NIORT Deux-Sèvres
Niort-Noron 21 boulevard
S-Allende (tel: 49790506)
Shady site by the river.
Open 15 April to 15 October.

LA FLOTTE Charente-
Maritime
Blanche (tel: 46095243)
North on D735 towards St-
Martin.
Open April to 15
November.

ST-MARTIN-DE-RÉ
Charente-Maritime
CM rue du Rempart (tel:
46092196)
At foot of ramparts.
Open 15 March to 15 October.

TOUR 8
NANTES Loire-Atlantique
CM Val du Cens-Petit Port
boulevard du Petit Port 21 (tel:
40744794)
In north part of town near Parc
du Petit Port. From town
centre follow Rennes road
(N137) then signs to camp
site.
Open all year.

CHOLET Maine-et-Loire
Lac de Ribou avenue L-
Mandin (tel: 41587474)
3km from town centre.
Open April to October.

SAUMUR Maine-et-Loire
Chantepie (tel: 41679534)
Access via D751 towards
Gennes.
Open 15 May to 15 September.

SABLÉ-SUR-SARTHE Sarthe
Hippodrome allée du Quebec
(tel: 43954261)
Open April to September.

TOUR 9
TOURS Indre-et-Loire
At Ballan-Miré (8.5km W
D751)
Mignardière 22 avenue des
Aubepines (tel: 47733100)
2.5km northeast.
Open 27 April to 29 September.

VALENÇAY Indre
CM Chènes route de Loches
(tel: 54000392)
1km west on D960.
Open April to September.

OLIVET Loiret
CM Olivet rue du Pont
Bouchet (tel: 38635394)
2km east. Signed from village.
Open April to 15 October.

BLOIS Loir-et-Cher
CM Boire boulevard A-Carrel
(tel: 54742278)
1.5km east on D751.
Open March to November.

TOUR 10
ARCACHON Gironde
Camping Club d'Arcachon
avenue de la Galaxie, Les
Abatilles (tel: 56832415)
1.5km south.
Open all year.

BISCAROSSE Landes
Bimbo 176 chemin de Bimbo
(tel: 58098233)
3km north towards Sanguinet.
Open April to September.

MIMIZAN Landes
Marina (tel: 58091266)
Take D626 from Mimizan
Plage. Signed from paper mill.
Open May to 15 September.

CASTELJALOUX Lot-et-
Garonne
CM de la Piscine (tel:
53935468)
Northwest on D933 Marmande
road.
Open 25 March to 30 October.

TOUR 11
PÉRIGUEUX Dordogne
Barnabe-Plage Boulazac (tel:
53534145)
Signposted from N89, 2km east
of town centre.
Open all year.

LES EYZIES-DE-TAYAC
Dordogne
At Sireuil (7km east off D47)
Mas (tel: 53296806)
North of D47.
Open May to September.

SARLAT-LA-CANÉSA
Dordogne
Périères (tel: 53590584)
1km north of town on D47.
Open Easter to September.

ROCAMADOUR Lot
Cigales (tel: 65336444)
Open 22 June to 5 September.

GOURDON Lot
Paradis La Peyrugue (tel:
65416501)
1.6km southwest off N673.
15 June to 15 September.

CASTELNAUD-LE-
CHAPELLE Dordogne
Maisonneuve (tel: 53295129)
10km south of Sarlat on D57.
Open April to September.

TOUR 12
BAGNÈRES-DE-BIGORRE
Hautes-Pyrénées
Bigourdan (tel: 62951357)
2.5km northwest at Pouzac.
Open May to September.

ST-BERTRAND-DE-
COMMINGE Haute-Garonne
Es Pibous chemin de St-Just
(tel: 61883142)
Open 15 May to September.

LUCHON Haute-Garonne
Beauregard avenue de
Vénasque (tel: 61793074)
Off N125.
Open April to November.

LUZ-ST-SAUVEUR Hautes-
Pyrénées
Pyrénées International route
de Lourdes (tel: 62928202)
1.3km northwest on N21.
Open June to September and
20 December to 20 April.

CAUTERETS Hautes-
Pyrénées
Mamelon-Vert avenue du
Mamelon-Vert (tel: 62925156)
Closed October to 10
November.

TOUR 13
LA CIOTAT Bouches-du-
Rhône
Oliviers route de Toulon (tel:
42831504)
Turn inland off N559 at Km34,
5km east of the centre ofg the
town and drive for 150m.
Open March to September.

BANDOL Var
Vallongue (tel: 94294955)
Camping card compulsory.
Open April to September.

SANARY-SUR-MER Var
Mogador (tel: 94741058)
2km northwest on N559, turn
off at Km15 and take next left.
Open Easter to 15 October.

HYÉRES Var
At Ayguade-Ceinturon (4km
southeast)
Ceinturon II (tel: 94663966)
4km southeast Hyères on D42.
Open June to August.

RAMATEULLE Var
Croix du Sud route des Plages
(tel: 94798084)
3km northeast of town. 80m
north of D93.
Open April to October.

GASSIN Var
Parc Montana Gassin route
du Bourrian (tel: 94561249)
2.5km east of N559. Access
from main road at Km84.5 and
84.9 on D89.
Open April to September.

GRIMAUD Var
At Port-Grimaud (4km east)
Plage (tel: 94563115)
Near Km59.6 on N98 on both
sides of road beside sea.
Open 23 March to September.

TOUR 14
CANNES Alpes-Maritimes
At Le Cannet.
Grand Saule 24 boulevard J-
Moulin (tel: 93905510)
Open April to 15 October.

ANTIBES Alpes-Maritimes
Logis de la Brague 1221 route
de Nice (tel: 93335472)
On N7.
Open 2 May to September.

UNFAMILIAR ROAD SIGNS

ACCOTEMENT NON STABILISE
soft verges

ALLUMEZ VOS PHARES
switch on lights

CHAUSSÉE DEFORMÉ
uneven road surface

CHEMIN SANS ISSUE
no through road

DOS D'ÂNE
humpback

FIN D'INTERDICTION DE STATIONMENT
end of parking restriction

ITINÉRAIRE BIS
alternative route

PASSAGE PROTÈGE
your right of way

PÉAGE
toll

POIDS LOURDES
heavy vehicle route

PRIORITÉ À DROITE/GAUCHE
priority to right/left

RAPPEL
warning!
(this literally means 'reminder', ie continue with the instructions given on the previous road sign)

ROUTE BARRE
road closed

SENS INTERDIT
no entry

SENS UNIQUE
one way

SERREZ À DROITE/GAUCHE
keep right/left

TOUTES DIRECTIONS
all directions

TRAVAUX
road works

VIRAGES
bends

GRASSE Alpes-Maritimes
Paoute 160 route de Cannes (tel: 93091142)
Open 15 April to 15 October.

CASTELLANE Alpes-de-Haute-Provence
International Plan de la Palud (tel: 92836667)
Signposted.
Open 15 April to September.

Nôtre Dame (tel: 92836302)
200m west on D952.
Open April to 20 October.

Verdon Domain de la Salaou, route de Moustiers/Ste Marie (tel: 92836129)
Below D952 towards Gorges du Verdon.
Open 15 May to 15 September.

MOUSTIERS-STE-MARIE
Alpes -de-Haute-Provence
St-Jean (tel: 92746685)
Open April to September.

MANDELIEU Alpes-Maritimes
Cigales boulevard de la Mer (tel: 93492353)
South on N7.
Open all year.

Plateau des Chasses (tel: 93492593)
Turn off N7 at Km4.2 and continue uphill for 1.2km.
Open 7 April to October.

TOUR 15
MENTON Alpes-Maritimes
Fleur de Mai 67 route du Val de Gorbio (tel: 93572236)
Exit from D23 at the Parc de la Madone.
Open April to September.

SOSPEL Alpes-Maritimes
Domaine St-Madeleine route de Moulinet (tel: 93041048)
4.5km northwest via D2566.
Open all year.

Tour 16
PONT-DU-GARD Gard
International des Gorges du Gardon route de Uzès (tel: 66228181)
1km from aqueduct on D981 Uzès road.
Open 15 March to 15 October.

REMOULINS Gard
Soubeyranne route de Beaucaire (tel: 66370321)
South on D986.
Open May to 16 September.

TARASCON Bouches-du-Rhône
St Gabriel route de Fontvieille (tel: 90911983)
Open April to September.

AVIGNON Vaucluse
Bagatelle Ile de la Barthelasse (tel: 90863039)
Travel alongside old town wall and Rhône on to Rhône bridge (Nîmes road). About halfway along turn right, follow signs.
Open all year.

CM Pont St-Bénézet Ile de la Barthelasse (tel: 90826350)
Northwest of town on right bank of Rhône.
Open March to October.

ARLES Bouches-du-Rhône
Rosiers Pont de Crau (tel: 90960212)
Access via autoroute exit 'Arles Sud' or N443.
Open 15 March to October.

AIGUES-MORTES Gard
Petite Camargue BP21 (tel: 66538477)
Access via autoroute exit Gallargues in direction of La Grande Motte.
Open 27 April to 22 September.

UZÈS Gard
At St-Quentin-la-Poterie (4km northeast)
Moulin Neuf (tel: 66221721)
Open Easter to 20 September.

TOUR 17
CORNY-SUR-MOZELLE
Moselle
Paquis (tel: 87520359)
0.7km north via N57.
Open March to September.

Verdun Meuse
Breuils allée des Breuils (tel: 29861531)
Southwest via the D34.
Signposted.
Open April to October.

TOUR 18
VILLARS-LES-DOMBES Ain
CM Autières (tel: 74980021)
Camping card compulsory.
Southwest off N83.
Open 20 April to 4 October.

THIZY Rhône
CM (tel: 74640529)
2km south on D504, route de Tarare. Access difficult for caravans.
Open June to 1 September.

TOUR 19
ST-PIERRE-DE-CHAR-TREUSE Isère
Martinière route de Grenoble (tel: 76886036)
Camping card compulsory.
2km southwest.
Open 25 May to 25 September.

ANNECY Haute-Savoie
Belvédère 8 route du Semnoz (tel: 50454830)
On south outskirts, on Semnoz road.
Closed 16 October to 19 December.

SÉEZ Savoie
Reclus route de Tignes (tel: 79410105)
Northwest on N90.
Open all year.

BOURG-ST-MAURICE
Savoie
Versoyen route des Arcs (tel: 79070345)
On south outskirts of town.

Access via the N90.
Closed mid-November to mid-December.

TOUR 20
KAYSERSBERG Haut-Rhin
CM rue des Acacias (tel: 89471447)
Camping card compulsory.
200m from the N415.
Open April to September.

RIBEAUVILLE Haut-Rhin
Pierre de Coubertin 23 rue de Landan (tel: 89736671)
Camping card compulsory.
Access via D106.
Open March to 1 November.

SÉLESTAT Bas-Rhin
CM Cigognes rue de 1-er DFL (tel: 88920398)
Open May to 15 October.

TOUR 21
CALAIS Pas-de-Calais
Peupliers 394 rue du Beau Marais (tel: 21340356)
Open April to October.

MONTREUIL-SUR-MER
Pas-de-Calais
CM (tel: 21060728)
North of town on the N1.
Open all year.

ARDRES Pas-de-Calais
At Autingues (2km south)
St-Louis 223 rue Leulène (tel: 21354683)
Turn off N43 approx 1km southeast of Ardres on to D224 and follow signs.
Open May to October.

TOUR 22
GUISE Aisne
Vallée de l'Oise rue du Camping (tel: 23611486)
1km southeast on the D960.
Open April to 20 October.

LAON Aisne
CM allée de la Chenaie (tel: 23202556)
Open April to October.

TOUR 23
REIMS Marne
Airotel de Champagne
avenue Hoche (tel: 26854122)
Approaching from north, turn

off on outskirts of town towards
Châlons-sur-Marne.
Open Easter to September.

STE-MENEHOULD Marne
CM de la Grelette (tel: 26608021)
East of town towards Metz.
Open May to September.

CHARLEVILLE-MÉZIÈRES
Ardennes
CM Mont Olypme rue des Paquis (tel: 24332360)
Well signed from town centre.
Open Easter to 15 October.

MONTHERMÉ Ardennes
Base de Loisirs
Départementale (tel: 24328161)
0.8km northeast beside the River Semoy.
Open all year.

Tour 24
BEAUNE Côte-d'Or
CM Cent Vignes 10 rue A-Dubois (tel: 80220391)
On the N74 on Savigny-les-Beaune road.
Open 15 March to October.

AVALLON Yonne
CM Sous Roche (tel: 86341039)
2km southeast by D944 and D427.
Open 15 April to 15 October.

MONTSAUCHE Nièvre
Mesanges Lac des Settons, Rive Gauche (tel: 86845577)
Camping card recommended.
On the left bank of Lac des Settons.
Open May to 15 September.

TOUR 25
RAMBOUILLET Yvelines
CM de l'Étang d'Or rue du Château d'Eau (tel: 30410734)
From railway station follow road southeast for 1km passing Camping Pont Hardy.
Open all year.

CHARTRES Eure-et-Loire
CM des Bords de l'Eure rue de Launay (tel: 37287943)
Signposted towards Orléans.
Open 22 April to 2 September.

INDEX

Index & Acknowledgements

The Automobile Association
wishes to thank the following libraries and photographers for their assistance
in the preparation of this book.

MICHELLE BUSSELLE front cover, main picture
BARRIE SMITH 77, 79, 80
SPECTRUM COLOUR LIBRARY 65, 81
TONY STONE IMAGES front cover, main picture

The remaining photographs are held in the Association's own library (AA PHOTO LIBRARY) with
contributions from:

P ATTERBURY 140, 142; A BAKER 83, 86, 87, 88/9, 91, 93, 95, 96, 98, 104; P BENNETT 76; S DAY 22, 23, 24/5,
84; J EDMANSON 20, 58, 59, 61; P KENWARD 32, 41, 42, 43, 44, 49, 62, 63, 66, 67, 68, 71, 73, 75, 78; R MOORE
5, 9, 11, 14, 17, 19, 33, 37, 51, 52/3, 54, 55, 57, 82, 106/7, 115, 117, 118, 120; R MOSS 15; D NOBLE 155, 156; T
OLIVER 34, 35, 38, 45, 101, 108, 109, 111, 114, 128, 130, 131, 132, 137, 138, 139, 143, 154; N RAY 99; D
ROBERTSON 110, 113, 133, 135, 141; C SAWYER back cover (a), 6, 7, 8, 10, 12, 13, 16, 18; M SHORT 134, 150,
151, 152, 153; B SMITH inside flap, back cover (b), 21, 30, 36, 39, 46, 47, 56, 60, 64, 69, 70, 74, 85, 94, 100, 103,
112, 116, 119, 122, 123, 124/5, 127, 129, 144, 146/7, 148, 149, 157; R STRANGE 2, 26, 27, 28, 29, 50, 90, 92, 97,
105, 126; R VICTOR 31.

Contributors
Copy editors: Audrey Horne, Dilys Jones   **Indexer:** Marie Lorimer